Thing
for Peace

Things That Make for Peace

A Christian peacemaker in a
world of war

Peter B. Price

DARTON · LONGMAN + TODD

First published in 2018 by
Darton, Longman and Todd Ltd
1 Spencer Court
140 – 142 Wandsworth High Street
London SW18 4JJ

ISBN: 978-0-232-53346-0

A catalogue record for this book is available from the British Library

Phototypeset by Kerrypress, St Albans, AL3 8JL

Printed and bound in Great Britain by Bell & Bain, Glasgow

Peace is the seed bed of righteousness,
and the peacemakers will reap its harvest.
(James 3.18, REB)

Contents

Foreword by Major General (Retd) Tim Cross CBE

Some years ago I was taking part in a media debate about the rights and wrongs of the various conflicts around the world since the end of the 'Cold War – including the invasion of Iraq in 2003. At one point the academic I was debating with argued: "Better an 'Unjust Peace' than a 'Just War'". My response was essentially to politely observe that it was easy for him to say that when he was nestled safely away in the confines of his university study; not so easy for those living under, or a refugee from, dictatorship; or being maimed or killed in conflicts around the world.

In many ways it was a cheap shot – but over my 40-odd years of service in the British Army I had experienced the reality and brutality of warfare and the consequences that flowed from it. I had seen behind the headlines – the gangsters and protection rackets; the greed and desire for power, along with the bitterness of religious, ethnic and cultural bigotry that divides our world – and watched enough mass graves being dug up to know that such bigotry isn't one-sided. I had seen at first hand the result of ethnic cleansing; seen enough to know that there are rarely 'goodies' and baddies' in this business – and never easy, glib answers. This is the stark reality of a world where mankind's primary sin is the declaration that we are our own god – and all that matters is 'self'.

By the time Peter and I first met I had been involved, one way or another, in many of the places that he examines in this extraordinary book. The so-called 'Troubles' in Northern Ireland broke out as I was about to receive my commission – troubles that didn't end until the year I left the Army, 37 years later. The 'Cold War' carried me through the 1970s and 1980s, and my three 'peace–enforcement' tours in the Balkans in the 1990s had followed a year 'peace-keeping' in Cyprus with the UN in 1981, and 'war-fighting' operations in the Gulf War in 1990/91. All of this prior to Iraq in 2002/03, when I had moved to Washington and then Kuwait before going into Baghdad as Saddam's statue came crashing down – and celebrating Holy Communion in the first service held there in St George's Anglican Church with Canon Andrew White.

Some years after I left the Army I met an ex-IRA terrorist who had planted some of the improvised explosive devices (IEDs) that I and others had tackled as bomb disposal operators. We met at a church in London – St Ethleburga's, Bishopsgate – which had been blown up by the IRA in 1993 and was now being used as a Centre for Reconciliation and a 'Maker of Peacemakers'. As I listened to his story I began to realise that if I had been raised in his circumstances I too may well have been planting those IEDs rather than taking them apart. Stories are powerful things – they help us to understand the 'baggage' that we and others carry; understand how we see the world around us and why we and they do the things we do – did the things we did.

What Peter has done in this book is to tell a series of extraordinary stories. Between them, they tell of a life well lived, with personal experiences few can match. His insights are rooted in his engagement in conflict resolution from the terrorism of Northern Ireland to the dirty wars in Central America and the seemingly never-ending conflicts in Africa and the Middle East – and in closing with such issues as nuclear disarmament. Honest about his own anguish and struggles, he doesn't avoid the ambiguities – he is rightly pretty strong on the subject of division and intransigence across the Anglican Communion and wider Christian church, which remains a scandal – but he is very challenging to us all in his conclusions, Christian or not. As he says, he and I have prayed about and debated many of the issues he talks about here – both one-to-one and when he led the Anglican Communion Pastoral Visitors facilitation, which I was privileged to be involved with. And through his challenges and arguments, he taught me to both explore and question my own story.

He acknowledges that he is not a natural peace maker; that he 'enjoys a good fight.' And the truth is so do I. I have often quoted Einstein's view that: 'the world is a dangerous place to live in not because of the people who do evil, but because of the people who sit and let it happen', and so does Peter. But he then rightly adds that peace is always more than the absence of war and violent conflict; it is also about the presence of justice. And in arguing that 'surely all prayer reveals our own complicity, our own prejudice, the complexity of the situation' he challenges me for one very deeply. 'Prayer', he writes, 'should lead us to repentance, a repentance that leads us to understand, to be better informed; to be enlightened. Any prayer for peace and reconciliation must have to do with our own responsibility to work for reconciliation. All prayer calls for action.'

What action? I may be convinced that justice in a fallen world sometimes needs enforcing but it is abundantly clear that simply stopping the fighting usually solves little or nothing – without forgiveness and reconciliation, the absence of overt violence is a false peace. As Peter argues, real peace requires the eradication of poverty, disease, lack of education and employment as much as the cessation of violence – 'wherever poverty is endemic, the mosquitoes of oppression, disease, abuse and violence swarm....'

I have consistently argued that the church as a whole may not have all the answers but it does at least understand the questions – and Peter understands them better than most. His answers are not lofty 'stuck in the clouds' aspirations, but grounded in hard-lived experience. Peter's journey from Parish 'vicar' to his time as the Bishop of Bath and Wells, and with it membership of the House of Lords, tells of a life lived in faith and courage. It ends with hope and challenge - a realisation that alongside the enduring truth that whilst in Jesus Christ we find an individual peace that the world cannot give – indeed doesn't understand – war and conflict is never 'the' answer to the world's ills.

The British Government's 'strap-line' for our Armed Forces is being a 'Force for Good' in the world. It is a good line but it – and we collectively – need to learn that those who pray, fast, hold vigil, demonstrate and debate reveal, as Peter says, 'a deep unease about the capacity of war to resolve historic divisions and conflicts'. What is surely needed is a world where there is a 'Just Peace' for all, which is essentially what Peter argues for.

Getting there is far from easy, but there is scant evidence that few, if any, politicians have taken any notice of the numerous articles, statements or reports that he and others have issued over the years – or listened seriously to the delegations that he has led and taken part in. They should take note and listen better. If Tony Blair, for one, had done so, then maybe he would have gone down in history for the right reasons.

Appreciation

An African proverb has it that 'the one who builds the path cannot build it straight'. I am grateful to all who have inspired, encouraged and wrestled with me in the production of this book. Without them it could not have been written.

It is somewhat invidious to highlight individuals and sources, but I want to acknowledge the influence of my wife, Dee, who has been a constant companion, wise counsellor and a passionate advocate of peacemaking. Jim Wallis and the team at Sojourners in Washington DC, together with editors and contributors to *Concilium* have provided nourishment and consistent theological reflection. In addition, Dr Teresa Dumasy along with others at *Conciliation Resources* have given substance to my journey in peace-building. To all of them I offer my profound thanks.

Sir Don McCullin has spent a lifetime photographing war zones. I have admired and worked with Don on a couple of occasions. He is a man of immense humanity. I asked him for a picture for the cover of this book that offered the possibility of a new dawn in human relationships. The result is the picture of Somerset countryside taken early one morning. I am grateful to him for his generosity and kindness.

Major General Tim Cross has written the Foreword. We have talked, prayed and struggled together over the 'things that make for peace' in arenas as diverse as the context of the Iraq War, and the Anglican Communion. He has been mentor, companion and friend and I thank him for his insightful words.

Without the team at Darton, Longman and Todd, this book would never have seen the light of day. I owe particular thanks to Ali Hull who helped give the book shape, pointed out its inconsistencies, and edited my overly verbose text. David Moloney has been a source of encouragement, particularly when self-doubt crept in over its viability. To all, my deepest thanks and appreciation.

In an age when most moral theology has focused on sexual themes, I have found inspiration and identity with the German Redemptorist priest Bernhard Häring who said: 'My main calling must be that of an untiring apostle for the elimination of war ... for a radical love that will not allow us to become enemies.' It is in this spirit I offer this little book.

Peter B. Price
Feast of the Presentation of Christ in the Temple

Introduction

The invitation to preach at St Paul's Cathedral was simple enough: 'We are asking four recently retired bishops to preach on a theme of their choosing under the title – "What do I want to say now?"' The implication of the request was that the speakers might offer a reflection on an issue on which they had strong views but had been constrained from expressing during their time in office.

I chose for my title, 'Can Christianity continue to sanction war?'. This was the subject of a symposium which took place earlier on HMS *Bulwark* between theologians and military personnel, in which I had participated. As I began my address in St Paul's in the spring of 2014, I told the congregation, 'What I want to say now', for integrity's sake, was an issue I had frequently addressed in 40 years of ministry.

2014 marked the centennial anniversary of the outbreak of the First World War, the so-called 'War to End All Wars'. Except that it was not. Rather it marked the beginning of a century or so of unprecedented wars, genocide and other violent conflicts. Over each of these the mantra has been cast: 'This must never happen again.' But inexorably, it does.

The failure to bring an end to war has meant suffering on a previously unimaginable scale, providing us with one of the greatest challenges of all time. It has caused humanitarians such as the Italian surgeon Gino Strada, the founder of Emergency which seeks to provide the medical care to victims of conflict to demand that war should be abolished.

When challenged, Strada replies: 'It has to disappear from history. … War should disturb us equally. It makes absolutely no sense. It's very particular to the human race and it's crazy because it is destroying humanity.'[1]

But his is not a new cry. As Jesus left the Temple in Jerusalem following his entry to the city, he wept and said: 'If you, even you, had only recognized on this day the *things that make for peace*! But now they are hidden from your eyes.'[2] And it seems we continue to suffer from such myopia.

This Introduction was written during a week in 2016 in which the current British Prime Minister, Theresa May, committed her country to the renewal of the Trident nuclear weapons system. When challenged in parliament about whether she would press the nuclear button 'that would kill 100,000 innocent men, women and children', she replied: 'Yes, and I have to say … that the whole point of a nuclear deterrent is that our enemies need to know that we would be prepared to use it.'

This question had been asked of previous prime ministers, but each had avoided a directly affirmative answer. Theresa May's candour might be shocking, but the truth is that weapons of mass destruction threaten the future of humanity as no previous weapons have. More disturbing is the affirmation that the potential destruction of '100,000 innocent men, women and children' is somehow acceptable in defence of the right of others to live, which raises huge questions.

Paradoxically, within a few days, the same Prime Minister pledged herself to bring an end to the 'barbaric evil' of modern slavery, arguing, 'Just as Britain took a historic stand to ban slavery two centuries ago, so Britain will once again lead the way in defeating modern slavery.'

The title of this book *Things That Make for Peace* comes directly from the lips of Jesus of Nazareth. He is the author and completer of the faith in which I have been brought up since birth, and subsequently chose to embrace as a teenager: Christianity. It is a faith with a complex history in relation to war and peace. Some have opposed it, such as the third-century theologian Origen, who declared: 'We will not raise arms against other nations; we will not practice the art of war, because through Jesus Christ we have become children of peace.' But as Christianity became the religion of governments, from the Roman emperor Constantine to the monarchies of Western Europe, and the presidents of the United States of America, arguments to justify war[3] have been required of theologians. Building on the ancient Greek theory of the 'Just War', enunciated by Plato and Cicero, Christian teachers such as Augustine and Thomas Aquinas provided the moral framework for Christian rulers to go to war.

These two positions still dominate Christian moral thinking on war. Early in my faith journey I embraced 'Just War' theory uncritically. It seemed to provide a conclusive rationale for engagement in the kinds of conflict that influenced me as a child of the Second World War.

In 1967 I married Dee, a woman from Northern Ireland. This was a community on the verge of what was to be a 40-year civil conflict. Increasingly I came to ask, as a disciple of Christ, how war could be justified. I began to ask what Origen meant when he said that 'through Jesus Christ we have become children of peace', and even more about what Jesus meant when he said: 'Blessed are the peacemakers, for they will be called children of God.'[4]

Around the time of our marriage, there were other conflicts as well as in Ireland. In South East Asia, in Vietnam and Cambodia, the USA was fighting a war against the Viet Cong, Communist insurgents. Britain was disengaging from its former colonies in Asia and Africa, often in conflict with dissident groups seeking independence. Across America, Britain and Europe, people were campaigning against war and nuclear weapons.

In America the Civil Rights movement was demanding racial equality, chiefly under the leadership of Martin Luther King and Malcolm X. In 1958, race riots took place in Notting Hill, London. During the 1960s, parliamentary legislation outlawed racial discrimination. It was an era of upheaval, threat and change.

On 17 May 1968, American Roman Catholic priests, Daniel and Philip Berrigan joined with others to make napalm, a weapon widely used by the US in the Vietnam War. Breaking into a military facility, protestors set fire to 378 files of people facing the draft into the US military. It was a controversial action receiving far from unanimous support within the peace movement. The perpetrators justified their action on the grounds that the Catholic Church had condemned as unjust the killing of civilians as unjust. Eventually tried, they were sentenced to jail. Daniel Berrigan was to write:

> We cry peace and cry peace, and there is no peace. There is no peace because there are no peacemakers. There are no makers of peace because the making of peace is at least as costly as the making of war – at least as exigent, at least as disruptive,

at least as liable to bring disgrace and prison and death in its wake.[5]

In 1972, it was the picture of a naked little girl, Kim Phuc, whose village had been napalmed, that was to touch the conscience of the world and begin the process to end the war.

The Established Church largely acquiesced over the conflicts that followed the Second World War, and did not take a stand against nuclear weapons. Protest was left to individuals and small groups of Christians joined in protests, notably the Methodist Donald Soper and Canon Collins, an Anglican.

The Irish crisis was portrayed as between Protestant or Loyalist citizens of Northern Ireland seeking to retain the union with England, and Catholic or Nationalists who wanted a United Ireland. As the first bombs exploded across the Province and nightly street battles of petrol bombs and riots dominated the news, newly married we faced the question, 'What are the *things that make for peace*? And if we can define them, do we have any role in seeking them?'.

One morning in the mid-1960s, walking through the Market Quarter district of Belfast, Dee was approached by a stranger who said to her: 'The man you are to marry will become a healer.' He then disappeared into the crowd. At the time we gave it little thought, though neither could we dismiss the encounter. As the challenges of peacemaking deepened, we increasingly wondered whether this was the work of healing to which the stranger might have been referring.

I am not a natural peacemaker. I enjoy a good fight. However, circumstances have frequently led me into situations where I have sensed an inner compulsion, a calling, to seek the *things that make for peace*. Those things are diverse, often disconnected, apparently insignificant, and their outcomes frequently questionable.

I owe much to the insights and accompaniment of others, living and departed, as I have sought to 'seek the things that make for peace'.

Among those in whose spirit I have walked alongside have been the famous: Dietrich Bonhoeffer, who died a martyr for his opposition to Nazism; Thomas Merton, a Trappist monk who from his hermitage taught contemplation and resistance; Mohandas

Gandhi, a Hindu who taught non-violent resistance as the way to oppose evil; and Dag Hammarsjköld, a former secretary general of the United Nations.

Lesser known saints include the German village farmhand, Franz Jäggerstatter, beheaded for his refusal to fight in Hitler's armies; Etty Hillesum, a Jewess from Amsterdam who died in the concentration camp at Auschwitz, whose diaries convey an awesome love of humanity in the face of inhumanity; and André Trocmé with the people of the Le Chambon, hid Jews, Communists and other enemies of the Reich, refusing to betray them. I have stood in the cell in Sachsenhausen where Martin Niemöller, a personal prisoner of Adolf Hitler, was held for four years, and been touched by his courage and faith.

Amongst contemporaries, accompaniers have been Jim Wallis of Sojourners; Father Jon Sobrino of El Salvador; Bruce Kent; Paul Oestrëicher, former director of reconciliation at Coventry Cathedral; John Morrow of Corrymeela; David Bleakley; and Hans von Sponëck, former UN humanitarian director in Iraq, as well as my good friend Canon Andrew White, sometime Vicar of Baghdad.

More than all these, it has been those *little ones* of the Gospel, the hidden brave, anonymous souls who have resisted violence in all its forms. Amongst these has been Dee, whose gentle, persistent radicalism, clarity of vision and reconciling heart, has encouraged, chivvied and nurtured me in sustaining a vision of a more peaceful world.

This book reflects a personal journey, but also attempts to offer some of the insights and understanding gained by exploring what it means to 'seek peace, and pursue it'.[6] It is not a 'how to' book, but one born out of experience. I do not judge others who disagree with my conclusions. There is a path to be taken together as Christians in seeking to discern how to respond to a world of increasing violence and human suffering. At the same time, I believe that we need to reflect together on what for me is an abiding question: 'Can Christianity continue to sanction war?'

Ireland: Silent testimony

'Loss is in our midst. Untold loss. Whilst identity or "label" is buried in the past it is my hope that the stories are not.' With these words, Colin Davidson introduced his exhibition 'Silent Testimony' at the Ulster Museum in the summer of 2015. His 18 portraits tell the stories of individual victims of the Irish Troubles, each of whom had experienced pain, suffering or loss.

'Look at their faces, study their eyes,' wrote Senator George Mitchell, one of the architects of the Northern Ireland Peace Process. 'There you will see the legacy of the sectarian conflict … and you will understand why it is important for peace to prevail.'

For more than 50 years, I too have been looking at faces, studying eyes, listening to stories of untold loss. Sometimes this has been in the context of violence and conflict, but also loss as a consequence of debt, poverty, sickness, lack of education and discrimination. I have borne testimony to loss in situations in Northern Ireland, Latin America, Africa, the Middle East, and the Anglican Communion. In each of these I have sought, like George Mitchell, to 'understand why it is important for peace to prevail'.

Peace is more than the absence of conflict. True peace exists where there is justice, restoration, forgiveness, and a desire to pursue reconciliation.

In June 2011 the Peace Bridge was opened across the River Foyle, linking the two sides of a city of two names, Derry/Londonderry, in Northern Ireland. Historically, Protestants lived on the east side of the river, and Catholics on the west. It remains much the same today, and people continue to live largely separate lives. Their children go to different schools, play different sports, and attend different churches.

The Peace Bridge is complex and beautiful. It is curved, not straight. It is not possible to see the end from the beginning. The span is suspended on a critically balanced fulcrum where the power to weight ratios are critical. Everything is held in tension. One miscalculation and the structure is potentially wrecked. It is a physical parable of the complications, intricacies and upheavals that peace processes entail.

Deep within Judeo-Christian Scripture and tradition lies the concept of the making of peace. The prophets spoke of the 'beauty of the feet' of the messengers who bring the good news of peace.[1] They in their turn, based their vision of peace upon the 'covenant of peace'[2], which they believed God had made with their ancestors. In the psalms, the *silent testimony* of the peaceable nature of God's intent towards humanity was re-emphasised in the directive to 'do good; seek peace, and pursue it'.[3]

The command to 'Pray for the peace of Jerusalem',[4] and for the nation's 'enemies to be at peace'[5] with them, is central to the covenant between God and people. For God is, by definition, 'Everlasting Father, Prince of Peace'.[6]

The achievement of peace lies in the beating of 'swords into ploughshares, and … spears into pruning hooks', leading to a time when 'nation shall not lift up sword against nation, neither shall they learn war any more'.[7] The prophets Isaiah and Micah make it clear that the leaders of nations have responsibility to both disarm and make peace.

The righteousness, or quality, of nations will be judged by God for their ability to make peace. Jesus reminded hearers that this is the criteria that defines true justice and humanity.[8] The ones who *bear silent testimony* to the needs of the *things that make for peace*, are the hungry, the thirsty, the stranger, the imprisoned, the refugee, the victim of war, the debtor and the slave. Only when we recognise them as truly sisters and brothers, can peace begin to be made.

Defining 'peace' is not straightforward, not least because it can be interpreted in different ways depending on context. 'Peace at last' declares the tombstone over the grave of someone whose body has been wracked with ill health through decades. 'Peace!' declares the newspaper headline at the signing of an armistice following years of bloody conflict. 'Be at peace among yourselves' counsels a wise voice over a squabbling community. Then there is the mystery of inner serenity, 'the peace of God, which surpasses all understanding'.[9] We could add many more.

Interpreting peace requires a deeper etymology. Peace is more than the absence of conflict, for non-violent conflict, which seeks a positive outcome, can be a force for good. Nor should peace be achieved 'at any price', through misplaced acquiescence, or weariness with fighting. Sheer battle fatigue can, however, provide a potential starting point for peace.

In Hebrew the word used for 'peace' is *shalom*. *Shalom* is a concept that carries the idea of the restoration, the making of harmony between people. It is an activity willed by God and directed towards creating unity.

An example of this came in 1980 when, in the light of the *Shoah*,[10] German bishops produced a Declaration on the Relationship of the Church to Judaism. They observed:

> Christians and Jews together can and should advocate what in Hebrew is called shalom. This is a comprehensive concept that signifies peace, joy, freedom, reconciliation, community, harmony, righteousness, truth, communication, humanity.[11]

This definition reveals that, far from being passive, true peace nurtures 'joy', 'freedom', 'community' and 'harmony' as integral to unity. A key aspect of making peace is 'reconciliation'. Reconciliation is a process of re-making or building relationships damaged by violent or ideological conflict. It is a term used freely in many circles, especially religious ones; however, as one contemporary observer has noted: 'Reconciliation is not an easy option. Reconciliation is tough, challenging, hardnosed. Reconciliation is not just for peaceful people.' It is neither 'soft [nor] non-contentious'.[12]

In the New Testament two pictures illustrate the meaning of reconciliation. One picture is that of the breaking down of a dividing wall to its foundations, so that every barrier is removed. The second illustration is that of creating a restored personhood out of multiple diverse and often conflicting personality traits. What St Mark calls being in a 'right mind'[13] – restoring people to their right mind.

Breaking down barriers and removing the foundations upon which they are built or being in a 'right' or common mind, requires both realism and application. True reconciliation requires patience, perseverance and a commitment to the values of *shalom* that enable the restoration of humanity to true unity.

In the Old Testament, Isaiah offered a vision of a reconciled future in which weapons of war could be fashioned into useful tools. Given the nature of early Iron Age weaponry, swords could be transformed into ploughshares and vice versa. The nature of modern weaponry does not provide for such possibilities, and disarmament as an integral aspect of peacemaking is much more complex.

Just because disarmament is complex does not mean it is impossible. We are not predestined to going to hell in a handcart. The voices of Isaiah, Micah, Jesus and other prophets such as Gandhi offer us testimony to another way. One writer, Pinchas Lapide, has interpreted their voices as offering 'the possibility of an international equalisation before God – "God will judge among the nations" – for which this symbolic re-forging of all swords into tools of peaceful bread winning could smooth the way'.[14]

Above all, reconciliation is the restoration of relationships. It was said that what made the Good Friday Agreement possible in Northern Ireland was the willingness of the parties to relate. In George Mitchell's terms to 'Look at their faces, study their eyes ... and see the legacy' of the dehumanising reality of conflict in people just like you and me.

As I have walked the Peace Bridge I have become aware that however beautiful the structure whether in critically balanced span or within the longings of the mind, the *things that make for peace* remain a challenge for Christian ethics, a demand that most Christians have not really faced. In an age when religion is perceived in the popular mind to be the source of too many conflicts (though this is only partly true), people of faith, particularly Christians, have a duty to commit themselves to building peace.

On 13 November 2015, alleged Islamic extremists attacked the Bataclan music venue in Paris killing and maiming many people. Amongst them was the wife of journalist Antoine Leiris. He later wrote: 'If this God for whose sake you kill blindly made us in his image, each bullet in my wife's body will have been a wound in his heart.' It is a sentiment that could be expressed over the stories of all of the silent victims of a million conflicts.

It is my hope that this book in its *silent testimony* to experience gained, as well as struggles both won and lost, will help to build bridges across chasms that divide, dig out foundations of broken down walls, and restore us to our 'right mind', so that God's kingdom of justice, love and peace may be restored amongst us.

2

Bystanders

Signs of unrest in Northern Ireland were evident between the Loyalist and Nationalist communities by the mid 1960s. The marching season takes place in July and August, to commemorate the victory of the Protestant King William of Orange in 1690, when he defeated the Catholic King, James ll. A sensitive and tense time each year, the marches frequently led to attacks on Catholics. In turn, Republicans would launch their own attacks, killing police in remote border areas. As always the question, 'Who started it?' raged. The outcome, however, was always more division, hate and further violence.

Through the late 1960s, the Northern Ireland Civil Rights Association (NICRA) was being formed. Its objective was to end 'gerrymandering' and abuses in housing allocation – an unfair electoral process that ensured Protestant or Loyalist supremacy in elections. In addition, NICRA sought to expose widespread discrimination in employment, particularly against Catholics.

In the spring of 1968, the Civil Rights Association organised its first march. Despite its claims to be non-sectarian, the Civil Rights movement stirred up anxiety and anger in the dominant Protestant community. Fear was palpable and violence soon erupted.

In October that year, a Civil Rights march was planned in Londonderry. Fearing confrontation, the Northern Irish prime minister, William Craig, banned the march. The ban was defied and the march was subsequently attacked by both police and Loyalists. The attack was filmed by an Irish television cameraman, Gay O'Brien, and his pictures shocked the world. For the following two days, pitched battles were fought between rioters and police, in the Republican areas of Derry. The 'Troubles', which had been brewing for a while, now began in earnest.

In the summer of 1969, my wife and I, now married with a one-year-old son, were visiting her parents' home on a Loyalist housing estate in Omagh. Rumours were rife over the intentions of Civil Rights marchers, and it was believed one march was to pass through the estate. People were gathering in the streets, erecting barricades and blocking off the various entrances and exits to the estate.

With my father-in-law, I too went out on to the street. The mood was tense as we walked around the barricades. We talked with vigilantes whose barely concealed guns brought an extra chill to the atmosphere. From time to time cars would arrive; hurried conversations with their occupants indicated that little sign of the march was evident, but they were sure it was on its way.

As the summer light faded and darkness fell, a vigil of watching and waiting began. Some, like us, returned home. On the way we had a conversation with a former 'B' Special policeman. A rumour surrounded this individual. Some years before, a fellow police officer had been shot and killed. A reprisal was ordered. It was alleged that this man had rounded up a number of Catholic men, put them in a barn and ordered it to be burnt. True or not, it was part of the local folklore.

That night no one slept. Just after midnight, I saw a police patrol instructing the dismantling of barriers. Drawing my father-in-law's attention to this, he raised his fingers to his lips. He had been badly shaken by events and though I could never get him to confirm or deny it, I believe he called the police.

A few days later, when the tension had dissipated somewhat, the truth began to emerge. Fearing internecine trouble between the Loyalist and Nationalist estates in Omagh, the police had circulated two rumours. The first, to our estate, warned of a Civil Rights march. The second, to the Catholic estate, warned of a Loyalist attack. The ruse worked.

Later on 12 August, 'The Battle of the Bogside' took place in Londonderry. The fighting followed the annual march of the Protestant Apprentice Boys, and continued for two days. Within hours, rioting had erupted in Belfast, Dungannon, Dungiven, Coalisland, Newry and Crossmaglen. Eight people were shot dead and nearly 140 injured. Loyalists set fire to hundreds of homes in Nationalist areas.

Anxiety surrounded our family. On the night of the barricades in our street, we had moved our son from the front to the back of the house in case of rioting and petrol bombing. The tension that we had experienced during the standoff, believing the rumours of impending attack, meant we were afraid.

Afraid but unharmed, we slipped across the border a day or so later for a seaside holiday. Seldom far from a radio we heard reports of bombings and riots, also that the British Army was to be deployed on the streets of Northern Ireland.

While we were away we had time to reflect on our reactions during our brief time behind the barricades. How were we to react in the future? These Troubles were not going away any time soon.

It would be easy to say at this point that we looked coolly at the situation and asked ourselves: 'What are the things that make for peace?' We didn't. Neither, at that point, did we recall my wife's encounter in the Belfast Market Quarter and ask how we might enter into this situation in ways that might contribute to a future peace.

As we sat in the caravan looking across the rain-sodden Donegal sands, with our son sleeping peacefully in his crib, we took stock. Dee had intuited from an early age that there was a deep sense of injustice at the heart of Northern Ireland. She had found the sectarianism and prejudice with which she grew up deeply disturbing, and knew it was wrong.

One afternoon, aged eleven, a road diversion took her and her father through a Nationalist housing estate. The estate was in an appalling condition with unrepaired houses and roads, and other signs of neglect. Disturbed by what she saw, she asked her dad why this was. Normally a moderate man, he nevertheless replied that it was the way such people were: they did not care for their homes and families in the way Protestants did. In her heart Dee knew this wasn't true, but did not feel she could confront her adored father over it.

Such attitudes reached back into the dark history of the Protestant settlement of Ireland, as Britain sought to subjugate its people. As the sociologist Allan G. Johnson[1] has pointed out, the frustration of the British 'in the face of stubborn resistance, gave rise to a cultural belief that the Irish were an inferior and savage people, not merely in the organisation of their societies, but in their very nature as human beings'.

This, he said, led to the British regarding the Irish as 'something like a separate species altogether possessing inferior traits that were biologically passed on from one generation to the next', and thereby 'inventing a concept of race' that made it 'easier to objectify them and more difficult to feel empathy for them as members of their own kind, both integral to the exertion of control over others'.

Recalling Dee's experience of the Nationalist estate, and witnessing the increasing violence in Northern Ireland, we talked about the present conflict and its causes. We had not read Johnson's insights, but intuitively understood their veracity.

These were early days, and we were in uncharted territory. Initially our response was that of any spiritually intuitive couple. We vowed to examine our attitudes to people who were different from us; the extent to which we had subconsciously objectified them, treating them, mentally at least, as inferior and different. We promised to teach our children to value everyone regardless of their gender, ethnicity, religion or background. We committed ourselves to pray for peace and work for justice, though we had little idea then of what this would mean.

Thus far, however, we had no further indication as to how, or whether there were things that we could do 'that would make for peace'; nor if any vocation existed to be peacemakers. Like children in a playground watching a fight, we were simply bystanders.

3

From bystander to witness

During the summer of 1970 in inner-city Belfast, it was almost possible to set a watch by the first crump of explosions that dinned the early evening air. Rioting, bombs, Molotov cocktails and burnings occurred most nights and went on for several hours.

Being teachers, we were able to spend much of our summer holiday in Northern Ireland, and some of it always in Belfast. Dee's uncle Terry Callan was the Rector of St Aidan's church in Sandy Row, a fiercely Protestant parish that bordered on an equally fervent Catholic neighbourhood.

The Boyne Bridge was the flashpoint between the two communities. Here around six at night, young people would gather as a prelude to the night's violence. This involved provocative taunts and acts on both sides, frequently involving police and soldiers.

Terry Callan was a deeply committed pastor. Each night he went to the flashpoint and placed himself between the protagonists. As he spotted someone he knew, he would gently tap them on the shoulder and say, 'Come on, son, I know where you live. Time to go home. You don't need to be here.' His intervention was remarkably effective. He *did* know them.

During our visits, Terry would invite me to join him. Still very much a bystander, I observed his one-man peace mission. When he had done all he could at the Boyne Bridge, he would make his way into the streets of monochrome rows of back-to-back houses that defined his parish.

Being summer and with the noise of conflict never far from earshot, people were out on their doorsteps, or queuing at the fish and chip shop. With gentle humour and warmth, Terry would engage everyone, listening out for bits of intelligence that might indicate the whereabouts of victims of the violence, or a warning of an attack.

Prior to our marriage, Dee had taught in Sandy Row, and witnessed the depth of indoctrination into Loyalist myths amongst even the youngest children. One day in her primary reception class, she told them she was leaving to get married. A five-year-old boy, Billy, asked her whether she loved her husband-to-be. 'Yes,' she replied. 'And who do you love, Billy?' 'Please miss. I love God and King Billy' the child answered.

Images are important in the making and maintaining of myths. Wall murals still adorn both areas: King Billy on one side and Republican martyrs on the other in the Nationalist roads. But, however at odds he was with the more extreme behaviour of his community, I noticed that Terry Callan did not decry the myths his people held. In his search for reconciliation, respect was integral.

One night in 1971, after a particularly notorious incident of house burning, Terry and I visited a terrace of apparently deserted and boarded up houses. Some piece of intelligence indicated that people might be taking refuge there. As we knocked on makeshift doors, frightened individuals cautiously opened them. Invited in, we listened to their accounts of being burnt out of the nearby, formerly integrated, communities.

For a young teacher brought up in comfortable London suburbia, such raw violence and inhumanity was profoundly shocking. But as I have discovered so often since, what brings out the worst in people also brings out the best. What moved me most amongst those displaced people was their lack of vindictiveness.

Initially, people spoke of how glad they were to be alive and in a place of relative safety. All told of how, over many decades, they had lived harmoniously with their neighbours. They spoke of the kindness, but also the impotence of those neighbours, who had feared for their own lives. Tears of grief were focused more on friendships torn asunder than by dispossession of chattels.

Accompanying Terry, I was gradually drawn from being a bystander to a participant in the search for peace. I'd learned most about the need to listen to folk, however obnoxious their views. Terry genuinely loved people, and was motivated both by compassion and a desire to open up possibilities for people to face the fears and hatred energised by their interpretation of history. His refusal to judge others, but to respect them however much he disagreed, provided some solid planks for my growing understanding of peace-building.

Our regular forays to Ireland over the succeeding years provided opportunities to build on these experiences, to become a witness, ready to speak about what had been seen and heard. Was I now ready for this? Through my time accompanying Terry, I had begun to be accepted and trusted a little. I had also been ordained, and though my parish was on a housing estate in the south of England, I was not to be immune there from the impact of the Northern Ireland Troubles.

In November 1974, the Provisional IRA blew up a pub in Birmingham killing and maiming many soldiers. One of my parishioners was an army major. His regiment had taken several bad hits in Northern Ireland during their recent tour. Feelings were running high, but I will always be grateful to him for coming to our house the morning after the bombing in Birmingham, and reassuring Dee that no one in the community felt that because she was Irish, she was in any way implicated.

It may sound ridiculous now to think such a possibility could be in anyone's mind, but in an atmosphere of fear, almost anything was possible. In September that year, Judge Rory Conaghan was gunned down on the doorstep of his home in Belfast. His brother lived a few doors away from us. I called on him that evening to offer my condolences. Before the door was opened, he shouted, 'Are you the IRA come to get me too?' I assured him that I was just the local Anglican priest come to express sadness at his loss. He let me in and we talked – but fear had stalked its way to all our doors.

I was now having to consider whether those anonymous words in Belfast had been prophetic. Was all this apparently coincidental witnessing of the Troubles suggesting that I should become a peacemaker? If so, I could not afford to be naïve about the implications.

I knew enough Greek from my reading of the New Testament to know that the word for 'witness' in Greek is 'martyr'. A 'martyr' is not necessarily someone who has to literally lay down their life, but nevertheless they must accept the consequence of commitment to the cause. Was I being called to do this?

4.

Accompaniment

By the mid 1970s, Northern Ireland was an armed camp full of combatants each carrying out their own deadly mission. Soldiers and paramilitaries, the police, civilians and bystanders were all victims of the deadly arsenals of increasingly indiscriminately used weapons. Each party perceived that victory or defeat could only be achieved by force. Talking or working for the things that make for peace seemed a lost cause.

I had never quite been able to describe myself as a pacifist. Yet as the Troubles erupted, I increasingly questioned whether as a Christian I had ever really understood what Jesus meant when he said: 'Blessed are the peacemakers, for they will be called the children of God.'[1] It is easy to be a 'peace lover', but to engage in *making* peace requires a willingness to accompany people in some very dark places.

Over the coming years, I took the early experience with Terry Callan into other communities across Northern Ireland. One of the best known communities was Corrymeela on the north coast of County Antrim. Meaning 'hill of harmony', Corrymeela was founded by a Presbyterian minister, Ray Davey, in the 1960s. He intended that people from both sides of the divide, as well as from all faiths and traditions, could meet there and find each other's common humanity, as they sought paths to reconciliation.

His inspiration had come from communities founded in Iona in Scotland by the late George MacLeod; and from Taizé in France by the late Brother Roger Schütz. MacLeod wanted Iona to become a centre of reconciliation for young people and families. Schütz saw Taizé as a place where the youth of European nations torn apart by war, could find hope and build peace. Each, in their own way, developed worship that re-built the common life, and served the cause of unity.

In 1975, I had befriended Corrymeela's leader, John Morrow and met with him regularly, visiting the centre on occasion. During such visits, I witnessed groups of Protestant and Catholic families from the ghettoes of Belfast and Derry, experiencing brief periods of respite in a common shared life together. Even the most casual of observers could see suspicion, fear and despair giving way to genuine friendships, and a desire to build a different kind of future.

In the ecumenical chapel known as the *crôil* (pronounced *cree*) – the name means 'hearth' or 'place of warming' – people shared their stories, songs and prayers. The experience was deeply touching. Later, as the families began to board the bus back to Belfast or Derry, there were many embraces, tears and a dawning awareness that all were going back to face danger, hostility and the ever-present reality of violence.

Buses left Corrymeela with all aboard. On the outskirts of each city, passengers would transfer to vehicles that would take them respectively back to their 'side' of the dividing walls of prejudice, hate and fear. This was the reality, and the impact of the Corrymeela experience would be severely tested on their return.

The peace movement grew out of such initiatives. My range of contacts expanded. The Franciscan Community on the Deer Park Road frequently offered me hospitality, and the opportunity to meet other courageous people determined to cross the divide in the pursuit of reconciliation.

On one such visit, following a particularly intense period, I got lost in an unfamiliar district. The road was littered with glass and debris and all the street lights had been shot out. I spotted a lone figure and called out, in my unmistakable English accent, for directions. I had been taken for a soldier once when ordering petrol in a Republican area. I feared being similarly identified again, but in the dark the consequences might have been different. But Ireland is Ireland and surprises are never far away. 'The boys have been havin' a bit of an ol' time,' said the stranger with a chuckle, before painstakingly explaining where I had gone wrong, and pointing me in a safe direction.

As the seventies unfolded and the initial panic of trying to end the violence gave way to more reasoned and considered activity,

I met the redoubtable Mary Grant, then a Roman Catholic Sister. Mary was facilitating groups along the so-called 'Peace Line' between the two communities, under a freshly constructed barrier of Berlin Wall proportions.

In such groups, some folk who had met at Corrymeela and elsewhere came together to pursue friendships and seek practical expressions of peace-building. 'We are somewhere between Good Friday and Easter Day in our lives,' remarked Mary one evening. At the time it felt more like Good Friday with the murders, abductions and bombings. Increasing numbers of people were emigrating.

By locating this space 'between Good Friday and Easter Day', Mary sought to hold out the promise of resurrection, of new life. These intentional groups were the living representation of that hope, even though in number they were small and apparently insignificant.

David Bleakley, a former Northern Ireland Labour Party Member of Parliament, and a doughty campaigner for peace, used to encourage people to become 'a one per cent peacemaker', and 'to make them an offer they can't refuse'. Groups such as those facilitated by Father Aidan of the Franciscans, Mary Grant and many anonymous community leaders were doing just that, and this gave energy to the nascent Peace Process.

One day, I stood outside a house on the frontier between two communities at the top of the Andersonstown Road and the Ballymurphy Estate. This convergence was something of a hot spot. The front door of this property was always open, yet the house was pockmarked with bullet holes. Occupied by one of the community leaders, the bullet marks were testimony to the danger they were in. It was a sign of their courage that they were prepared to risk assassination, in order to provide a place of refuge. 'Blessed' indeed are such peacemakers.

What touched me most amongst these groups were people's openness and humility. There was also something wonderfully naïve. One night we were sharing people's favourite hymns. A Protestant might say, 'I love "The Lord's My Shepherd"', and, before the words were out, one of the Catholics would say, 'Me too! We didn't think you knew *our* hymns.' Or when talking about Bible stories, a Catholic would say, 'I like the story of the Prodigal Son', and a Protestant would respond 'We didn't think you Catholics read the Bible – and that's my favourite too'. It was out of such ignorance that misperceptions and prejudice led to distrust, hatred and violence.

By the very nature of my life and work, the time I spent there was always limited. But however limited the time I had, it was about sticking with the task, not until I thought it had been completed, but when those being accompanied thought so. Being present, walking with, supporting, and sharing - in some measure - the fate of those being accompanied, was both a privilege and a growing vocation.

5

Prayer

There is a 'time to every purpose under the heaven',[1] observed the author of Ecclesiastes. That is certainly true of peacemaking. Knowing when to act, and when to wait to act, are matters of fine judgement.

By the mid 1980s, the most recent 'Troubles' had been continuous for nearly two decades. Throughout that time, successive governments had made various attempts to secure their ending. On 15 November 1985, Margaret Thatcher, prime minister of Great Britain and Northern Ireland, and Garret FitzGerald, the *taoiseach* of Ireland, signed the Anglo-Irish Agreement.

At first sight, the Agreement appeared a step forward. However, many people in the thick of it felt it was too soon. Fifteen Unionist Members of Parliament resigned over what they saw as an act of betrayal. On the Nationalist side, Fitzgerald's involvement was seen by Sînn Feîn as a ploy to exclude them from a future role in government, as well as reneging on the Republic of Ireland's constitutional commitment to a United Ireland.

Meanwhile, the firebrand preacher Ian Paisley held a mass rally to form 'Ulster Resistance' with the specific commitment to 'take direct action' to bring an end to the Anglo-Irish Agreement. This threat was perceived as including possible armed intervention.

I received a number of phone calls from contacts pleading for intervention by the government. I had several conversations with my MP Bernard Weatherill, then Speaker of the House of Commons. I explained the fears of those who had been courageously and painstakingly building support for resolving conflict at the local level. I said that if the Agreement was not to lead to further violence, people in those neighbourhoods would need tangible support and protection. It was not to be.

Over the coming months and years, the Provisional IRA intensified its campaign, and this was epitomised by the Remembrance Day bombing in Enniskillen in 1987. A young woman, Mary Wilson, was killed. In an emotional interview with the BBC later that day, her father, Gordon, offered forgiveness to his daughter's killers and begged that there would be no revenge.

A few months later in March 1988, two British army corporals were pulled from their car in Andersonstown and killed by the Provisionals. The justification for the murders was that the soldiers were suspected of being Loyalist gunmen. It was a bleak moment, and with the exception of the actual moment of killing itself, largely captured on television.

I went to Belfast to meet with different groups, but chiefly to talk with Cahal Daly, the Roman Catholic bishop of Down and Connor. Daly was pastorally responsible for the Catholics of West Belfast. In the aftermath of the killings, he issued a strong statement of condemnation of the Provisionals. He appealed to the Catholic population 'to turn to peaceful and constructive ways of promoting justice, peace and human rights'.

On the day of my visit, Daly had been subject to excoriating criticism by Sinn Feîn. Its spokesman had declared on ITV's *World in Action* that 'Bishop Daly no longer speaks for the people of West Belfast'. Such accusations were not new to Daly. He rarely challenged them, believing that despite their propaganda, the Provisionals did not lead a popular armed struggle in the way the IRA had in 1916.

Softly spoken and mild-mannered, the bishop who would soon become cardinal welcomed me into his home for an hour or so of conversation. He saw the murders as a potential tipping point. 'If there were a United Ireland tomorrow,' he said of Sinn Feîn, 'they wouldn't know what to do with it.'

Daly described the bloodshed as a moment of 'grave spiritual danger for sections of our Catholic community'. He called on Sinn Feîn to repudiate violence in its pursuit of a United Ireland, and to take a political route. He explained that whilst Sinn Feîn required its supporters to 'give unambiguous support to the armed struggle', the Church could only declare such activity to be sinful. 'Evil must be rejected totally and unequivocally. There must be no ambivalence, no double standards, no selective indignation.'

It was brave talk. The funerals of IRA volunteers took place in Catholic churches. At one such funeral, the parish priest Father Tom Toner, himself a critic of the IRA and on their 'hit list', called for the congregation to 'love their enemies'. Pointing to the dead man's brother, a boy with Down's syndrome, he asked, 'Would you have the courage to follow his example, he who does not know how to hate?'

Despite his criticism of the murders, Daly passionately argued against the conditions that he saw leading to the recruitment of people into the paramilitary organisations. 'Too many were born into the Troubles, raised on the streets by violence, unemployed, harassed by the security forces. Is it any wonder that people turn to violence?' he concluded.

As our conversation continued, Daly reflected on a series of events that while having no intrinsic intentional connection, nevertheless had a bearing on the tragedy of Andersonstown. He cited the failure of the appeal of the Birmingham Six, various shootings by security personnel, gun and grenade attacks by Loyalists in the Milltown Cemetery, and the apparent cooling of British support for the Anglo-Irish Agreement. He said that all these events spoke of a beleaguered and neglected people.

I asked him, 'Apart from prayer, what can ordinary Christians do for reconciliation in Northern Ireland?' 'Apart from prayer?' he queried. 'Surely all prayer reveals our own complicity, our own prejudice, the complexity of the situation. Prayer should lead us to repentance, a repentance that leads us to understand, to be better informed, to be enlightened. Any prayer for peace and reconciliation must have to do with our own responsibility to work for reconciliation. All prayer calls for action, and part of that action is to call on the British government to act responsibly towards all the people of Northern Ireland.'

Bishop Daly asked me to say the Lord's Prayer with him, and asked, 'Will you pray for me as I will pray for you?' I assured him that I would.

Whether or not the Anglo-Irish Agreement was timely, paradoxically the murder of the soldiers in Andersonstown was something of a watershed. At the time Bishop Daly's call for Sînn Feîn to reject the armed struggle and work for a political way forward seemed to fall on deaf ears. Yet it was eventually the path chosen by the Sînn Feîn president Gerry Adams and chief negotiator Martin McGuinness, and eventually led to the Good Friday Agreement in April 1998.

The encounter with Cahal Daly convinced me that no matter how little we appear to change things, yet as we should still try. As Albert Einstein put it: 'The world is a dangerous place to live in ... not because of the people who do evil, but because of the people who sit and let it happen.' Being in the company of Cahal Daly, and those like him, was giving me hope that there would indeed be – as Ecclesiastes remarks – 'a time for peace'.[2]

6

Hidden curriculum

'People say it's no worse than it was. If it's no better, it's a lot worse.' These words are from a play, *Hidden Curriculum* by Graham Reid, staged during 1994 whilst I was on an extended visit to Northern Ireland. The play was about Protestant paramilitaries and how they were recruited. Though written some 12 years earlier, the play was timely, and its sentiment 'the same is worse' depressingly accurate.

1994 offered the first hints of a tipping point in the conflict. Indications of the possibility of talks about talks were emerging from Sînn Feîn. The pre-requirement was a ceasefire, something often discussed, occasionally implemented, but easily broken. Tiny fragments of hope were emerging. Two such 'fragments' occurred in conversations I had with David Bleakley and John Morrow.

Both men spoke of a new mood within the churches. The 'apocalypse' that had raged across the working-class communities had largely passed by the middle classes. The word 'apocalypse' means 'to reveal'. Long-held hatreds, frequently expressed in violence, had been revealed to many in both Loyalist and Republican neighbourhoods.

During 1993, 'An Inter Church Symposium' was called together in Armagh by the Anglican archbishop Robin Eames, and his Roman Catholic counterpart, Cardinal Tomás Ó'Fiaich to address the challenges of sectarianism. This event and its subsequent documents offered a new direction for theological and political thinking; a kind of political theology.

Bleakley and Morrow sought to share this thinking with me. Bleakley described it as 'a window of opportunity - a *kairos* moment' in the long-running peace process. Both men remarked on a change in tone. People from both sides of the community began to speak of 'An All Island of Ireland' or an 'Agreed Ireland', rather than a 'United Ireland' solution to the conflict.

Writing in *The Guardian*,[1] Will Hutton reflected that 'An All Island future will not be the old Nationalist dream.' Bleakley spoke of how both parts of Ireland had shared an 'Island of Ireland' identity. 'Northern Ireland is distinctively Irish,' he said, and for him this was one of the keys to the future. For both Bleakley and Morrow, this insight provided a sign of hope that might lead to peace.

Bleakley noted that the recent ending of apartheid in South Africa, and the emerging moves towards conflict resolution in Latin America, offered lessons to be learned. Hope, rather than optimism, surrounded rumours of a ceasefire. Paramilitaries appeared increasingly weary and resentful of the armed struggle. Yet there was reluctance by such groups to give up too easily, because of the difficulty of relaunching violent campaigns.

Although the signs were very weak, Bleakley's perception of a *kairos* moment did seem to be true. John Morrow spoke of the impact of the ecumenical communities such as Corrymeela, Cornerstone, Columbanus and others that had sprung up in search of reconciliation and unity.

Morrow also referred to the impact of the pacifism of Quakers and Mennonites, and the quiet presence of their witness in households on the frontline between communities. He called it, 'A recognition of the God given nature of diversity, but also the God intention of unity and harmony: a unity in diversity.'

Through these small, apparently insignificant groups of diverse individuals, common bond was being made, and a growing sense of the need for peace and conflict resolution was gaining traction.

Despite these 'straws', the prevailing mood was discerned in the title of Seamus Heaney's poem, 'Whatever You Say Say Nothing'. Still, passwords, winks and nods conveyed people's real feelings and allegiances. This spirit so often dominated relationships. Something understood was conveyed in silence or gesture. 'Polite relationships should not be confused with trusting relationships', observed the authors of *Sectarianism – A Discussion Document*.[2]

Morrow reminded me that any attempt to understand division requires people to recognise the extent to which lives are lived defensively in divided societies, dominated by 'the realism of fear'.

Too often the stories speak of 'what has been done to us', rather than mutual trust.

'We are represented towards each other by rival self-righteousness, and any awareness that the other has reason to fear us is concealed from my view,' observed one contributor, Frank Wright.[3] All of this was the very antithesis of the teaching and person of the Christ whom both Catholics and Protestants sought to defend.

To move from such intransigence to truly embracing God's love in Christ was indeed a radical assault on the boundaries of fear and prejudice. Yet as St Paul puts it: 'while we were enemies, we were reconciled to God through the death of his Son.'[4]

It is all too easy to judge. The irony is, of course, that fear and discrimination impact upon us all, particularly when we perceive our security to be threatened. What Morrow and Bleakley bore testimony to was the theo-politics of small steps that were beginning to address such fears and hurts.

The Sectarianism symposium had provided something of a stepping stone towards new possibilities: 'Contempt and hostility do not bring people to the truth; and surely no Christian should have such an attitude towards anyone, least of all those who acknowledge that Christ died for them.'[5] Many were recognising that if hope nourished by the Spirit of God was to be realistic, practical politics had to go hand in hand with faith.

Church and communal vocabularies were increasingly including words and phrases such as 'security', 'interests', 'identity', 'equal understanding', 'non-discrimination', 'participation in the common life'. Questions too were emerging. 'How might people be given security?' and 'How can interests and identities be maintained whilst securing equal understanding of each before the law?'

Given the history of discrimination in Northern Ireland from person to person, as well as in institutions and structures, only legislation could bring an end to the culture of superiority and inferiority. Elsewhere in the United Kingdom, the Race Relations Act of 1965 was in force, prohibiting discrimination on grounds of race, gender, or religious conviction. It did not apply in Northern Ireland.

Addressing such matters in law, as well as enabling and empowering people to re-learn how to live together, was no mean task. How might differences be addressed, without wanting to hurt, destroy, dominate, or separate from the other? What would peace look like? Morrow concluded that the Hebrew concept of *shalom* – a word I have mentioned earlier, often interpreted 'peace' – might hold a key.

Shalom means 'integral wholeness'. It brings together the political, social and religious.

> Thus welfare and salvation, wellbeing, peace of mind, good fortune and social harmony are mutually complementary components of one and the same *shalom*, itself as indivisible as the biblical oneness of politics, society, nature, and theology – all parts of a single world order under one Creator God.[6]

John Morrow and other church leaders were seeking to re-engage with the truth that ultimate loyalty was not to the flag, tradition or tribe, but to God. This, the God who in Jesus Christ revealed our status as children of God, commands us to act boldly, seek peace and take risks for building a just society through the making of good relationships.

John reflected that none of this was possible if a spirit of forgiveness did not emerge from the process. Forgiveness is seldom easy, and it cannot be demanded. It is always an act of grace. Only if forgiveness is offered and received does it make possible and true that phrase so beloved of the media: 'This must never happen again.'

David Bleakley was always a source of accounts of forgiveness and healing. One such example, which he told often resonated with many, including me: Mary Kylie was a Catholic, whose son Patrick had been killed because of his friendship with a Protestant girl. One night she had a 'visitation' from her dead son. She thought she heard him ask her for a cup of tea, something he frequently did when alive. She made the tea and then, realising the 'voice' was only in her head, threw the tea at the wall which held a crucifix. 'Jesus,' she shouted, 'why did you let them kill my son?' As the tea dripped down the crucifix she again heard the voice: 'Ma, make me a cup of tea, but never again like that.'

Her clairvoyant experience led her to write to other bereaved mothers, and to establish Women of the Cross, a support group for women from both sides of the conflict. Included were mothers of military personnel and paramilitaries, as well as civilians and children. These gestures were small signs of hope in the process of creating a wider peace.

Following one of David's radio broadcasts a woman, a cleaner, phoned him. She spoke of how every time she heard of the death of a soldier 'her stomach would fill with warmth'. She would call the regimental chaplain and ask for the address of the dead soldier's wife, or girlfriend. Then she would write a short loving letter and, enclosing a gift, sign it simply: 'An Irish Mother.'

Many women replied to her, but one in particular touched Bleakley. It was from a woman named Valerie. She wrote, 'I gave Arthur to Ireland, and it killed him. I felt nothing but bitterness until I read your letter and received your gift. I will buy a present for my child, not yet one, and I will tell her it was from you, and how you taught me to love. Signed Valerie, aged 19.'

Both these women understood the gut compassion that Jesus experienced in the face of loss or need. These 'one per cent peacemakers' became the foundation of the more elaborate political peace processes.

David Bleakley would constantly remind us to:

Pray Peace
Think Peace
Speak Peace
Act Peace

This was the true *Hidden curriculum*.

7

'It's going to be all right'

It was a cool summer's evening in 1970 when a loud bang interrupted the balmy calm. It was clearly a bomb, and nearby too. It was the first of the bombs that was to blight Omagh, my wife's hometown, over the coming 40 years. A house and home had been destroyed a few short streets away from where we were staying. Thankfully, on this occasion, no life was lost.

On a Saturday afternoon in August 1998, nearly thirty years later, a car bomb was detonated in the town, killing 29 people, two unborn children, and injuring 200. It was the worst single atrocity of the Troubles. It came a few months after the people of Northern Ireland had agreed to a peace process widely known as 'The Good Friday Agreement'.

I heard the news of the bomb in a small Donegal village some forty miles away. On advice, we left travelling to Omagh until the Sunday. We arrived to a scene of terrible devastation. An eerie silence had descended upon the town. Five of my mother-in-law's neighbours were among the dead. Her own punctilious habits had saved her as she had shopped in the morning as usual.

The Archbishop of Canterbury asked me to represent him at the Memorial Service, held a week after the bombing. Prior to the service a reception was held for relatives of the victims, local dignitaries and political leaders. It was a tense occasion. There was much fear and anger from both Loyalist and Republican communities. Each queried why the other had representatives present. Yet it was a first in that both communities were together in the same place. Despite the anger, the overall emotion was of a deep sense of loss.

Dee and I mingled with groups and individuals, offering condolences, listening to remembrances of loved ones, affirming support. After the service, we accompanied the President of Ireland to the Tyrone County Hospital. Here, we met the medical teams who a short week before, had managed the trauma of the atrocity with professionalism and skill.

This was also the first time that I was to meet political leaders, with whom I would dialogue in subsequent years. The most significant conversation was with Martin McGuinness.[1] As we shook hands, he held mine for a few moments and looked me in the eye. 'Bishop,' he said, 'we are in the peace process for the long haul. Omagh is the abyss into which we have looked, and there is no going back. Nothing like this must happen again.'

For McGuinness and Sînn Feîn, the decision to join the peace process had been a radical one. McGuinness' remark about the 'abyss' was as spiritually incisive as it was accurate. For four long decades the conflict had been binding all sides into an abyss of nothingness and evil. Out of the darkness each now faced the choice of freedom from the past.

Omagh was a defining moment in the Peace Process. Despite moves towards a ceasefire in 1994, attacks continued on both mainland Britain and in Ireland until 1997. Following an intense bombing campaign in 1996, David Bleakley and I had been involved in a postcard campaign. People were invited to send a postcard to a postcode address with the words 'Stop the Violence'. It was a brief but successful action.

Steps towards a more lasting peace were orchestrated by the US Senator George Mitchell. In 1997 the Provisional IRA, through its political wing Sînn Feîn, signed up to what became known as 'The Mitchell Principles', the forerunner of the Good Friday Agreement of 10 April 1998.

Gerry Adams, president of Sînn Feîn, and Martin McGuinness participated in the talks. Signing up to the principles did not bring an immediate resolution to the conflict. It did eventually lead to the Provisional IRA putting its arsenal of weapons beyond use.

The towering figure of the Reverend Ian Paisley was not present at the Omagh Service. For more than 40 years, he had dominated the Northern Irish scene, as the strident voice of Protestant loyalism and founder of the Democratic Unionist Party. Shortly after I was appointed Bishop of Bath and Wells, Ian Paisley visited the Bishop's Palace. During the summer months the house and garden were open to the public. Having been told of his presence, I invited him and his wife, Eileen, in for tea.

It was surreal having this man, whose influence had been so significant, sitting in the drawing room, drinking tea and reminiscing with Dee, who had taught in his constituency during the sixties. We did not talk peacemaking that day. However, something very surprising happened. As he prepared to leave, Paisley turned to me and said, 'Bishop, you know, when you get to my age, you begin to wonder whether you have done it all right.'

It was an extraordinary admission from a man whose public persona pervaded certainty. Later he was to explain that during a severe illness from which he nearly died, he believed God told him to do all he could to make peace. He had not welcomed the Good Friday Agreement, and many at the Omagh Memorial Service had been distressed by his absence. Times were moving on – and new initiatives were essential if there was to be real peace.

The encounter in our home was to lead to regular contact between us. Over the next few years, as the setting up of the Northern Ireland Assembly was happening, a number of problems appeared to threaten it. Whenever one of these occurred, I would call his home at breakfast time and talk through the concern. More often than not there would be a jovial response, 'Oh! Don't you worry, Bishop; it's all going to be all right.'

In due course Ian Paisley was elected First Minister of the Northern Ireland Assembly, with his former nemesis, Martin McGuinness, as Deputy First Minister. I had been invited to Stormont to meet both men, though due to a more pressing engagement Martin McGuinness was unable to be present. As I entered the newly decorated suite of the First Minister, Dr Paisley greeted me warmly, and as we sat over tea remarked: 'You know, Martin McGuinness is a very fine Catholic boy.'

I believe he meant it. What had become clear in public, at least, was that these two old foes had become reconciled, and a real warmth and affection existed between them. The media christened them 'The Chuckle Brothers', not entirely a compliment, but it stuck. When Paisley died, McGuinness paid a generous tribute to him, and I was privileged to be invited to his family Memorial Service.

Of course, the temptation existed to ask why such a rapprochement had not been possible 40 years before, and how much suffering and death could have been prevented. But people can only move at the pace at which they are able. Overcoming historic prejudice and fear requires a change of heart, and such things cannot be forced. At the same time it must be recognised that historically both men had contributed to much hurt and sadness through their previous intransigence.

Many people were unable to accept their reconciliation, some seeing it as little more than a search for power and status. Undoubtedly political deliverance is not the kingdom of heaven, and motives are always difficult to determine. But if these two men, representing the views they did, had not sought the 'things that make for peace', the conflict would still be raging, and much further pain, suffering and loss experienced.

Since 2005 much has been happening at the grassroots towards building a lasting peace. Former paramilitaries on both sides have found ways of working towards coexistence. Rivalry and internecine squabbles still occur, and occasionally overflow into violence, but much of that is criminal rather than ideological in origin.

One example of this occurred a few years ago when a peace activist friend and I were invited to visit a Loyalist group. Since the Good Friday Agreement they had done some innovative work in conciliation. Inevitably, historic tensions would emerge and renewed conflict was always a possibility. Our visit took place after one such local intra-Loyalist incident, and a real possibility existed that arms might be taken up again. For several hours that morning we witnessed fear, anger and vitriol pouring out from those present.

Listening patiently, we occasionally asked a question that drew attention to their experience in their reconciliatory work. We hoped to encourage them to reflect on how they had defused such situations before. As the hours went by, reason began to emerge out of rage. Within a few days, equilibrium had been restored, but the occasion served as a reminder that peace-building is a process, not a panacea.

During six years as a bishop in the House of Lords, I contributed to debates, the All-Party Parliamentary Group on Northern Ireland, and maintained contact with groups and individuals on the implementation of the Good Friday Agreement. Issues remain that could derail it: the historic feuds, when and where the flags should be flown, and the issue of criminality.

Whenever people have said to me 'how good it is that there is now peace in Northern Ireland', I counsel that peacemaking is a process. Achieving it calls for patience, tolerance, endless acts of forgiveness and 'forgetteries'. For people to be truly reconciled is not simply a matter of an armistice or peace agreement.

It is encouraging that many groups from other conflict areas now visit Northern Ireland to learn from the peace process. Much remains to be done. Aspects of the Good Friday Agreement remain to be implemented. 'Addressing the past' still remains politically sensitive and there has been no equivalent of the South African Truth and Reconciliation Commission.

Yet there is forgiveness. The German pastor Martin Niemöller, a victim of the Nazis, often visited Northern Ireland during the early days of the Troubles. He observed to Bleakley: 'Every day hundreds of acts of forgiveness are carried out in this country. Far more than anywhere else in Europe.' It is a grace that simply must continue if everything is 'going to be all right'.

8

The nuclear issue: 'Farther on and further in'

6 August 1945 marked the moment when the first atomic bomb, codenamed 'Little Boy', was dropped on the city of Hiroshima in Japan. A blinding transfiguring white flash was followed by the deaths and terrible suffering of thousands of men, women and children.

On 6 August 1968 our eldest 'Little Boy' was born. We named him David, meaning 'Beloved'. He came and has remained as a light in our lives. At the time we did not make the connection with Hiroshima. Neither did we make the connection that in Christian tradition, 6 August is a celebration of the Feast of the Transfiguration of Christ. In this mystical moment of divine revelation, Jesus is affirmed by God in the presence of witnesses with the words: 'This is my Son, the Beloved; listen to him!'[1]

On the thirtieth anniversary of the dropping of 'Little Boy', our family and friends sailed from Tenby to Caldey Island to visit the Benedictine monastery. Media coverage and growing numbers demanding nuclear disarmament gave the occasion particular significance.

Leaving the boat, something drew me towards the chapel away from the others who were visiting the gift shops in search of the cheese, shortbread and perfumes manufactured by monks. That day I did make the connection with the Feast of Transfiguration. In the church built on the site of a sixth-century foundation, I lit a candle and sat alone in silence. In my head echoed the words, 'This is my Son, the Beloved; listen to him!' Wistful questions arose: why have we not listened? What have we not heard?

On Caldey, I reflected on the paradox of the mystery of the Transfiguration of Jesus on the mountain, and the blasphemy of atomic warfare. I thought on the 'belovedness' not only of my son on his birthday, but of us all, by the Christ who was transfigured in dazzling white to be the Light of the World.

Something was beginning to dawn on me then that I would not able to articulate for several more years. My moment of disclosure came in early 1980 when I visited another island, Cumbrae in the Clyde Estuary. On a retreat at the Cathedral of the Isles, I gazed out of my bedroom window at the black hulls of the Polaris submarines moored across the river Clyde at Faslane.

I had taken the retreat to try to address my complicity in a time of conflict and confusion with others with whom I was in ministry. It was not an easy time, and I realise with hindsight it was more important for me then to want to be right than to love others simply for who they were. During a period of quiet reading and reflection, I was pulled up short by some words of the Trappist monk Thomas Merton, in his *Seeds of Contemplation*.[2] He was writing about spiritual pride, the danger of becoming isolated in self-satisfaction, of even thinking of 'oneself as a prophet of God', with a mission to reform the world.

The words cut through me like a sharp pointed sword. Then Merton observed: 'I must look for my identity, somehow, not only in God but in other men (*sic*). I will never be able to find myself if I isolate myself from the rest of mankind as if I were a different kind of being.' The message to my soul could not have been clearer.

My journeying in peacemaking on the fringes of the Northern Ireland conflict had challenged my 'closed system' view of sin. I was beginning to see sin as structural as well as personal. As I reflected on the conflict I had witnessed, I saw it beset by structural injustice, violence, powerlessness, poverty, unemployment and meaninglessness. Now I had to face how both the personal and the structural were intertwined in my life.

Instead of loving what you think is peace, wrote Merton,

> love other men (*sic*) and love God above all. And instead of hating the people you think are war makers, hate the appetites and the disorder in your own soul which are the causes of war.

> If you love peace, then hate injustice, hate tyranny, hate greed
> – but hate these things in *yourself*, not in another.

Across the river, glinting in the sunlight, lay the menacing long black hulls of the nuclear submarines. Wisps of innocent steam billowed from the pipes on the conning towers. Around them fussed naval pickets, protecting, supplying. Such awesome power, so apparently at peace, yet resting like the dragon, ready to strike and wreak havoc upon humanity.

Contemplating this activity, I reflected on my internal struggles. I saw myself with a heightened sense of awareness as part of the self-centred, self-destructive, God-hating humanity, which Christ came to confront with love and power. In one of those 'God incidences', I was facing the cost of being a peacemaker.

On the coffee table in my room lay a copy of *Sojourners*, the magazine of a radical Christian community from Washington DC which is led by Jim Wallis, widely known as a preacher and prophet, gaining the ear of presidents and prime ministers around the world. We were to become friends in years to come.

In what seemed to me a first for a Christian journal, were questions such as: 'Can the use of nuclear weapons be reconciled with the gospel of Jesus Christ?'; 'Can their existence be reconciled with the command, *Love your enemies*?'. These began to challenge the unquestioning reliance I had made on deterrence as the basis of my security. I had accepted too readily the argument that 'if we are attacked, we should retaliate'.

What was beginning to become apparent was that trusting such weapons for security might well be pragmatic, but it was not the way Jesus called his followers to live. Neither was it the way of life he practised. Countering the prevailing wisdom of his day, Jesus declared: 'You have heard that it was said, "An eye for an eye and a tooth for a tooth." But I say to you, Do not resist an evildoer. But if anyone strikes you on the right cheek, turn the other also...'[3]

I had seen the futility of 'an eye for an eye and a tooth for a tooth' as a means of resolving conflict on the streets of Belfast. In the coming years, I was to witness dead bodies in the streets of cities across the globe, all as a result of so-called 'conventional' weapons – whether home-made, or the product of the burgeoning arms trade.

Subsequently, through reading and film I explored the destructive impact of the atomic bombing of the Japanese cities of Hiroshima and Nagasaki. By the standards of today's nuclear weapons, such weapons were minuscule. Increasingly I questioned how as a Christian I could accept even remote the possibility of their use.

Jesus took the title 'Prince of Peace'. How often had I taken this title and reduced it to being Prince of Peace in my heart, my life; or held it out as a pious hope of a kind of 'pie in the sky when you die'? *If* Jesus had made his dwelling place amongst humanity, as St. John[4] seems to indicate, then such a Divine Ambition is to be reckoned with here and now.

In one of the last speeches before he was murdered by the Provisional IRA off the Sligo coast in Ireland, Earl Mountbatten reflected: 'In the event of a nuclear war there will be no chances, there will be no survivors – all will be obliterated.'[5] Albert Einstein, one of the inventors of the atom bomb, wrote: 'When we released the energy from the atom, everything changed except our way of thinking. Because of that we drift towards unparalleled disaster.'[6] After a visit to the Auschwitz concentration camp, Billy Graham asked:

> Is nuclear holocaust inevitable if the arms race is not stopped? Frankly, the answer is almost certainly, yes. [...] I think many Christians are only just beginning to see that the nuclear arms race is an entirely new factor in human history, and that we cannot be complacent about it, or treat it as just another minor issue. We need to educate the Christian community about the moral and ethical issues that are involved.[7]

These were powerful questioners of the morality of nuclear weapons. But a deeper question was arising: Jesus told his followers that they should seek security in God alone, as he did. But there were consequences. Confronting the raw power of pagan Rome, and the ambivalence of an acquiescent religious elite, Jesus faced judicial execution. To a cowardly individual like myself, such a placing of 'confidence' was hardly appealing!

On Cumbrae, I re-read the gospel accounts. I wanted to see if, and how, they could help me address the challenges I was beginning to face. To understand anything of the meaning of the Transfiguration, I needed to look at the accounts in context.[8] Jesus had been feeding the hungry, healing the sick and blind, and warning his hearers of how the religious and political elites corrupt truth. He challenged his disciples to come off the fence and say who *they* thought he was. They came up with the claim that he is the Messiah – 'The Promised One' who would 'save his people'.

Already harassed by the authorities, Jesus warned his followers of the impending judicial execution that awaited him. They did not want to hear it. The disciples failed to hear Jesus say 'and after three days [he will] rise again' and come 'in the glory of his Father with the holy angels'.[9]

The gospels recall that a few days later, with his core team of four, Jesus climbed a mountain. Here in the words of one writer, 'he was transfigured before them, and his clothes became dazzling white'.[10] By any stretch of the imagination, what followed was mysterious. To the onlooking disciples, the imagery would have been clear: in Scripture it is the martyrs and the just who are clothed in white. Jesus is now identified with these.

Appearing with Jesus on the mountain were Elijah and Moses. In addition a voice was heard: 'This is my Son, the Beloved; listen to him!'[11] The scene was reminiscent of a court. Judgement was being made. But who or what was being judged? To understand this more fully, I reread part of Daniel.[12] He depicted a struggle between 'beasts', representing the powerful of the earth, and the white-robed 'saints'. Eventually there is a trial. At the trial, the beast was judged, and final victory was handed over to the saints (or 'holy ones').

The Transfiguration confirmed two things. Firstly, Jesus was to suffer crucifixion and die. Secondly, he would rise from the dead, come again and judge the powers that have destroyed humanity through the ages. The Transfiguration provides the bridging point between Jesus' warning to his disciples that he is to suffer trial and persecution, and the vision of resurrection and return. The mystical experience on the mountain, and the vision of the 'resurrected' ones – Moses and Elijah – is to reassure those who 'deny themselves and take up the cross'[13] that resurrection, return and judgement are their ultimate hope.

Jesus 'took up the cross', bearing the burden of peacemaking in a hostile world. His invitation for followers to do the same was in order that they too should be peacemakers, 'bearing all things, believing all things, hoping all things.'[14] Increasingly, I was convinced that turning from the acceptance of nuclear weapons towards peacemaking was a task not just for me, but for the Church. Such action would be costly, not least because of the divergence of views between fellow believers.

This came with surprising clarity on my visit to Cumbrae. I had come with personal conflicts to be resolved, but the insights gained in those brief few days were to set a course for wider engagement of what it meant to be a peacemaker.

'Unilateral disarmament'

The effects of the conflict that I had brought with me to Cumbrae remained unresolved for some time. Yet the apparently coincidental choice of a retreat venue with its proximity to the nuclear submarine base was to prove significant in its subsequent resolution. Equally significant was the serendipitous encounter with Sojourners, and the starkness of the question as to whether the use of nuclear weapons could be reconciled with the Gospel of Jesus Christ. All I knew at that moment was that something must be done.

At the time, the Campaign for Nuclear Disarmament (CND) was coordinating a number of rallies across the country. I attended my first in Leeds, joining a group of around a thousand people demanding that Britain must unilaterally disarm. This was to be the first of a number of occasions over the coming years when I took to the streets with others in the cause of nuclear disarmament that would include demonstrations and 'sit downs' at Upper Heyford, and in London.

One of the more intimate occasions organised by clergy, doctors and nurses was on St Luke's the Physician's Day. We walked from St Martin-in-the-Fields to Westminster Abbey, calling at the Ministry of Defence and Downing Street, where we were to present a petition. Those of us leading the procession were so engrossed in conversation that a policeman politely pointed us in the direction of the Ministry of Defence.

I knew that many people engaged in protest over nuclear weapons were prepared to risk being involved with, and indeed be arrested for, offences from wire-cutting and entry to bases to more symbolic actions such as pouring files of blood on replicas of weapons, or taking hammers to military hardware. This was not something I had either the courage or vocation to do. Such action is a matter of conscience. For me, I believed that damage to property was in itself a violent act, and contrary to the spirit of peace of doing unto others as you would have them do unto you.

When the Berrigans burnt draft files in 1968, it was a deeply considered action. They and their collaborators had fasted and prayed at length before undertaking it. Yet for many in the peace movement, including Thomas Merton, the 'violence' of the breaking and entering and burning was 'useless if it is merely pragmatic'.

Writing in the *Catholic Worker*, Merton counselled realism and political moderation. As their spiritual director, he wrote to the Berrigans:

> The whole point of nonviolence is that it rises above pragmatism and does not consider whether it pays off politically ... I admit that may sound odd ... Someone once said, did he not, 'What is truth?' And the One to whom he said it also mentioned, somewhere: 'The truth shall make you free.' It seems to me that this is what really matters.[1]

What the Berrigans, and others who have acted similarly, understood, was summed up again by Merton:

> The standard doctrine of nonviolence says that you can disobey a law you consider to be unjust, but you have to accept the punishment ... In this way you are distinguished from the mere revolutionary. You protest the purity of your witness. You undergo redemptive suffering for religious – or any way ethical – motives. You are 'doing penance' for the sin and injustice against which you have protested.[2]

I never found demonstrating easy. On the night before, I rarely slept well. To my shame, I even hoped and prayed I might be a little bit sick. Once on the street and in the company of others, and to some extent re-energised in the cause, anxiety dissipated and a sense of comradeship and common purpose returned.

In his reading of T.S. Eliot during the First World War, the author E.M. Forster wrote: 'For what, in that world of gigantic horror, was tolerable except the slightest gestures of dissent?'. Commenting on this, Thomas Merton observed: 'We tend to think that massive protest is all that is valid today. The massive is also manipulated and doctored. It is false. The genuine dissent remains individual.' Merton advised to 'not line up with the manipulated group. But to the group that looks like defeat. It looks like futility'.[3]

The significance of this observation came home to me on another Transfiguration day. I was standing by the war memorial in the town where I was a vicar for a silent vigil commemorating the victims of Hiroshima and Nagasaki. I regularly wrote on such issues in my parish magazine, not always to the delight of some of my church members.

After the vigil was ended, a fellow demonstrator, a member of the Socialist Workers Party, whom I knew a little, approached me. 'Your piece on the bomb was OK,' he said referring to an article in the magazine. 'However, brother, you are not in line with the party on abortion.' I explained that I was not a member of 'the party', nor any political body. I said too that my opposition to nuclear weapons was based on my growing belief that they were contrary to my understanding of Jesus Christ, and his mission of reconciliation. Further, I reflected that I believed that God had given humanity creation to steward, protect and nurture, not destroy. I had extended this to the issue of abortion. I trust what I wrote was both simple and sensitive. Clearly my interlocutor did not think so. After a few minutes he went off mumbling something like, 'Well, it still isn't the party line.'

This little incident revealed, and perhaps continues to reveal, something of the tension of being a Christian and peace activist. Much peace activism takes place within the framework of non-sectarian and political bodies. Yes, there is the Christian CND; and there are movements such as the Fellowship of Reconciliation, the Society of Friends – the Quakers, the Anglican Pacifist Movement, of which I have been Bishop Protector, the Catholic *Pax Christi*, and many others. It is in groups such as these, rather in the church as a whole, where support and theological reflection on peacemaking have been found.

Ultimately peacemaking has to be an activity that has integrity. This is not a question of seeking to be right, nor of being a prophet of God nor, as Merton reminded me so forcibly, isolating 'myself from mankind as if I were a different kind of being'.

What lay at the heart of my own struggle in becoming a peace activist was the inconsistency in my own life; the failure of relationships in a leadership team, the need to be right or at least to justify myself, and the disorder in my own soul. Certainly in the early years these realities ate away at my inner core, and distorted my motives and actions.

One warm summer day during a conference amongst people with whom I shared something of my inner struggles, I finally had to face up to the inconsistency in my life and action. 'When,' asked a wise older friend, 'are you going to unilaterally disarm?' He was referring to the ongoing resentment and hurt that had marked out what I perceived at the time as failure in my life and ministry. 'You must be joking!' I cried. 'If I do that, they'll have me!'

'Precisely', he said, 'and if this is hard for you, how much harder must it be for those who have to make the political decisions.' We talked for some time. I knew within his question lay the kernel of an answer to my own spiritual struggle.

I had planned a retreat at a convent near my home soon after. I took Jim Wallis' *Agenda for a Biblical People* with me as well as notepaper, envelopes, stamps and a Bible. Taking in the deep breaths of silence and solitude, I prayed and slept. I began to feel at peace.

The following morning after prayers, some biblical reflection and breakfast, I took pen and paper. For the next few hours, I wrote letters to each of those who had shared in the hurt of disunity in the past. I asked folk to accept that I recognised my contribution to our shared hurt. I said I was sorry for the devastating impact this had on our relationships.

I prayed and walked through the village to the post. It felt like the 'unilateral disarmament' my friend had challenged me to make. All I could do now was wait. In the meanwhile, I began to have I clarity over the wider task to which I was being drawn. I turned to Wallis' book almost at random and read:

> A commitment to Christ entails a radical relationship to money, possessions, violence and war, power, status, success, leadership, ideology and the state. Our relationship to Christ gives us a new relationship to persons and especially to the poor, the weak, the broken, the outcasts, the 'enemies', and the victims of the various systems of this world.[4]

Several days later, replies began to arrive from those to whom I had written. Most expressed appreciation, some acknowledged their own fault. Only one rejected my overture. Sad though that was, I knew that I had nothing else to 'lay down'.

Following this, we would meet in threes and fours from time to time, and share the good memories – and much had been good. Perhaps the most significant conversation was around 30 years later, when we discussed what our common experience of pain and disunity had taught us. We recognised what passed between us was not good – but good had come from it. We reflected on the text in Hebrews where the writer says of Jesus that 'he learned obedience through what he suffered'.[5] The word 'obedience' comes from the Latin *obedire* – meaning 'to listen'. In the intervening years we had all learned to listen: to God, and to our hearts, both with their sin and their desire for reconciliation, forgiveness and peace. We each agreed we had come through what had been bad to a greater listening to God, to our true selves, and to the needs and aspirations of those around us, towards something good.

Jim Wallis also helped me face afresh what commitment to Christ meant:

> The biblical vision provides a vehicle for personal transformation and the emergence of a new people who embody the basis for social liberation. To challenge the system, we must be willing to have our own lives changed, and become radical ourselves. To repudiate the old is not enough; we must act on the basis of a new reality that we have experienced.[6]

I have risked a certain vulnerability here because, firstly, it is not institutions who decide to destroy, or make peace: it is people like you and me. Secondly, to engage in a non-violent opposition to structural violence, we first need to address the inner violence of our own hearts. Only when we grasp the reality of these two truths can we be effective in the task of peacemaking.

Under what sign?

Outside the United Nations building in New York is a remarkable statue of St George and the Dragon. It is constructed from the remnants of rockets that once had the capacity to carry nuclear weapons. The dragon is depicted as a weapon of war. Even more remarkably, this sculpture was given in 1990, during the Cold War, before Mikhail Gorbachev brought in *glasnost*.

At that time, atheism was the official creed of the Soviet Union. Yet taking things at face value is not always wise. I was once told a story that during a visit to the United States, when he was the Soviet president, Gorbachev was overheard saying: 'When I was a little boy, there were two pictures in my bedroom; one of Lenin, the other an icon. My grandmother asked me one day, "Mikhail, when you are Lord of all the Russias, whom will you serve?"'[1]

Ironically, the highest point of the gifted statue was a cross atop St George's lance. In Russian tradition, the legend of St George has played a significant part in nurturing nationalism, as well as faith. The image is simple and powerful. It represents the struggle against evil and fear.

'What the real dragon George fought against was panic', observes Jim Forest, and the sword 'rests lightly in his hand – meaning that it is the power of God, not the power of man that overcomes evil.'[2]

Today, because of fear of terrorist attacks, increased security measures mean that the statue of St George is not so visible from the sidewalk. It is symptomatic of a kind of universal panic. Yet when I visit New York I still search for a glimpse of what has become something of an icon: a reminder that the defeat of evil ultimately lies in the power of God and not human beings. Whilst Christians believe that the defeat of evil lies in the power of God, humanity has to take responsibility for disarming and preventing nuclear annihilation.

For me, Jim Wallis articulates the contradiction of the cross and the bomb well:

> The sign of the nuclear age is the Bomb … The sign of Christ is the Cross. The Bomb is the countersign to the Cross, it arrogantly threatens to undo the work that the Cross has done. In the Cross, all things are reconciled; in the Bomb, all things are destroyed. In the Cross violence is defeated; in the Bomb violence is victorious. In the Cross evil has been overcome; in the Bomb, evil has dominion. In the Cross, death is swallowed up; in the Bomb, death reigns supreme. Which will hold sway in our times? Will we choose to live under the sign of the Cross or the sign of the Bomb?[3]

This is a matter of conversion. The term 'conversion' is not just that moment of turning to Christ. It is both a moment and a continuous experience. It is an action that does not simply save souls for the future, but as a direct means by which believers bring the kingdom of God in to the world, here and now.

Much contemporary Christianity has lost itself in the labyrinth of its own internal debates, becoming acquiescent on nuclear war. Sadly, Jim's observation of some 30 years ago still holds true: 'A Church that places its trust in the Bomb is a Church that no longer trusts in the Lord.'[4]

In a rare moment of nostalgia over dinner in Washington recently, I shared with Jim Wallis the extent and influence of Sojourners and his book *Call to Conversion* had upon my own spiritual life. Through *con*-versation, self-examination and prayer, I had undergone my own *con*-version in respect of nuclear weapons. This truly had become an issue of 'serving God, and not mammon.'[5]

'God does not punish sin. Sin punishes sin,' said Julian of Norwich. The activity of God is always towards redemption. We should not be surprised that in God's economy good comes out of evil; learning from sin. When we see ourselves as 'sinners', we open ourselves up to the possibility of compassion for others like us; we gain understanding, we learn humility and we grow in perception.

A few years ago, I was invited by Channel 4 News to participate in a debate on the renewal of the Trident nuclear weapon system. On the programme was the then Labour Minister of Defence, Des Browne. The debate was lively and yet friendly. During it Browne turned to me and said, 'The trouble with you is that you are an "absolutist".' I think he thought it was a put-down. To me, it is a badge of honour.

Sometime later when I was a bishop in the House of Lords, Browne formed a cohort of former Defence Secretaries and Chiefs of Staff to work on a process for nuclear disarmament. I wrote him a cheeky note asking who was the 'absolutist' now – and could I join the group? One of their number, Lord Tom King, a churchwarden in my diocese, was detailed to explain that the group was limited – but I'd be welcome at all open discussions the group held.

Over recent years in parliament, I have been quietly impressed by the thoughtfulness and commitment of many, particularly in the House of Lords, to issues such as nuclear war. It is a deeply moral question, and the ambiguity of the Church on this issue has been inexcusable. Weapons that threaten the destruction of God-given creation have an immorality about them that far exceeds the other moral issues the Church takes a stand on.

It is all too easy to shift the moral responsibility for nuclear war onto others. We forget that moral responsibility is not selective. When I was chaplain of Scargill House, I had on my study wall a poster which read, 'It's a Sin to Build a Nuclear Weapon'. A friend in the military asked me to positively vet him for promotion. The interviewer, a former nuclear weapons base commander, arrived and saw the poster. 'Do you believe that?' he asked.

'Yes,' I replied.

A friendly, challenging and lengthy discussion followed. At the end he said, 'I used to defend my base from people like you.'

'Dangerous, aren't we?' I quipped.

He paused thoughtfully. 'I too am a believer in Jesus Christ. What you have said today has made me think. I promise to do so.' He left. My friend got his promotion. I don't know what the outcome of the encounter was, but it comes back in essence to what Mahatma Gandhi once said: 'Whatever you do in life will be insignificant, but it is very important that you do it...'

There can be nothing just or secure about nuclear war. Here the challenge of Jesus' words to love our enemies becomes particularly pointed. Whenever we hear of mass murder, we know it is wrong. Yet we are prepared to contemplate mass murder on a cosmic scale in the name of freedom, security and 'our values'.

In 2006, when the government was contemplating the renewal of Trident, a group of 19 bishops co-authored a letter to *The Independent* in which we declared that such weapons were 'profoundly anti-God'. They 'threatened long term and fatal damage to the global environment and its people'. Although we did not state this, as soon as radioactive fallout drifted beyond the country being attacked, a war crime would have been committed. Whatever the original justification for pressing the nuclear button would thereby be de-legitimated. Our letter concluded, 'As such their end is evil and both possession and use profoundly anti-God.'

Although it was secondary, we made the wider moral point that 'the cost (of Trident) could be used to address pressing environmental concerns, the causes of terrorism, poverty and debt'. None of this provoked a debate within the Church itself. There was no talk of the arms race, pleas for prayer for nuclear disarmament or an end to political violence; no response from Church or State to suggest that this issue was, and remains, a deeply spiritual, as well as human, matter. It is as if our hearts are hardened on this issue. Our security in God seems to be established by a morality that is determined only by honesty at work, sexual faithfulness and financial probity. None of those things are wrong *per se* but I cannot recall any debate in the churches' synods that have faced Jesus' injunction of what it means to love enemies in a nuclear age.

In the public arena, little has happened. Arms reduction is at best cosmetic. The threat of nuclear annihilation is not one whit reduced by the nuclear arsenals of the major powers, let alone the silos of Pakistan, India, North Korea and Israel, nor the resources of terror groups that may be able to create 'dirty bombs'. As Thomas Merton has shown:

> We face moral responsibility for the destruction of civilisation or even global suicide. Much more than that, we are going to find ourselves gradually moving into a situation in which

we are practically compelled by the 'logic of circumstances' deliberately to choose a course which leads to destruction.[6]

Opponents of nuclear weapons, whether from an ideological or religious perspective, are seen by the state as foolish at best and unpatriotic at worst. The morality of placing the power to destroy what they have neither created nor can sustain into the hands of a tiny elite, is never debated. The closest we get is the mantra: 'But they are a deterrent, once they are used deterrence ceases.' The trouble is nuclear clocks tick – and times change and the likelihood of deterrence giving way to weapon usage increases.

Sometimes, dealing with an issue as big this, it is helpful to reduce it to something simple – individual, almost. Imagine Jesus as a victim. The bomb obliterates him – gone is the mystery of love, forgiveness, grace, mercy. Gone is the 'love of neighbour', and 'love of enemy' is utterly denied. Gone too is the Jesus who identified himself with the suffering – the one who claimed to count each hair on our heads. To kill another is always to kill Jesus, who represents the Creator and sees the destruction of his creatures, their environment and destiny. As Jim Wallis has concluded, 'He will be there with every father, mother, and terrified child in thousands of infernos. He would feel every death.'[7]

Can we, in the name of Christ, believe that a loving God could contemplate, or permit as moral, the use of such weapons of mass destruction? The challenge for Christians still lies in Jim's question: 'Do we live under the sign of the Christ or the sign of the Bomb?' To date, the question has not been addressed.

The Dirty Wars – Central America: 'To uproot sins...'

One night in the spring of 1987, I stood in the transit hall of San Salvador airport on my way to the Central American country of Nicaragua, surrounded by armed guards from the Treasury Police. Our stopover was for little more than an hour, but the sense of intimidation and latent violence was palpable.

Much of Central America was in turmoil during the 1980s. In El Salvador, Guatemala and Honduras, these conflicts became known as 'The Dirty War'. In Nicaragua, a similar period of conflict had ended with the triumph of a popular uprising.

At the time, I was vicar of a south London suburban parish on a three-month period of study leave. I was researching the impact of theologies of liberation on a resurgent grassroots church.[1] It was my first visit to Nicaragua. Here the Church was in a post-revolutionary situation. In 1980 the overthrow of the ruling elite by Sandinista revolutionaries had led many priests, Religious and laity to radically reappraise their understanding of the Church's life and witness.

Central America has not featured particularly strongly in the Anglican tradition. However, the impact of so-called 'liberation theology' emerging from the Roman Catholic tradition was impacting all contemporary efforts at mission. One particular individual had caught the attention of the wider world, a Catholic archbishop, Oscar Romero. On 24 March 1980, he was murdered in San Salvador by an unknown assassin. His death changed the course of history in the region, but not before conflict had torn countless lives apart, leaving, even today, a legacy of poverty and oppression.

The region had been 'Christianised' by the Catholic Church, during the Spanish and Portuguese colonisation of the fifteenth century. The rapacious nature of the colonists led to six centuries of unholy alliance between the ruling powers and the Catholic Church. The alliance remained in place until well into the second half of the twentieth century.

During the 1960s and 1970s a wind of change began to blow through the Catholic Church. In the mid 1960s, Pope Paul VI called together a meeting of cardinals and bishops to the Second Vatican Council. He died before its fulfilment, and the radical change the Council was to present to the world was overseen by Pope John XXIII.

Many within the Church saw this as a period of revolution that would ignite a new spirit of hope for all humanity, particularly the poor. The Latin Mass was replaced by use of the vernacular. Bible reading was encouraged amongst the laity, with new translations. Historical intolerance of other Christian bodies was replaced by a new mood of ecumenism. Priests and Religious discarded clerical dress. Pastoral plans were drawn up to empower people to be what Jesus called 'yeast in the dough'. A 'commitment to a preferential option for the poor' refocused the Church's mission.

In Latin America, Catholics and some Protestants began to embrace what Romero had called the Church's 'difficult mission': 'to uproot sins from history, to uproot sins from the political order, to uproot sins from the economy, to uproot sins from wherever they are'. Brave representatives of this vision had emerged throughout Latin America; Romero in El Salvador and Archbishop Helder Camara in Brazil, articulated this vision with growing radicalism.

Romero reflected: 'When we struggle for human rights, for freedom, for dignity ... we are not straying from God's promise.' Camara said: 'When I give food to the poor, they call me a saint. When I ask why they are poor, they call me a communist.'

Salvadoran Lutheran bishop Medardo Gomez summed up what was increasingly an ecumenical challenge in the region: 'The first thing I want to impress upon you is that in our desire to be faithful to the gospel we have to come close to the people, to get to know the people the better to communicate God's love.' From both a Protestant and Catholic perspective, this insight into the Gospel was to prove timely and relevant for Christians experiencing political ferment. However, such an outlook was not universal. In Nicaragua the conservative Archbishop Obando y Bravo continued to support the status quo, and real anxieties were expressed from the essentially conservative Church about this 'revolutionary doctrine'.

The initial purpose of my visit to Latin America stemmed from a desire to witness the impact and growth of base Christian communities.[2] At the time I had little knowledge of the history of the region and its conflicts, a situation that was to change as I engaged with the impact of the conflict, and the witness of Christians.

Readers who are aware of the history of revolution in the region may wish to skip the brief summary that follows.[3] The primary cause of conflict lay in the ownership of land that in the 1980s was largely owned by ruling elites, native peoples and religious orders.

During the nineteenth century, native groups and religious orders were perceived by ruling elites as 'obstacles to progress'. Land owners and governments wanted to produce more bananas and coffee. The government ordered that to facilitate such growth, the lands of native peoples were to be 'freed'.

Despite an era of modernisation and development in the mid twentieth century, bananas and coffee remained the mainstay of the economy. Towards the end of the century, as US multinationals gained an increasing grip on world markets, demand for land for the production of beef and cotton grew. This in turn led to further exploitation of land.

Growing more cotton meant a wider use of pesticides, and beef production required the felling of forests. As Phillip Berryman has observed, both meant: 'The situation of many people worsened, especially the growing numbers of the landless poor. The development model that produced growth brought little improvement to many people.'[4] Migration increased, chiefly to the United States, Mexico and Honduras. Locally, it led to the rise of revolutionary movements; the Sandinistas[5] in Nicaragua and the FMLN[6] movement in El Salvador. Though formed at different times, it is generally agreed that 1979 was the critical year in which both movements became notably militant.

These bodies were influenced by Marxist ideologies, as was Fidel Castro's Cuban revolution in the 1950s. As with Cuba, this was seen by the USA to threaten democracy, leading it to support various dictatorial governments, offer covert military training and assist in repression, including torture.

The growing political ferment and repression of the dispossessed was paralleled by the theological and pastoral earthquake in the Catholic Church that followed Vatican 2. In 1968 Latin American bishops met in conference in the Colombian city of Medellin. Here the Church's 'preferential option for the poor' was reaffirmed, and wide-ranging debate as to how the Church, its clergy and Religious should respond to revolutionary activity.

Questions such as: 'What does Christian love mean in a class society?'; 'How should the mission of the Church be defined?'; 'What does Jesus' saying "Blessed are the poor" mean today?' were posed. Berryman reflected: 'For centuries "God's will" had seemed to be that the world remain as it is: now suddenly "God's will" was re-interpreted to mean that people should work together in community and solidarity for a more just world.'[7]

The combination of political insurgence, together with an 'option for the poor' being widely expressed by Christians of all traditions, led to the first modern revolution to be carried out with the active participation and support of Christians. Unsurprisingly, it provoked controversy and was eventually to lead to bloody conflict.

Solidarity

I first arrived in Managua, the capital of Nicaragua, late one June night in 1987. Prior to leaving the USA, I had spent the few days in Miami with friends of friends who treated me with great kindness. It was a challenging time. Devout Christians, they supported the US policy of covert war, and its role in the training and financing of counter-revolutionary movements. Deeply opposed to my intended visit to Nicaragua, they did everything they could to dissuade me, including taking me to a meeting led by the leader of the Contras,[1] who were seeking to overthrow the Sandinista government. I was warned that my life would be at risk, and I would be treated as a spy. I was frightened by all this. Briefly I wondered anxiously whether I was too much an 'innocent abroad'.

A couple of days earlier, I had visited the Sojourners community and met Joyce Hollyday from Witness for Peace, and other agencies committed to seeking peace and justice for the people of Central America. I shared in their practical commitment to 'welcoming the stranger, feeding the hungry, and clothing the naked', and gave out post-dated supermarket food on the Sojourners food line one Saturday morning.

I heard the prayer of Mary Glover, 'That God would feed the hungry, and stay the hand of the mugger and rapist today, and bless God's holy name. And when we meet you in the line today, help us to treat you well.' This solidarity was expressed to me as 'a sign of tenderness between people who are all united in the same struggle but in different fields of conflict'.

In Washington I had been amongst people of like mind. But groups like Sojourners, and the theology of a 'gospel option for the poor', were anathema to my hosts in Miami. In Washington, I had been briefed on the current US foreign policy in Central America.

A policy that, in the words of Morris Morley, was based 'on the notion of violence as the ultimate arbiter of power and guarantor of basic U.S. interests – political, economic and strategic'.[2]

I was worried about the flight to Managua. I would witness both the reality and aftermath of military conflict. I would have a spiritual struggle of my own. My Miami hosts could easily identify with the sign outside an Alabama store 'Jesus is Lord – We buy and sell guns',[3] but would see Christians taking arms against the established power as unscriptural. Perhaps in their conservatism lay a little of my own.

I had to trust my judgement, and rely on some words of the poet Rilke:

> Strangely, I heard the Stranger say
> I am with you.

The layover in San Salvador's airport, surrounded by the Treasury Police armed with guns, did little to allay my fears. Once we had reboarded the plane, the atmosphere changed from the previous tense anxiety into a party mood. People laughed and joked. I was included in the sharing of food and drink, and told I would be very welcome in Nicaragua. Mother Julian of Norwich's mantra echoed in me: 'All shall be well, and all shall be well, and all manner of things shall be well.'

It was. At Managua airport the passport and immigration facilities were perfunctory. I was smiled at by the receiving officers, welcomed, told to 'Have a good stay'. My host was the local Anglican theological college principal, Ennis Duffis, whose first question after a night's sleep was: 'Did you bring any toilet paper?' I hadn't. But I quickly learned that, as a visitor, I could have access to diplomatic supplies, and he could accompany me.

'Toilet paper' became a euphemism for little luxuries that the inflationary economy of Nicaragua did not permit most of its citizens, and evidence of President Reagan's trade embargo. Access to this store remained a symbol of privilege, cushioning, as Phillip Berryman has said, 'some high officials from truly experiencing the plight of the poor majority whom they wished to serve'.[4]

In 1987 the Sandinista government had been in power for some six years. In the countryside, the US-backed Contra attacks on villages meant that the military budget was consuming ever increasing amounts of government money. Despite this, many of the promises made by the Sandinistas had been fulfilled. Education, literacy campaigns, health care for the masses, the redistribution of land and the establishment of a mixed economy for the benefit of the people rather than foreign investors, were all significant achievements.

Further, the lot and status of women was changing during this era. On a visit to the Catholic University, during a conversation with Professor Veronica Campanile she revealed the extent to which the revolution had begun to deal with historic discrimination and violence against women. She spoke of greater equality, better sex education, learning about nutrition and child care, particularly for those with special needs. Despite the dangers of military conflict, an atmosphere of hope was permeating the people.

Yet the infrastructure in Managua was fragile. An earthquake in 1972 had virtually ruined the city. Years of conflict, and lack of investment meant sporadic supplies of water and electricity. 'The water will be off for two days,' my host had warned me over my first breakfast. Getting adequate supplies of safe drinking water, and storing sufficient for washing and flushing the loo during cut-offs, became priorities.

I was discovering that amongst the 'things that make for peace' are utilities we all take for granted. Restoration of infrastructures, water, sanitation, electricity; the status of women, health care, security and education are all integral to peacemaking.

Although I did not directly witness fighting, the impact of the Contras attempts to overthrow the government were increasingly evident. Ron Sider[5] quoted that during the 1980s 'approximately 30,000 Nicaraguans were killed, thousands more maimed and wounded and 350,000 internally displaced'. Such action, he argued, was 'contrary to the Just War's prohibition against targeting civilians, (and) the Contras almost daily kidnapped, tortured, mutilated and killed noncombatants'.

I was to learn more about the impact of this on communities and individuals through an encounter with Norma Galo, a remarkable woman. I had initially intended to learn from her experience of base Christian community formation. In the end, she was to teach me something more about the challenges of 'the things that make for peace' in an environment of oppression and terror.

Non-violent action

I met Norma Galo in her house on the edge of one of the many *barrios*[1] in Managua city, sited around the corner from a marker stone where a girl of twelve had been raped and killed by two soldiers during the uprising. It was a sobering reminder of the lives of so many dispossessed people prior to the Sandinista victory of 1980. Norma, a housewife and mother, became a community organiser and a voice of the people during the closing years of the Samoza government.

During the 1960s and seventies in the *barrios*, drugs and prostitution were rife, and many suspected the government of controlling the black economy that financed these activities. Illiteracy and lack of education impacted upon 70 per cent of the population. Oppression of women and girls was simply seen as the way things are in a macho society. Poverty was endemic and violence, both by state forces and drug barons, a frightening and frequent occurrence.

'You cannot imagine what we had to suffer,' Norma told me. 'Samoza had one of the best trained and resourced armies, and they would march into our neighbourhood with guns and tanks to frighten us. And they did so because our kids didn't have guns with which to fight back.'

She had been one of the many catechists and community enablers who had facilitated the growth of the base communities in the light of Vatican 2 and its objective of 'a preferential option for the poor'. These Christian communities had been critical in laying the foundation for the ultimate victory of the Sandinistas.

During the 1970s, a new priest from Spain had come to the *barrio*. The Samoza regime was at its most repressive. The priest spoke of building a church not of bricks and mortar, but of people and community. It was the language and approach of Vatican 2. He sought to encourage community organising, which provided a template for the revolutionary cells that facilitated the success of the uprising.

'We didn't understand,' said Norma, 'and we didn't intend to. But the priest asked us to get people together and visit all the houses along the dirt road in our neighbourhood. We did and we formed cells. Each person was invited to try to convince one or two others about the point of being community which the priest had explained to us.'

Everyone knew the problems that young people faced. These included the scale of violence, drugs and the exploitation of women and girls for sex. Many in the *barrios* of this traditional Catholic country had stopped attending church. The new cells attracted both young and old. The young people in particular began making demands of the priest and the religious missioners who frequented Nicaragua. One of their demands was that they would go to Mass if the priest did not wear vestments. They told him too that they would not go to confession, nor did they want him to preach to them. And within the Mass itself, they wanted words that would say something about Nicaragua.

Maura Clarke, an American nun later to be martyred in El Salvador, was working with the communities and said, 'If the boys (and by that she meant priests) are saying these things, is it not time for me to jump out of this habit and help to rescue these young people?' Norma and others like her increasingly saw their vocation as working with the addicts, and the street gangs.

Despite the growing division and violence in Nicaragua, these were signs of hope. The influence of the Brazilian educator Paulo Friére was transforming literacy, reading and writing amongst the illiterate. The translation of the Bible into the vernacular and a reading of the Bible from the 'perspective of the poor' gave fresh impetus to its truth. All contributed to a growing awareness among a people long regarded as of no consequence, that they could find the courage and resources to become the future for their nation.

'One thing about the Bible we discovered,' said Norma, 'was that it helped us to understand how we were being exploited. We reflected on the captivity (of the Hebrews in Egypt) and discovered it was not so different from our experience – in fact the only thing was the names – instead of Pharoah, it was Samoza. The situation we were living in was the same. We discovered that we were going to have to do something about it. God was not going to do it from heaven. In Exodus the people had to do their thing, and God had to do his. The Israelites through Moses were the subject of their own liberation. Otherwise they would have been parasites. We discovered this too.'

The composition of the Peasant Mass by the folk singer and composer Carlos Mejia Godoy was to prove a magnet to the young, but at the same time the Samoza government saw it as evidence of a growing politicisation of the Church. The composer was arrested before the first public presentation[2].

Both government and Church hierarchy perceived such movements as subversive. The archbishop banned the Mass. In protest the young people went and sang it outside his door. 'What a beautiful Mass,' he is alleged to have said, but refused to approve it. The young people took this as a refusal by the Church to accept an offering from the poor. Many were tempted to leave the communities. Norma and her colleagues sought to persuade them to follow Jesus Christ and not the bishops.

Banned from the churches, the Mass began to be sung in the streets and in people's homes. It became a subversive anthem of what was to become, in time, a revolution. Already the signs of revolution were present as members of the Sandinista Liberation Front were giving their lives in conflict. Voices were emerging calling for 'Overthrow through violence'.

Norma and her colleagues began to realise that the Church of the *barrios* would not be protected in the coming social and political struggle. Many of the young, including her daughter, saw no option but to take up arms. A crisis was happening in the communities. 'The Bible speaks of being patient, turning the other cheek,' said Norma. 'But the people who colonised us fooled us and misused the Bible. They put the cross to us, and when it was not accepted, they put the sword in.'

It can be argued that the Sandinista revolution would not have happened had it not been for the base communities. The *barrio* Church taught the Sandinistas how to organise cells. These became the primary unit of resistance against the authorities. Underground newspapers announced the killing of peasants in the villages and mountains. In the *barrios*, students began protests. In response the National Guard moved in, tear-gassed the students and carried out summary arrests.

By now there was no way out for the *barrio* Church communities. The government accused the Christians of being atheists, mocked their theology of justice and, more seriously, began killing young people. On one occasion, five young people organised a march to a local church with guitars, singing elements of the banned Mass. The National Guard moved into the church and shot all five dead.

In 1973 Rosario Murillo, wife of the leader of the *Sandinista* National Liberation Front (FSLN), Daniel Ortega, sought to politicise the base communities. The people refused. Rosario was an educated woman who talked a lot about Marx and Lenin, but the people would not listen. Murillo was at a loss. Norma Galo explained to her the people understood a God who did not make alliances with the powerful.

Gradually, however, an alliance grew between the base communities and the Sandinistas. The Church was being sucked into the conflict. Many members were arrested during the frequent incursions by the military, and were tortured and beaten. Inexorably the protests and violence grew. Home-made bombs and weapons dropped by frightened soldiers formed a crude armoury for the insurgents' cells. Safe houses were organised. Guerrillas were hidden, as well as those suspected of violent activity. Raids were frequent and many people disappeared.

One demonstration in particular spooked Norma. She said she was brave, but she would not join one that was almost certainly going to end in bloodshed, not least of unarmed women and children. A few days before the demonstration, she got a fever and prayed. 'The troops went away,' she said. 'God acted at the right time. It was a miracle.'

People like Norma were convinced that the revolution had to go through death and blood. Much was made of the valour of the Sandinista fighters, but the Christian communities played their part, many opting for acts of non-violent resistance. Though Norma herself said, 'There is no pacifist struggle against injustice. When we started out we thought it might be possible, but we gradually moved to violence.'

My encounter with Norma had been powerful. Her testimony was dramatic and moving. It raised many questions for me about the relationship of faith to politics and violence. Back in 1987 the inadequacies of the Sandinista government were not so apparent, and today I hold something of a revisionist view on its approach. But the important achievements mentioned earlier stood.

From the perspective of the 'things that make for peace', I must say the suffering experienced by the poor and oppressed was evil. The theological 'option for the poor' emerging from Vatican 2 provided the ground for re-engagement with those left behind by a Church that supported the political status quo. Literacy campaigns, and increased educational provision and health care became valuable resources building peace.

Undoubtedly the base communities in Nicaragua enabled people to find the courage for 'non-violent resistance'. Far from being 'pacifist', this 'passive resistance' in the words of *The Times* of 1861, 'can be so organised as to be more troublesome than armed rebellion'. Initially, and for some time in the 1970s 'non-violent action' in the *barrios* was the chief form of resistance. Many Christians steadfastly refused to take up weapons yet played their part against oppression.

Defining such action, Ron Sider[3] argued, 'Nonviolence is not passive nonresistance; nor is coercion always violent. Non-lethal coercion (as in a boycott or a peaceful march) that respects the integrity and personhood of the "opponent" is not immoral or violent.' Non-violent activism means, says Sider, 'an activist confrontation that respects the personhood of the "enemy" and therefore seeks both to end the oppression and to reconcile the oppressor through nonviolent methods.'

The perfectionist in me would have loved to have brought the story of this encounter to a close by testifying that such non-violence won the day. It didn't, but it did contribute, and provides a challenge to Christian 'Just Warriors' in Sider's words: 'to explore, in a more sustained and sophisticated way than ever before in human history, what can be done nonviolently.'[4]

Contradictions

Early one Saturday morning I met Ernesto Cardenal in his office in the palace of the former dictator Anastasio Somoza. A priest and poet, Cardenal was one of three priests appointed to be ministers in the revolutionary Sandinista government. Their appointment was the cause of considerable controversy. Over the coming years Pope John Paul II ordered each to resign.

In the late 1970s Ernesto Cardenal, together with his brother Fernando and Miguel d'Escoto, a Maryknoll Father, served as priests among a group known as the Twelve. The Twelve were widely admired Nicaraguans. Prior to the outbreak of armed conflict, they had proposed that the Sandinistas should be involved in resolving the crisis engulfing the country, seeking to ensure a peaceful transition to a more democratic government.

Protestants also opposed the Somoza dictatorship. Evangelical Gustavo Parajon, director of aid and development agency CEPAD,[1] supported democratic government. All their pleas failed, and by May 1979, the Sandinistas launched a military insurrection.

Then something totally unexpected happened. The Catholic bishops of Central America, with the exception of Archbishop Obando y Bravo of Nicaragua, drew up a document which laid down conditions for the Church's support of insurrection. In the encyclical *Populorum Progressio*[2] Pope Paul VI wrote: 'Revolutionary uprisings engender new injustices and bring new disasters except where there is manifest, longstanding tyranny which would do great damage to fundamental personal rights and dangerous harm to the good of the country.'[3] With these words the revolution was effectively endorsed.

Minister of Culture Ernesto Cardenal was an impressive figure with a gentle, strong face, clear blue eyes, white hair and beard.

'For us to contribute to the revolution is significant,' he observed. 'Former revolutions have been against the Church, against Christians.' This Marxist-led revolution broke the mould with its slogan: 'Between Christianity and the revolution there is no contradiction.'

In 1990 when the Sandinistas had been in power for a decade and were, to the surprise of many, defeated in elections, Father Miguel d'Escoto, who had served as foreign minister, reflected:

> The issue was not the revolution but the failure of the church – specifically the bishops – to oppose a war waged against Nicaragua 'by the greatest power in the world', a war that had been condemned by the World Court. The church was up to its ears in the blood of the people.[4]

The conflict raged between the Church hierarchy and the revolutionary priests throughout the Sandinistas decade in office. When Pope John Paul II visited, and publicly rebuked the obeisant Ernesto Cardenal on the tarmac at the airport, he was, as Ernesto put it: 'not upset because we are revolutionary. He does not believe we should govern. But many priests and nuns are involved in the process of government, and will continue to do so.'

Around Ernesto Cardenal's office, the walls were covered with oil paintings by members of his base communities in Solentiname, an island on Lake Cocibolca. They were scriptural scenes, based on the peasants' experiences and made famous in Cardenal's *The Gospel in Solentiname*. The faint smell of drying oils, the bright sunlight and the almost mesmeric presence of Father Cardenal, gave the room a sacred feel.

It was hard to imagine that it was in this room Somoza had ordered and supervised the torture of Tomás Borge. Equally hard to imagine was the fighting going on in the villages and remote hills. In increasingly brutal raids, the US-backed Contras wrought havoc. Ernesto and I discussed the chances of a Sandinista victory. 'We will win in military terms,' he confirmed. 'But we are concerned about the economic consequences. Of course we want to stop spending on the military, but if we do the Contras will be at the gates of Managua within an hour. We need help from other countries, we are not just defending Nicaragua, we are defending Latin America and helping to contain the threat to this region.'

I acknowledged these were very real dangers. In 1979 the Bishops' Pastoral Letter condoned the right of people to take arms and defeat Somoza in armed insurrection. Following the Sandinista victory the bishops changed their mind. In a second pastoral letter they stated that any Catholic serving in the military of the Sandinista government was tantamount to a denial of Christian faith and an embrace of Marxist ideology.

Cardenal said divisions were deep over the bishops' *volte face*. 'They say that people should obey the commandment not to kill,' he remarked. 'That was a dangerous idea while we were having a war. But it is a conflict within Catholicism. The Church is making too many hard decisions.'

In the second pastoral letter, priests were instructed to dissuade young people from joining the military. Many young people who refused to join the military were spirited out of the country by friends and relatives, although many feared they were secretly being recruited into the Contras and participating in the insurgency.

Polarisation was total. Those like the Cardenal brothers understood 'sin' as refusing to fight against oppression from an external power, thus preventing the adequate defence of the country. But if God was a God of justice, a justice which directly related to the daily needs of the Nicaraguan people in terms of economics, politics and military aggression, then it was legitimate to fight, because the fight could be interpreted as being for the kingdom of God.

I was uneasy with the argument that fighting for a revolutionary cause equalled fighting for the kingdom of God. Images of '*Gott mit uns*' ('*God with us*') engraved on military belts went through my head. The decision by the priests, and even the bishops, to justify fighting oppression was one thing. Sanctifying it as some kind of 'holy war' was another.

Miguel d'Escoto, the third of the priests in government, stood against violence, despite his commitment to the cause. During my visit, he was travelling around the country striving to lay non-violent foundations for a post-revolutionary society. The war would be over one day, he said. When that day came, Christians must be prepared to lead a new phase of the revolution through non-violence, and it should start now.

Ambiguities

On 1 August 1986, the Contras killed four church workers, leaving four wives, 12 children and 51 members of extended families bereft. 'The first question I asked was, "Where was God?"' reflected evangelical pastor Gustavo Parajon. Though the Sandinistas were in power, the violence was far from over. Miguel d'Escoto's campaign for non-violence to 'start now' still had no political traction. Though not a party member, Parajon, like many Christians, Catholic and Protestant, identified himself with the Sandinista cause. For this, commitment he was accused by the Religious Right in the United States of 'being a Marxist and guilty of un-American activity'.

When I met Parajon he had recently returned from giving evidence to the United States Institute of Religion and Development (IRD). In his testimony, he spoke of the impact of the low intensity conflict that daily brought stories of brutal violence, rapes and murders. He criticised the United States' support of the conflict through the training and arming of the Contras.

In the comfort of his home, we began our conversation talking about God. Where indeed was God in the midst of such events that had caused the deaths of the four church workers? It is a question that constantly faces believers. There are no cheap answers. Parajon said that when he visited victims of violence and killing, he often found a firmly held faith in God. 'This was not God's doing,' they would say. 'He is with us. God shares our suffering our pain. We know he is with us.'

'At the funerals,' said Gustavo, 'as I listened to and talked with the relatives, I experienced a kind of tangible empowering. I had expected a desire for revenge. What I discovered was that the relatives expressed no bitterness, no desire for revenge. They were convinced of the love and power of God.' It is hard to argue with such conviction.

Yet Parajon was a realist. He anticipated the future with deep anxiety. He was fearful that the US government and the Contras could destroy the good achieved so far by the revolution. He feared that the poor who had benefited most from the changes would once again be marginalised and lose hope.

In a childcare centre in the Nicaraguan border town of Octal, teachers played a game with the children. From time to time one of them would come into a room banging a pan with a wooden spoon. Immediately the children would drop to the floor, slithering on their tummies towards the centre of the school. Heads down, mouths open, they were playing at being fish. Theologian Raymond McAfee Brown, comments:

> What the children do not know is that the game is deadly serious, and is designed to save their lives next time the U.S. backed *contras* conduct a terrorist assault on the village, where (as a member of the U.S. embassy told us) it is perfectly justifiable to attack child care centers, since that is where the 'ideologues' of the future are being trained.[1]

Parajon spoke of the experience of church workers, coffee pickers, children and *campesinos* who were attacked by the Contras, and the many who were brutally killed. The excuse for such attacks was that many believed that US Congress funded humanitarian aid had been distributed to village communities. By destroying villages, the terrorists sought to obtain money and other resources with which they could bargain and obtain arms.

'These were the "powers and principalities" of which St Paul spoke in Ephesians,'[2] said Gustavo. Then, with barely restrained anger, he remarked, 'This war is not God's fault. I believe in prayer. There are no wrecked lives that start in prayer. The words "Vengeance is mine, I will repay", says the Lord[3] are still good news. Stop the war!'[3]

A kind of serenity came over him. 'There is something very powerful in hope. Rationally you cannot justify this. I am reminded that the powerful, God will render powerless. Justice *will* prevail. At this time crucifixion is strong in our lives. We send teams to clinics for four or five days. They may be ambushed or killed. What we have to remember is that when St John records Jesus raised Lazarus from the dead, they (the authorities) decided to kill Jesus. Such a possibility exists in the lives of all of us.'

It was not to be the United States or the Contras who would bring down the revolution. It was corruption of power within the Sandinista movement. In 1995, Fernando Cardenal spoke of how he had come to love the Sandinista revolution, and was willing to sacrifice anything for it. Nevertheless, he concluded, after what he called the 'debacle' of the 'acts of corruption (that) broke the traditions of Sandinista honesty', along with the accompanying leadership power struggle, he concluded that he would out of 'conscience and principles' resign.[4]

Good things were achieved by the revolutionary government. Fernando led the national literacy campaign that, in five months, reduced illiteracy amongst *campesinos*, poor farmers, from 50 per cent to 13 per cent. Initially, the revolution facilitated better education opportunities for women and girls, a decrease in sexual abuse and exploitation, whilst health care and welfare benefited the poorest.

One tragic effect of the revolution's failure is evidenced in the ongoing abuse of women and girls today. In 2011, Amnesty International reported that 'over half of the rapes reported between 1998 and 2008 involved girls of 14 and under'.[5] The government's 'No abortion' ban meant that sexual violence condemns girls and women to unbearable suffering. 'The stigma associated with sexual crimes', continued Amnesty's report, 'means that it is often the survivor – not the abuser – who is blamed. For women who speak out, the struggle for justice can be traumatic. Failure and lack of resources in the justice system often mean the case collapses and attackers walk free.'

Nicaragua offered no easy answers on the 'things that make for peace'. I was impressed and moved by the convictions of many victims of violence, that 'God was with them'. It echoed Jesus' identification with the suffering of humanity. For someone like me who has never resisted to the point of shedding blood,[6] witnessing the courage of those who speak of God's presence in the midst of suffering is deeply moving.

With hindsight, I can see a legitimacy in the revolutionary struggle against oppression, injustice and violence perpetrated by a brutal regime propped up by a paranoid superpower. Observing, as I did, the revolutionary government when it enjoyed popular support, with its good intentions, programmes and campaigns, I, and others like me, were perhaps too uncritical and naïve. Maybe Pope John Paul II was right when he criticised the priests for their role in government. However, the priests might not have done so had they not had the authority of Pope Paul VI's encyclical, *Populorum Progressi*. We shall never know.

The things that would have made for peace, and still should, in the Central American republics, is an all-out international endeavour to end the abject poverty that breeds abuse, violence and oppression. Trade barriers, inequality of land ownership, the marginalisation of poor farmers and mass migration create the swamp for the mosquitoes of violence and revolution to breed.

If the Sandinistas can be criticised for their corruption that decimated their cause, then the international community must also be held up for judgement, particularly the United States in its failure to both perceive the causes of the revolution in human rather than ideological terms, and to seek in the name of Christian democracy to bring an end to poverty and its causes.

A single photograph I took encapsulates my feelings about Nicaragua. It is of a young woman sitting on a gate post with her young son on her lap. A large puppy stood by them. The woman gazes contemplatively into the middle distance. The child and the dog are both still. I was captivated. What was she thinking? Why was she there? What hope did she have for her future and her child's?

Today the picture hangs on my study wall, reminiscent of Madonna and Child images in a million churches around the world. What was her Magnificat? What for her did the 'mighty being brought down from their seats, and the humble and poor being lifted up' mean? Gustavo Parajon asked in the light of the killing of the church workers: 'Where is God?' At the funerals it appears he received an answer. But what of the woman with her child: where are they?

'The Land of the Saviour'

In the summer of 1988, I was invited to join a group of international church leaders to visit El Salvador – 'The Land of the Saviour'. From 1980 to 1992 a vicious civil war raged in this tiny country between a military-led government under President José Napoléon Duarté, and a coalition of rebel groups, the strongest of which was the FMLN.[1] The Duarte government, backed by the USA, was receiving, at its height, some $1.5 billion a day in military and economic funding.

For decades, tensions existed between military-backed land-owning elites, and the majority of the population of *campesinos,* and native groups. Between 1961 and 1975 landlessness among the peasants increased from 12 per cent to 41 per cent of the rural population. In one region, five landlords had incomes equalling that of 7,000 local families. Sixty-five per cent of the population was illiterate, 98 per cent lacked sanitation, 50 per cent had no potable water and 35 per cent lacked adequate housing. Agricultural workers expected to be employed on average for 141 days a year.[2]

During the 1970s, under pressure from opposition groups and the churches, most notably the Jesuits, attempts were made to 'transform' land allocation. Refusing to use the term 'agrarian reform' because of its perceived 'communist terminology', the government reneged on any reform. This decision was to lay the foundation for the 'Dirty War', which raged from 1980–92.

Much of the violence from 1981 was carried out by the notorious Atlatacatl Battalion. Torture and killing were commonplace in their headquarters, which had a sign over its gate reading: 'Welcome to Camp Hell.' Until the late 1970s, the Salvadoran army was incompetent and ineffective. It took the 'low intensity conflict training and support' from the United States to turn this group in to a deadly fighting force against perceived Communist penetration. This became something of a Faustian bargain for the United States. Whilst US aid supported the military 'containment' of the people, many unauthorised reactionary groups roamed the cities and countryside as 'death squads'.

Night by night, squads attacked slum neighbourhoods across the country, butchering and murdering those seen as opponents, whether members of rebel groups or not. Morning light revealed the mangled remains of the dead.

Written in Spanish on the walls of the US Embassy, were the words, 'Here they plan the deaths of our people' yet the United States, in all fairness, was concerned at the resurgence of 'death squad' activity. The US Ambassador Thomas Pickering, himself subject to death threats, expressed deepening concern at the growing disorder.

By 1984, US military aid helped increase the Salvadoran army from 12,000 to 41,000. Rebel activity by the FMLN and others was recalibrated to guerilla warfare. A kind of stalemate emerged; neither side could defeat the other. By 1992, a report to the US Congress seeking to justify involvement concluded that the US had 'assumed responsibility for ameliorating the pathology produced by centuries of abuse perpetrated by the very armed forces and governing elite that its policy now supported'.[3]

As a consequence of US foreign policy in El Salvador during this period:

> some 10,000 people, including Archbishop Romero and four American church women were murdered in 1980, and in 1989 six Jesuits and their housekeeper and daughter were killed. Church leaders and workers were particular targets for arrest, rape, torture and disappearance. Meanwhile in a similar conflict in neighbouring Guatemala, over 50,000 died, more than 100,000 disappeared and 626 village massacres took place.[4]

El Salvador, like many Latin American countries, was colonised and named by the Spanish in the fifteenth and sixteenth centuries. On the 500th anniversary of the arrival of Christopher Columbus, two contemporary writers reflected: '12 October 1492 was the beginning of a long and bloody Good Friday for Latin America and the Caribbean. It is still Good Friday, and there is no sign of Easter Day.'[5]

History is chiefly written by the winners, not the victims. 'The invasion represented the biggest genocide in history. The destruction affected around 90% of the population' of Latin America observed Leonardo Boff and Virgil Elizondo, attempting to redress the dominant perspective of history. The destruction of the sixteenth century included the population of El Salvador. Its colonisation caused a Mayan prophet to reflect: 'Alas, we were saddened because they came,' one Mayan prophet wrote. 'They came to make our flowers wither so that their flower might live.'

El Salvador has a complex yet complementary history to that of Nicaragua. From the nineteenth-century, small numbers of land-owning elites ruled El Salvador. Stealthily over the past 100 years, land was requisitioned from natives and the Church to grow staples of the nation's economy, coffee and bananas. Few of the dispossessed *campesinos* benefited either from their labours, or the economy.

The economic and political influence of the United States steadily grew in the region following the Spanish-American War of 1898. That influence culminated in its increased support of ruling elites during the 1970s and eighties, ostensibly to prevent the spread of Communism.

It was against this background that the 'Dirty War' was fought. As in Nicaragua and elsewhere, a growing commitment by Catholics and Protestants to 'make a preferential option for the poor' was perceived as a direct threat to the ruling elite. This re-evaluation of the Gospel of Jesus Christ, theologies of liberation, the growth of base communities, offered to many the hope that El Salvador could indeed become 'The Land of the Saviour'.

Whilst not supporting the armed struggle, one of the Jesuits articulated the plight of landless and peasant farmers:

> The *campesino* has three options, dying of hunger, as indeed happens and there is no work nor land and a lot of repression; dying fighting, in the worst instances; or the hope of living in a different society, a society that will be good for himself

and his sons. He has chosen, the third, with the risk of falling into the second.[6]

In 1988 our visit was facilitated by the late Guillermo (Bill) Cook. A Protestant missionary theologian, Bill had worked in Latin America for many years. Since the late 1970s we had been in correspondence because of a shared interest in the development of base communities.

Our party was to travel in two groups. One would visit Guatemala, the other El Salvador, and subsequently we would meet in Nicaragua and conclude our mission in Costa Rica. Our visits would enable us to hear stories of many affected by the violence, and to express solidarity with them. In my group were two people with an additional motive, to rescue people whose lives were in particular danger through the 'Underground Railway'.[7]

Those arriving at immigration in El Salvador were advised to say that we were 'tourists'. Tourists were not notable by their presence at the time. I had been asked to report for the BBC World Service. In my hand luggage was recording equipment with 'BBC' written on it, hardly the baggage of a holidaymaker. Bluffing my way through passport control and customs, I covered the small recording equipment with books and clothing. I planned to open the bag while engaging the immigration officer in polite conversation. I tried not to show my anxiety and the ruse worked. My bag was given a cursory examination, my passport stamped and I entered 'The Land of the Saviour'.

Crucified people of God

The atmosphere was tense inside the terminal at San Salvador airport. Here I met some of my fellow travellers.[1] As our minibus left the airport, we spotted a group of people beside the road spread-eagled against a wall. Surrounded by the infamous security police, who brandished heavy-duty weapons, they stood a few short metres away from the spot where the bodies of four women had been found in 1980. Maura Clarke and Ita Ford had been Maryknoll Missioners, while Dorothy Kazel was an Ursuline Sister, and Jean Donovan a lay worker. All of them had been tortured, two raped, and all brutally killed.

Maura Clarke who had been in Nicaragua before her assignment to El Salvador, and like the others believed God had called her to live in solidarity with the poor, wrote: 'One cries out, "Lord, how long?" And then too what creeps into my mind is the little fear or big, that when it touches me personally, will I be faithful?' [2] Together with her companions, Maura had indeed been 'faithful', ministering to the needs of refugees, protecting people on the run, providing comfort to widows and orphans, and paying the ultimate price of laying down her life in the cause of the Christ who had laid his life down for her.

'Don't rubberneck' Bill Cook warned us as we passed those under interrogation by the roadside. Bill had spotted that those being held were others from our party. We had been warned of the risks, but had not expected that we would receive the attention of the authorities quite so soon.

We headed for a remote beach hut on the shore of the Pacific Ocean. Here we could be safely and confidentially briefed. An hour or so later, the remainder of our party arrived. Released from their interrogation, they were clearly shaken. An indication that the security forces were on to us came when a Hué helicopter gunship passed low over the beach looking for us. Once we had been sighted the helicopter flew off, leaving us all wondering what next.

We stayed overnight in a hotel in San Salvador. Warned that our rooms were bugged, we kept our conversation light. The following morning the hotel was surrounded by the feared Treasury Police. Carrying guns, within a few short minutes they had arrested several members of the group, including Mark Gornik. Being slothful, I arrived late for breakfast to be greeted by Mark's cry: 'Man, I've just been arrested.'

The next few hours were tense. Almost everyone was detained, their passports checked, and faced with the same question: 'Why are you here?' Eventually all were released. We were beginning to get some sense of what Bill had meant when he said to us, 'If you are for life here, you are in danger of losing your life.'

We left the hotel for a series of encounters that would confirm some of the harsh realities we had heard about. Yet there were lighter moments. That evening, we returned to the hotel and were confronted by a hostile group of young Americans, supporters of the government. 'After you left,' they said, 'we were arrested and interrogated for five hours. Then they realised they had got the wrong people.'

President Reagan's 'low intensity conflict' strategy left most Americans ignorant of the contempt in which many El Salvadorans held the United States. This group was no exception. Perhaps in those few hours, they had a small insight into what many El Salvadorans were facing daily. Increasingly, we watched our backs. This was a regime that, night by night, murdered people and left their gruesomely butchered bodies on the streets as a warning of the dangers of opposition

One visit was to the Misquital *barrio*, one of the many squatter camps on the edge of San Salvador. Here we met with the Catholic and Protestant leaders of base communities. Housing was in shacks built from discarded building materials, wood and corrugated iron sheeting. Sewage ran in gutters frequently contaminating water sources. Here the infant mortality rate was 65 per cent of live births. Education for children was nonexistent. Everyone scavenged the city dump to make a living. Armed gangs controlled the 'turf' and violence was endemic.

Signs of hope were evident, not least in the growing ecumenical commitment to the people. A former Roman Catholic priest and his wife, Rachel, worked together with evangelicals and Protestants. We were to witness this unity frequently, most notably when we visited the remote country village of Panchilmalones, high in the hills beyond San Salvador.

To reach this isolated community we travelled for some hours by minibus. We stopped on a cart track that narrowed into a footpath, beginning a two-mile walk into the wooded hillside, occasionally emerging on to fertile farmland. A little under an hour later, we were greeted enthusiastically by the villagers. We listened to their stories, wiped tears, and sought to comfort those witnesses of violence, rape and kidnap by the militia groups. It was hard to hear, let alone to experience.

Every month the military arrived, burnt the huts of the people, stole food and set fire to standing crops. The villagers were driven out by machine guns, and those who could not run fast enough were often killed.

During the raid of the previous week, a thirteen-year-old girl and her mother had been murdered. The military arrived by helicopter and demanded all the food stocks in the village. The commander then lined up the villagers and said, 'We know you are storing food for the bandits.' They detained a boy who would be forced into the military. Others too were taken away, tortured and if not killed, returned bruised to the community as a warning. It was one such person that members of our group were seeking to save through the 'Underground Railway'.

It was the welcome feast following these harrowing accounts that amazed and moved me. In the communal hut tortillas, chicken, beans and other food had been prepared for us. Given the raid of the previous week, such a feast represented immense generosity, love, gratitude, and no little sacrifice.

After lunch and deeply affected by everything, I walked to the edge of the village. As I passed one of the wattle, daub and straw-roofed houses, I heard a radio playing the Beatles song, *Hey Jude*. It seemed incongruous, yet some of the phrases resonated. Here were people who had much to make them afraid, whose lives seemed the very echo of the lyrics of this song. 'If one suffers, then all suffer,' as St Paul has it.[3]

In those brief hours we stood in solidarity with the 'crucified people of God'. We heard no calls for revenge or retaliation; no appeals for weapons or violence; but rather a humble and deep hope in God and a time of liberation. They testified to suffering that produced endurance, character and hope. In the midst of deep testing, they understood that St Peter's words 'because Christ also suffered for you, leaving you an example, so that you should follow in his steps'[4] could have been written for them.

I can never hear *Hey Jude* without thinking of those brave and beautiful people of Panchimalones, and of how in their humility, endurance and fortitude, I had witnessed 'things that make for peace'.

18

Do not kill this man

Harsh political realities faced us each day of our visit. Meeting with the Lutheran bishop Medardo Gomez at his church in downtown San Salvador gave us one of the most poignant and powerful encounters with the suffering of the people.

The Lutheran Church did not appoint bishops in El Salvador. However, Gomez's persistent opposition and criticism of the powers and their murderous death squads led to numerous arrests and periods of imprisonment. His congregation became concerned that their pastor would one day be among the 'disappeared'. They pleaded with the Church authorities that he be made a bishop, believing that such status might protect him from arrest or death.

Gomez was accused like Archbishop Romero, and other priests and pastors, of subordinating the Gospel to politics. His dilemma and that of others, such as the Baptist Carlos Sanchez, Catholic priests and Religious whom we met was: how is good news of resurrection life in Jesus to be proclaimed in a culture in which poverty means death? Jesus' statement in Matthew's gospel, 'Whatever you do unto the least of these brothers and sisters of mine, you do to me',[1] they argued, was a commission to act in solidarity with the poor, and share with them a 'hunger and thirst for justice'.

The evident unity among Christian leaders was a response to the Roman Catholic bishops' conference in Medellin, Colombia in 1968. Addressing the challenges of Latin America, the conference stated a 'profound conversion' was necessary for a 'true liberation' from 'sin, ignorance, hunger, misery and oppression'.[2]

Medellin seemed a God-given preparation for the realities of conflict. A Christian community was uniting to 'Strengthen the weak hands, and make firm the feeble knees' and 'Say to those who are of a fearful heart, "Be strong, do not fear!"[3] This 'profound conversion' amongst church leaders led to a renewed spirit of service to the poor, and an attitude summed up in Oscar Romero's words: 'With this people it is not hard to be a good shepherd.'

In the months following our visit, repression against the people and persecution of the Church increased significantly. It came as no surprise when the following spring I received a phone call from San Salvador telling me that Bishop Gomez was in prison. He had confided in us that being a bishop would not protect him and if he was arrested again he would be killed. My caller was insistent that his life was in immediate danger.

An international campaign was quickly mobilised, drawing attention to the danger he faced. Phone calls and faxes crisscrossed the globe. I wrote an impassioned plea for his release in *The Independent* newspaper in the United Kingdom. We held vigils, prayed and waited.

Later that week on Saturday evening, the phone rang in my Croydon vicarage. 'Gomez has been released,' said the caller. It transpired that evening two men had been sent to his cell with orders to execute him. On their way, an urgent message was sent from a higher authority: 'Do not kill this man.' As they opened the cell door, one man said, 'We were coming to kill you, but you have too many friends around the world. You are free to go.'

It was to be 23 years before I was to see Gomez again. On 22 September 2011, together with Mark Gornik, we were reunited with him in San Salvador. Our reunion was deeply emotional and unforgettable. A supper had been arranged at which Gomez and many others who had passed through what the Book of Revelation calls 'the great tribulation' were present. Many had experienced the brutality and inhumanity of the 'Dirty War'. It was humbling to listen to the testimonies of courage and faith, and witness the fortitude of living martyrs. Many tears were shed, but much joy too was shared.

When Gomez spoke, he reflected on the story of St Peter's imprisonment for subversion, and how he was released from prisons by angels following prayers by the Church. Looking across at Mark and me he said: 'I believe in angels, but sometimes they come in human form. That is what happened in my case.' We tasted heaven that night.

It was later in our 2011 visit that I heard the full story of Gomez' arrest. Both Sanchez and he had been warned of the possibility of arrest. Sanchez surrounded himself with members of the international community in San Salvador, believing that this could offer some immunity. Gomez meanwhile took refuge in the German embassy.

Unable to arrest their quarries, the authorities took 50 of the congregation hostage. Imprisoned in a church, they were left pondering their fate for several hours. All knew the dangers they faced, and began preparing themselves for the worst. In the church was a large cross. Taking pieces of paper each in turn wrote an account of their sins and the sins of the nation. Confessing to God and to one another, they placed their testimonies on the cross and prepared to die.

The security forces eventually returned and took them to prison. Seeing the cross with its testimony of confession, the soldiers decided it was evidence of their guilt and carried the cross to prison with the people. Gomez had been smuggled to the airport, although he knew of the arrests of the people and the cross. Here he met US Ambassador Pickering who was returning from the states where he had been arguing against US policy in El Salvador. Recounting the story of the incarcerated men and women, and the cross, Gomez pleaded for his help in obtaining their release.

Some days later when it was deemed safe for Gomez to return, he discovered that all the people had been released. The cross meanwhile had been transferred to the presidential palace, its own silent witness to the powers of a Greater Power. Gomez was invited to retrieve it. It was a trick and he was arrested.

What these accounts reveal about 'things that make for peace' are deep and complex. Gomez's conviction that prayer and human activity had both played a part in his release is clear. In the Christian tradition, we are used to praying for people in such circumstances. It is not, however, slot machine praying, or indeed bargaining. It is prayer both 'for' the victim, and 'against' the oppressiveness of the powers. Believers see 'the hand of God' in such coincidences. I certainly do.

However, integrity requires us to struggle with the situations such as in the murder of Oscar Romero, Maura Clarke and her companions, and in 1989, the six Jesuits and their housekeeper and her daughter. Undoubtedly people prayed here too, but like Jesus in the Garden of Gethsemane, these were called to the ultimate sacrifice.

The testimony of the 50 hostages revealed a faith that few of us are called to express. Their chances of survival were slim. Yet their actions seemed to indicate that if they were released, then 'God be praised'. If they faced martyrdom, then their witness would speak of trust and confidence in the grace of God, and the assurance of resurrection life.

Jesus prayed, 'My Father, if it is possible, let this cup pass from me; yet not what I want but what you want.'[4] It was possible, but it still happened. Taking up the cross is not being poor, sick or isolated; these are just facts of life. Taking up the cross is to make a conscious choice for change, for the will of God to be done 'on earth as in heaven', as the Lord's Prayer has it.

Such choices hold risks, which is why Jesus advised his would-be followers to 'sit down and count the cost'.[5] 'Things that make for peace' are rarely soft and fluffy. Prayer, confession, holding to account, and being open to life or death with equanimity, these are what truly 'make for peace'.

19

Companions – each one of us

'We remember moments, not days' declared a poster in my study. This was certainly true during my first visit to El Salvador in 1988. We had been engaging in a tough schedule of meetings in different parts of the city of San Salvador. It was hot, tiring and stressful. I had nodded off to sleep in the coach, before being wakened by Mark Gornik. We were outside the hospice chapel of the Divine Providence where Archbishop Oscar Romero was assassinated in 1980.

We stepped down from the coach and entered the small, cool building. Alone I walked up the aisle and for a few solitary moments stood behind the altar. Romero had stood in this same spot celebrating Mass, when a lone gunman rode up on a motorcycle and entered the west door, shooting at him, killing him instantly. I have stood there once since, and on each occasion I experienced a deep sense of being on 'holy ground'.

When he was shot, Romero had been offering the words of the consecration prayer: 'On the night he was betrayed, Jesus took bread, and after giving thanks, broke it and said, "This is my body which is to be broken for you."'

Someone had indeed betrayed the Archbishop.

Previously Romero had addressed the perpetrators of violence, pleading for an end to the killings. 'Brothers, each one of you is us ... We are the same people. The *campesinos* you kill are your own brothers and sisters. When you hear the words of a man telling you to kill, remember words of God, "Thou shalt not kill." God's laws must prevail. No soldier is obliged to obey an order contrary to the law of God. It is time for you to come to your senses and obey your conscience rather than follow sinful commands.'[1]

Most of the recruits to the death squads were young men without prospects, yet many were deeply religious. It was said that part of the daily pay was four ounces of cocaine. This was to give them courage to undertake the acts of violence demanded of them by their superiors. Romero hoped that his words might touch the drug-numbed souls of his hearers. It was not to be.

When in 1988 we left the Divine Providence chapel, we travelled the short distance to the cathedral. At the time inside the main entrance, Romero's body lay in a simple tomb. Romero had ordered a halt on the building's restoration, seeing the needs of the people as the priority. At the tomb people prayed, posted messages, laid flowers and left all manner of detritus, all bearing testimony to miracles alleged to have been performed by Romero. It was deeply touching, and there was rawness to the grief, as well as a sense of expectation of answer to the prayers that the suffering would end.

It was not until 1992 that the Chapultepec Accords were to be signed, bringing peace to El Salvador. In the cathedral square there were rapturous celebrations to mark this event. Signatories to the treaty included representatives of the government, the FMLN who agreed to the disbanding of their fighters, and the United Nations. The process was formally observed by representatives of the Roman Catholic Church. The various military and paramilitary units of the El Salvadoran government were reduced by 70 per cent in size, and the intelligence agencies were to come under the auspices of the president.

In 1988 all of that was to come. The civil war still raged. Early one morning we headed for the mountains. Here we were to have a clandestine meeting with FMLN representatives. At 6 a.m. we stopped for breakfast at a hill-top village. From the street café restaurant we could observe the road leading from the valley. It would be from here that any pursuing security forces would come.

As we finished our beans and tortillas, a large truck was heard grinding up the steep hill towards the village. Soon it was in sight and evidently filled with soldiers. We hurriedly boarded our minibus as the heavily loaded lorry entered the village square. We glimpsed armed boys, press-ganged from the streets and *barrios*, climbing down from the truck, as we sped out of town.

An hour or so later we stopped in a clearing on a hillside. We walked into a small field and onwards into a stand of trees. Soon a group of FMLN fighters appeared, some of them armed. For a little over an hour we talked together. We discussed the state of the nation, the ambitions of the would-be liberators, and listened to their accounts of success and failure in the military campaign.

Before we left, one of the guerrillas asked how they should behave when they came to power. A number of positive stories were circulating of how the Sandinistas had behaved in victory. In Nicaragua the previous year I witnessed something of the spirit enunciated by Romero, of the need to see former enemies as 'Brothers, each one us'.[2]

Ernesto Cardenal had spoken to me about the magnanimity of Sandinista commander, Tomás Borge. In prison he spoke to his torturers, promising them that they would be shown 'the justice of our revolution'. Cardenal said that when the Sandinistas proclaimed victory, Borge went to the prison, took the guards to the gate and, reminding them of his promise, had the gates opened and released the guards.

I offered this account to the young men and women on the hillside. There was attentiveness, and a sense that they wanted to do right by all the people, even though many had experienced great wrong by the government and its organs.

A few days later, when I returned to Nicaragua, I met up with Espéranza Guévara, a young woman who had been a guerrilla at the age of twenty. She had witnessed her brother being tortured and killed by the Somozans. Visiting her house, there was a picture of her and her brother on the wall. 'Today I am a teacher,' she said, 'and former Somozan guards are my pupils. Sandinistas teach forgiveness after the manner of Christ.' Much time has passed since then, and as we saw earlier, the Sandinista period was tainted by corruption. Yet there was a genuine desire to bring something alternative, something that would give hope to all. It was this spirit that we sought to encourage in our answer to the question from our guerrilla hosts.

The 'holy ground' of Romero's martyrdom offers 'things that make for peace'. Romero's personal transformation from a conservative prelate to a defender of the poor and oppressed was undoubtedly a work of grace. It provided the bedrock for all that was subsequently to follow. His appeal to 'Stop the oppression', and his reminder of God's law, 'Thou shalt not kill' that trumps all commands to the contrary, culminated in a manifesto for peace:

> When we struggle for human rights, for freedom, for dignity, when we feel that it is a ministry of the church to concern itself for those who are hungry, for those who have no schools, for those who are deprived, we are not departing from God's promise. He comes to free us from sin, and the church knows that sin's consequences are all such injustices and abuses. The church knows it is saving the world when it undertakes to speak also of such things.[3]

It seems likely that Romero spotted his assassin as he prayed a few seconds before he died: 'May this Body immolated and this Blood sacrificed for Mankind nourish us also, that we may give our body and our blood over to suffering and pain, like Christ – not for Self, but to give harvests of peace and justice to our People.'

'We need help'

The morning of 16 November 1989 was a dark day in El Salvador. The international press corps had been called to a scene of unspeakable horror in the garden of the University of Central America. The mutilated bodies of six Jesuit priests[1] lay scattered between the lawn and their residence. The night before a unit from the Atlatcatl anti-terrorist battalion had come to kill those alleged to be 'the intellectual authors' of the revolution in the country. The squad also killed the housekeeper, Elba Ramos and her sixteen-year-old daughter, Celina.

A further member of the community, Father Jon Sobrino, was out of the country that night. As a warning of what awaited him, the body of fellow priest Ramon Moreno was dragged into Sobrino's bedroom. On the floor of the room lay a book. Stained with Moreno's blood it had been knocked down as his body was dumped by his attackers. The book, entitled *El Dios Crucificado – The Crucified God* by the German theologian Jürgen Moltmann stands today as testimony in the memorial hall to the martyr priests and their companions.

During a visit to the site of the killings, Moltmann was to write that he made 'a pilgrimage to the graves of the martyrs and found my blood soaked book there, behind glass, as a symbol of what had really happened there'.[2] In September 2011 Mark Gornik, a Presbyterian pastor, and a Catholic lay man, Mike Hard and I also visited the memorial and were privileged to spend time with Jon Sobrino.

Those murdered in 1989 were neither Communists, nor advocates of the armed struggle. They were seeking to be faithful to the challenge of 'a preferential option for the poor' through a 'service of faith and promotion of justice'. One of those killed,

Ignaçio Ellacuria had described those whom they ministered amongst as 'the crucified people of God'.

'What is it to be a companion of Jesus today?' Ellacuria had asked. 'It is to engage, under the standard of the cross, in the crucial struggle of our time: that struggle for faith and that struggle for justice which it includes.' He and his companions lived and died in this spirit. The deaths of these eight people undoubtedly became the tipping point that would eventually lead in 1992 to the signing of the Chapultepec Peace Accords.

'We need help,' said Jon Sobrino as he began our conversation. 'No one has addressed the question of the poor.' Typically forthright, Sobrino's fiercely independent and prophetic voice was born out of his witness of the sufferings of his people. As the sole survivor of his community, his words had both authority and integrity.

Our return to El Salvador had been marked by none of the anxiety our first visit in 1988. Now we were welcomed by government representatives, educationalists and businesspeople. On the surface there was greater prosperity. Supermarkets, multinational companies, luxury stores and new gated residential communities seemed to evidence increased well-being.

At the same time, hotels and businesses away from the new centres of affluence all had armed guards. We were warned of endemic violence and told to travel everywhere by car. The *barrios* of the city still lacked clean water and sanitation. Unemployment, muggings, rape and drug-related killings were endemic.

In the countryside we witnessed poverty too, as well as military patrols once again taking young men off the streets. Sobrino confirmed the shockingly high murder rate in 2011, but more recently he commented: 'During 2015 it has been increasing, and some days it reaches 20. The week before I gave this talk there were 85 murders in three days, and when I came to revise it for publication I found that in August 2015 there were 907 murders.'[3]

There have been changes since 1988. Democratic government replaced the terror regime of the elites. Human rights form part of the nation's constitution. Nevertheless, girls and women made pregnant following rape cannot have abortions, and many such victims are twelve or thirteen years old. One night over supper, a pastor's wife cried out angrily of how little had really changed.

'People are still poor, violence is endemic, women are abused, and there is no adequate health care or education for our children.'

In 2016, *The New York Times*[4] reported that the failure of successive governments to deal with the reality of the poor of El Salvador has led to fear and terror. 'The gangs that make El Salvador the murder capital of the world are not sophisticated global cartels but mafias of the poor,' creating 'a level of deadly violence unparalleled outside war zones: 103 homicides per 100,000 residents last year, compared with five in the United States'. With a population of some 6.5.million, 'the gangs hold power disproportionate to their numbers. They extort about seventy percent of businesses. They dislodge entire communities from their homes, and help propel thousands of Salvadorans to undertake dangerous journeys to the United States'. The cost to the economy was around $4 billion per year. 'El Salvador has been brought to its knees by an army of flies. Theirs is a criminal subsistence economy; even many of their leaders are barely solvent.' As one former prosecutor, Rolando Monroe who oversaw money-laundering investigations until 2013, observed: 'The gangs are like an anthill. They are all after the same thing: something to eat.'

None of this justifies gang violence, with their recruitment of vulnerable, poor and unemployed children into processes of extortion and violence. Neither does it justify indiscriminate arrests and detainment of teenagers by the police and military so reminiscent of the bad old days of the 'Dirty War'.

One story illustrates the bind of so many of the young: 'I was a kid: I was stupid,' he said about joining. 'A bunch of crazy guys were messing with me because I was a kid, smacking me in the head, knocking me around. It made me think: I have had enough. Since I joined up, nobody screws with me.' Who of us would know how we would respond in such circumstances?

The cry of the pastor's wife back in 2011 still echoes in the misery of too many people.

It was against this background that Jon Sobrino spoke: 'God is against a world that gives death to others. Until the question of the poor is addressed, there is no salvation.' From the 1970s through to the 1990s, the Church's 'preferential option for the poor' had, despite oppression, war and death, provided a vision of hope in

Jesus Christ that would 'create decent humanity in a decent world', said Sobrino.

The cost of seeking God's liberating justice during that period led many to accept the possibility of martyrdom. With the signing of the peace accords, and a growing conservatism amongst the Catholic hierarchy, came a decline in the Church's commitment to a 'preferential option for the poor'.

Sobrino spoke of the emergence 'light religion'. This is when Christianity 'does a deal' offering private faith in exchange for security and conformity. 'Light religion' ignores the messianic Jesus of Nazareth and the cross, and refuses to engage with harsh realities; of the blasphemy against the Spirit, of seeing need before your eyes and ignoring, or refusing to acknowledge, or address them. 'That is why I ask,' he said, 'who defends the poor? God defends the poor and loves them. It is the main work of God to make people human. That is why Jesus of Nazareth is so important. We can argue about his divinity and much else, but it is his humanity that leads us to learn how to become human – and defend the poor.'

When Sobrino spoke of needing help, he had in mind the painful memories of the 'Reagan offensive' that had supported the ARENA government attacks on what one commentator had called 'an affinity of liberalist Christianity and Marxist socialism'.[5] This calumny, said Sobrino, sought 'to make terror among Christians who were seeking to empower people to resist poverty, violence and abuse'. To many in the US this made Christians a threat not only to the security of El Salvador, but the 'fatherland' of the USA itself.

'Things that make for peace' require the eradication of poverty, disease, lack of education and employment, as much as the cessation of violence. Wherever poverty is endemic, the mosquitoes of oppression, disease, abuse and violence swarm. Ignaçio Ellacuria would say that not only is a different world possible, but a different world is necessary. 'To have this *different* world there is a need for a *different* civilisation,' said Sobrino, 'but not just one that is different, but the opposite of and superior to the civilisation of wealth that shapes the present world of sin.'[6]

Enabling a civilisation of poverty demands a universal understanding that depriving people of necessities and essentials is morally wrong. No society can describe itself as civilised unless it guarantees all basic needs, the freedom of individual opinion, and the possibility of individual and community creativity that make for new relationships, with nature, with human beings and with God. 'What on earth is the Church?' queried Sobrino as we concluded our visit. 'If it is the "People of God", and God defends and loves the poor, then who are we to defend? Surely the poor. That is why the main work of God is being human. The Gospel is a tiny plant but it exists to bring the possibility of a new future.'

'Does it work with garlic bread?'

One of the great scandals of humanity is the disunity of Christians. Jesus is called the 'Prince of Peace', yet for too long his disciples have been divided and frequently the cause of violent conflict. Disagreement over Jesus' teaching, as well who is 'in' and who is 'out' of God's love, has polarised countless generations of Christ's followers. Neither is this a recent phenomenon. Arguments and divisions from the start are recorded in the New Testament. Amongst the most toxic of debates is over who should be welcome at 'the Lord's Supper'.[1]

Disagreement and conflict are part of life. Argument, debate and conversation are modes of seeking to discern truth. Visiting the Orthodox Jewish enclave of Mia She'arim in Jerusalem, on a Friday night at the beginning of the Sabbath, I have frequently watched diligent young men reading the Torah, discussing, what a given text, or *midrash*[2] might mean. The argument is often heated, but does not give way to violence.

Our visit to El Salvador in 1988 evidenced Christians and churches working together. One of the contributing factors to this unity was the shared experience of indiscriminate state-sponsored violence towards all perceived as critics and opponents. Theological heft towards unity was provided by the directives of Vatican 2. Its emphasis on Christian unity led to a new mood of reconciliation, acknowledging that unity was divinely ordered, and a necessary witness. The prayer of Jesus's in John's Gospel, that 'all be one ... so that the world may believe',[3] was the key to unity.

During the 1970s and eighties, one of the most influential aspects of Vatican 2 was the engagement of lay people and clergy in a common mission. This was expressed in vernacular liturgies, contextual biblical interpretation, the formation of basic Christian communities and social action. Key to its impact was the leadership of local catechists and animators.

Sadly, following the signing of the peace accords in El Salvador, during the papacy of John Paul II, the new structures and accompanying freedoms came under scrutiny from the hierarchy. Gradually authoritarianism began to be reasserted. The people were put back in their box; priests and Religious were required to reclaim their traditional teaching and dominical role, and base communities were discouraged.

Some brave souls, including bishops, resisted this recidivism. As dusk drew in on our final evening in San Salvador in 2011, we found ourselves in the company of two such resisters, Armando and Eva. They were catechists still working with some of the remaining base communities. Throughout the civil war they experienced persecution. Now within an increasingly conservative Church, they were experiencing harassment and isolation.

Recounting their experience, Eva said: 'The Spirit of Jesus said, after we had been thrown out of one church: "Come back and work with your people, because good news to the first disciples begins with talking about what saves us."' Armando spoke of infiltration and opposition from within the Church, but expressed the determination to '... keep on going, not as a different church, but in the Roman Catholic Church, or in others, if Mother Church won't have us.' They spoke of how they were facilitating a Lent programme in the villages on 'The Ethics of the Kingdom in the Gospel of Mark'. This topic they said had been 'dreamed up by the people'.

It was getting late, and travel at night was dangerous. We invited them to dinner before they journeyed home. Entering the empty dining room, I had an overwhelming sense that we should share the Eucharist together. We were a motley crowd of Anglicans, Presbyterians, Baptists, Catholics and people with no particular allegiance. I asked the waiter for bread and wine. We were brought garlic bread. I found myself asking, 'Does it work with garlic bread?' I concluded that it did, and we shared a simple breaking of bread and the cup of blessing. I used the words of Jesus, 'This is my body, this is my blood.' As the 'bread and cup' were passed around the table, people ministered to one another. I noticed tears in the eyes of the participants, especially Armando and Eva. It was as if those who had been on the outside for so long, felt themselves to be drawn in.

Over the years I have been in the company of the discarded in big cities around the globe. I often asked: 'Where would Jesus eat?' I concluded then, as I would now, that Jesus would have broken bread and shared the cup with *all* present, regardless of their state of grace. If he could eat with people who would deny and betray him, who could possibly be denied?

Prior to my return to El Salvador, my attention was drawn to a dialogue between the Protestant theologian Jürgen Moltmann, and the Catholic Hans Küng. Moltmann told of his long time membership of an ecumenical Bible study group. Protestants and Catholics, they wanted to share Communion together. Moltmann and a Jesuit member of the group were charged with the task of working out 'how'. To their mutual surprise, they quickly developed a form of liturgy, which the group was to practise, albeit amongst themselves, for many years.

Küng reflected that the Eucharist,

> was not given to an individual, but to everyone. 'Do this in memory of me' are the words that refer to celebrating the Eucharist ... in principle; a group of Christians can come together and celebrate the Eucharist, even though others will contest it is not a valid Eucharist ... Normally, of course, the priest, the president of the community, presides over the Eucharist ... I would want to keep that ... (But) if an increasing number of parishes have no priest, then we have to ask, what are they to do about it?

Küng concluded that the agreements in the 'Lima Declaration', published by the World Council of Churches Faith and Order Commission in 1982, resolved all real difficulties between Catholics and Protestants concerning inter-Communion, but they have never been enacted. 'If they are not,' said Küng, 'then (w)ell, we'll have to take the law into our own hands again, if we want to go forward.'[4]

Whether it is a case of 'taking the law into our own hands', as Küng has it, or something more organic, I sense there is a new kind of ecumenism, often untidy, unstructured and deinstitutionalised. Division over who can sit and eat with us at the Lord's Table remains a scandal. It is the antithesis of Jesus' dream of the common table, 'at which the unequal can all sit', reflects Sobrino.[5]

Those seeking to build foundations for peace often invite protagonists to share a meal. If Christians are to be 'peacemakers' as Jesus requires, we too should begin at the eating and drinking place. Just as the question, 'Does it work with garlic bread?' can only be answered in the affirmative, so it is for 'the Body given up for you'. If we are to participate in the 'things that make for peace', we must learn to sit down and eat and drink the body and blood of our Lord Jesus Christ, together.

The Middle East: Cradle of the holy?

The transit sheds at Southampton docks were crowded with soldiers, and filled with the noise of shouting, and the smell of cigarettes. This is amongst my earliest memories. In 1947, with my mother and sister Liz, we prepared to board the troop ship *Otranto*. She would take us first to Libya for nine months, and then we would travel by warship to the Suez Canal Zone of Egypt. Aged three, this was my baptism into the Middle East.

The countries of this region – Iran, Iraq, Israel, Syria and Egypt – are referred to as 'The Cradle of Civilisation'. From earliest recorded history it has also been a place of conflict. The so-called 'Holy Land' of Israel/Palestine has been the focus of some of the region's bitterest tensions and wars. In religious terms, the city of Jerusalem the sacred site of Judaism, Christianity and Islam, has provided the nexus of internecine conflicts. Today the region as a whole has provided the stage for proxy warfare between superpowers.

In 1947 I was unaware of such matters. A 'Christened' child of God, I attended Sunday school for children of military personnel in the Uaadan Hotel in Tripoli. Apparently I sat solemnly with a hymnbook on my head singing, 'Jesus loves me, this I know, for the Bible tells me so.' It was a truth yet to be learned through subsequent years of catechetical teaching, Scripture reading and moments of disclosure.

The terms 'Cradle of Civilisation' and 'Holy Land' appear euphemistic today amongst nations armed to the teeth with world's most sophisticated weapons of destruction. Human rights records in many states provide little evidence of any understanding of either what it means to be 'human' or indeed what it means to have 'rights'. Despite the presence of world religions ostensibly committed to peace and equality, there seems to be little perception of a humanity loving God whose mission is to save it from hell-bent destruction.

Our sojourn in Libya and Egypt in the aftermath of the Second World War was at a time of great regional upheaval. In the 'Holy Land', the State of Israel was being established. Palestinians were being displaced. Along the Suez Canal Zone conflict flared, and there was internal dis-ease culminating in a desire to see the British ousted from their occupation of Egypt. The years after the Second World War saw the rise of nationalism amongst countries which had been under colonial rule since the ending of the First World War and the break-up of the Ottoman Empire.

It was events from 1990 that drew me into the region as an adult. In August, Iraq invaded Kuwait an action that led to the first Gulf War. This followed a bitter conflict between Iraq and Iran from 1980–88. During this the West had supported Iraqi president Saddam Hussein. In the midst of attempted ceasefire negotiations, Saddam chose to invade his smaller neighbour. In turn a coalition of Western nations mounted 'Desert Storm', leading to the removal of Iraq's forces from Kuwait. The coalition forces did not seek to remove Hussein from power in 1990. This was not accomplished until the second Gulf War in 2003.

On 11 September 2001, Al-Qaeda, a little-known terrorist group based in Afghanistan, launched an attack on the United States. The event, known as '9/11', witnessed the destruction of the World Trade Center in New York, as well as further attacks in Washington and Pennsylvania. Subsequently, US President George W. Bush gathered a new coalition of Western powers attacking provinces in Afghanistan where Al-Qaeda's leadership had been located. This 'war against terror' began in October 2001 and formally ended in 2014.

During 2011, civil war broke out in Syria. This followed a period in which a number of North African and Middle Eastern countries had experienced what became known as the Arab Spring. Peaceful demonstrations against Syrian president Bashar Al-Assad had been ruthlessly put down by the military. Armed opposition had been growing for some time by various rebel groups. Conflict seemed inevitable.

US president Barack Obama, who had previously shown reluctance towards putting boots on the ground, now sought allies. However, the British prime minister, David Cameron, was unable to achieve the required majority in parliament for such action. Both nations elected instead to provide covert operational support to the rebels.

Initially the Syrian Army suffered considerable loss to both territory and personnel. At one point Assad controlled only between 30 to 40 per cent of the country. Support of the rebel groups was complicated for the West by the rise of fundamentalist Muslim groups who sought to form an Islamic Caliphate.

These groups, known as Daesh and ISIL emerged as a consequence of the wars in Iraq and Afghanistan.

Attempts at ending the conflict in Syria and defeating Daesh have at the date of publication been unsuccessful. In the various conflicts in the region over nearly thirty years, tens of thousands of men, women and children have died and millions have fled. Islands like Lampedusa in Italy and Lesbos in Greece have become, in the words of one observer, 'a symbol and snapshot of our divided world and its victims, and indeed of a moral and political disgrace'. The same observer also reflects that the 'Migration crisis may cause panic; but it is a wake-up call to the magnitude of inequality and exclusion in our contemporary world'.[1]

Meanwhile, the bubbling cauldron of the Israeli/Palestinian conflict shows few signs of moving towards peace. The whole region has been described by the BBC Middle East editor, Jeremy Bowen, as the site of 'a proxy World War between the superpowers'. On the face of it, there is little reason to hope that the 'things that make for peace' can prevail in this region. The risk of all-out war between the nations, a possible Third World War, remains.

Despite the evident lack of success in bringing peace to the region, it is not for want of trying. Geneva Conferences in 2012–14 sought to provide a basis for ending the conflict. In January 2014, I was invited to participate in the World Council of Churches Ecumenical Conference in preparation for the Geneva II talks on Syria. Participants came to Switzerland from France, Germany, Italy, Iran, Lebanon, the Netherlands, Norway, Russia,

Sweden, Switzerland, the United Kingdom and the United States. Ecumenical partners included the ACT Alliance, the Community of Sant'Egidio, the Lutheran World Federation, *Pax Christi* International, Religions for Peace and the World Student Christian Federation.

After three days of discussion, the conference issued a Statement, acknowledging the presence of Christians in Syria since the dawn of Christianity. In addition we highlighted the role of churches, humanitarian and refugee agencies amongst the people of Syria. Concern was expressed for all affected by indiscriminate violence and the consequent humanitarian calamity.

The report argued that no military solution to the crisis was foreseeable and called for a recognition of our common humanity under God, and respect for international humanitarian law, as guidelines for building peace.

We called upon participants in the forthcoming Geneva II conference to pursue an immediate cessation of armed conflict within Syria; the release of all detained and kidnapped persons, and for the United Nations to strive to end the flow of weapons and foreign fighters into Syria. Additionally we sought assurances that vulnerable communities in Syria and refugees in neighbouring countries would receive appropriate humanitarian assistance in accordance with international humanitarian law.

Finally we sought a comprehensive and inclusive process towards establishing a just peace and rebuilding Syria.[2] The Statement was unanimous, and whilst it is regrettable that the Geneva II process – despite considerable efforts by various parties, including the churches – was unable to establish any of these goals nor the subsequent UN objectives, it was not for want of trying.

In the succeeding chapters, I offer some reflection on aspects of peace-building in this region in which I have had some small part. They reflect on the need for religion to be reconfigured, to acknowledge that the answer to bad religion is not no religion, but better religion. Equally, it is to recognise that realism demands that it is better to strive to 'fight the long defeat',[3] than to throw up one's hands in despair.

Towards the end of 2016, some sixty-nine years after first arriving in North Africa, in another hotel and a neighbouring country I attended a conference in Hammamet, Tunisia. The theme was 'Building Bridges of Hope for the Future'. For several days we listened to people speak movingly of their attempts to bring peace in conflicts in North Africa and the Middle East. I was particularly touched by the testimony of a Libyan woman strategist and peace activist, who through the Libyan Women's Platform for Peace, had coordinated the first meetings between armed groups, parliamentarians, and civil activists, a courageous and brave act. Subsequently the same person, partnering with the United States Institute for Peace, undertook a mapping process that sought to understand the role that religious actors of various hues could play to counter extremism and build peace.

The little boy who in 1947 sat with a hymnbook on his head singing 'Jesus loves me' had embraced and sought to live out that experience in the intervening years. At Hammamet I was humbled by the compassion and desire for peace of peoples of other faiths, and none. I wondered at the price many were prepared to pay to overcome evil and violence. I could only believe that what motivated them was the Mystery of Love.

War is not the answer

It was in February 1991 when *Sojourners* magazine dropped on my doormat with a headline declaring 'War Is Not the Answer'. Preparation for 'Desert Storm', the codename for the first Gulf War, was almost complete. A coalition of Western powers had carried out a relentless air and ground assault on Saddam Hussein's forces and the city of Baghdad since early January that year. At first sight, the content of this edition seemed to be too little, too late. But things are not always what they seem. This was certainly the case over the crisis that had been building since Saddam Hussein had invaded Kuwait with some one hundred thousand troops in August 1990.

From early September 1990, following Iraq's August invasion of Kuwait, Jim Wallis and I talked about whether the churches could effectively oppose war, whilst seeking to offer realistic alternative strategies for a peaceful but just outcome. Jim had expressed the view that a certain momentum toward destruction was gaining speed. Coupled with dangerous brinkmanship, this appeared to be the operative policy of the conflicting parties. Deadlines were drawing nearer. There was a fear that George W. Bush and Saddam Hussein might be miscalculating each other's resolve, leaving a high stakes game of 'chicken' to see who would back down first.

Jim was organising a high-ranking international and ecumenical Church delegation to Baghdad. He wanted Robert Runcie, then Archbishop of Canterbury to join the group which already included the American presiding bishop, Ed Browning. I was serving as Canon Chancellor of Southwark Cathedral when I wrote to the Archbishop outlining the delegation's intent and encouraged him to join. Sir Edward Heath, a former prime minister of the United Kingdom was also planning to go to Iraq to seek a non-violent solution to the crisis, and I hoped that this might influence the archbishop's decision favourably.

Robert Runcie was gracious and appeared to give the matter serious thought if the raft of faxes and phone calls between Lambeth Palace and Southwark Cathedral was anything to go by. In the end he decided not to go. I conveyed the archbishop's decision to Jim, who was disappointed. The delegation went ahead, and besides the Americans included representatives of the Middle East Council of Churches.

Travelling via Amman in Jordan, the party arrived in Baghdad. 'The irony and promise of Christmas carols over the radio accompanied us throughout our journey,' Jim commented. The delegation met with Iraqi government representatives. Though the encounters were far from easy, nevertheless the parties reached some measure of agreement on alternatives to war.[1] On their return, Bishop Ed Browning met with George W. Bush and secretary of state James Baker, himself an Episcopalian. Browning reported what they had seen and heard. He urged the president not to go to war, otherwise 'the Middle East will be scorched beyond belief, and the recovery of such destruction would be almost impossible'.

Following their return, the church leaders outlined why they believed 'War is Not the Answer'. They spoke of the clarity of the voices from Iraq that 'War would be a disaster for us all', with unspeakable loss of lives, not least of civilians. They expressed their view that the United States itself would be 'ravaged here at home by a war in the Middle East. Given the make-up of US volunteer armed forces, we know that those who will do most of the suffering and dying in the Gulf War will be disproportionately low-income people and people of color' (*sic*).

The delegation appealed to the United Nations to provide an Arab contribution to help facilitate a resolution of the Gulf Crisis, and to work for a refusal to 'submit to the inevitability of war'. Churches and the nations were called upon 'to fast and pray for peace, and to pursue every means available of public dialogue and popular expression to find a way out of certain catastrophe, to resist the war option and help point the way to peace with justice'.[2]

In London, Washington and across the world, large demonstrations and vigils were held resisting the possibility of war. I took part in one of the marches through London having participated in nightly ecumenical vigils opposite Downing Street through the preceding weeks. In addition, one of my neighbours was a senior civil servant responsible for preparations for war. On a number of occasions we were to meet and talk through the issues.

Despite the protests and delegations, war was declared. 'Desert Storm' was launched in January and raged for 42 days. The war had killed an estimated one hundred thousand people with more than one third of a million injured. These figures included Iraqi combatants as well as civilians; Kuwaitis and members of the coalition forces. It was reckoned as the most intensive death toll in a single conflict since the Second World War.

At its end, President Bush claimed, 'There is no anti-war movement,' and exclaimed, 'By God, we've kicked the Vietnam[3] syndrome once and for all.' Jim Wallis commented: 'Well maybe, but not "By God".' The fact that President Bush felt impelled to declare there was no 'anti-war movement' was significant. Peace activism in the churches of the USA at least had seldom been more evident than in the months leading up to 'Desert Storm'. It had raised a salient question: who is the Christ of the so-called Christian West? Why did George Bush end every speech during the conflict with 'God bless the United States of America'?

The religious leaders had noted in their Statement that 'Given the history of the "Christian" West and the "Muslim" East, war would do nothing to unite Arabs with the West, and the price Christians would pay in a cycle of revenge would be significant'. Jim was to observe: 'Is God's blessing only especially, or mostly for us? Is the peace of Christ to become synonymous with the peace of the "new world order" – *pax Christi* become *pax Americana*?'

Whilst Christians had openly debated the morality of nuclear defence for decades, more immediately than at any other time in modern history, the Gulf Wars and the Afghanistan conflict raised the question, 'Who is the Christ whom Christians follow?'

The Jesuit priest, Daniel Berrigan warned of how the gentle face of Christ 'of new beginnings has become a clock face, warning of mere minutes before midnight, the face of nuclear countdown'. Berrigan continued:

> In America the face of Christ, like a brand on the soul, is impressed in fire on the incumbents of the Christian White

House, the Christian Pentagon ... In such places Christians ... are 'doing their thing.' Within walking distance of the living, highly qualified scientists and engineers seriously envision the end of the world. Their ideology and weaponry are hyphenated horrors.

He concluded: 'We must resist with all our powers the apocalyptism that would make of the gentle Christ the warrior of a mad Christian star war.' [4]

Pursuing 'things that make for peace' sometimes involves asking uncomfortable and politically unpopular questions. Such 'things' also mean standing up for a costly radical alternative. Christ died rejected and abused by enemy and friend alike. He was not the Christ of 'cheap grace' or comfortable church-going that lacks discipleship.

Jesus called would-be followers to 'repent'. The first century Jewish historian, Josephus, translated this as: 'Give up your agendas and trust me for mine.' In his first article for the *Catholic Worker*, the Trappist monk Thomas Merton observed:

> At the root of all war is fear: not so much the fear men (*sic*) have of one another as the fear they have of everything. It is not merely that they do not trust one another; they do not even trust themselves ... They cannot trust anything, because they have ceased to believe in God.

The invitation to trust God's agenda, as expounded by Jesus Christ, has since been confused with the political intent of the so-called Christian West. The Church in its various forms has all too readily confused Western democratic values with those of Jesus Christ. The effect has been compromise and support of the political status quo, particularly in respect of state-sponsored violence. The German theologian Karl Barth, an opponent of Nazism, reminded his audiences: 'If we wish to hear the call of Jesus, then we must hear it despite the church.'

'War is not the Answer' – but it happened nonetheless. Prayers, fasting, demonstrations and debates apparently made no difference. We are living with the predicted consequences. But something *did* happen. The mass movements that resulted in those same demonstrations and vigils revealed a deep unease about the capacity of war to resolve historic divisions and conflicts. Attempts by Christian leaders and others to seek alternatives to war were perhaps more marked than at any other time in recent history. Voices within the Church and elsewhere seemed to say, the Bible may tell us to be obedient to the authorities, but it also tells us that there are limits to that obedience.[5]

The challenge that the first Gulf War presented to many Christians was the challenge to go on 'fighting the long defeat', as Dr Paul Farmer has it. Whilst most people appeared to accept the inevitable outcome, others continued to work, pray and strive for a different outcome in the future. Resisting war and violence requires as much commitment and energy as is expected of those who have the responsibility to make war.

'In your struggle against sin', argued the writer to the Hebrew Christians, 'you have not yet resisted to the point of shedding your blood.'[6] 'Fighting the long defeat' involves many lost struggles, many failures, but it is always so in the pursuit of true humanity and justice. It is a day-by-day choice to 'take up the cross of Christ – and follow' – step by step, moment by moment. It is not the falling down that is defeat, but the staying down.

Martin Luther King did not live to see either justice for his people nor the end of segregation. But he believed with all his heart that though 'the arc of the moral universe is long ... it bends towards justice'. 'The things that make for peace' call for the willingness, as Merton has reminded us, to walk in the path of another, to discover what we have in common with our enemy, and to recognise that God reaches out to both of us.

It is better to light a candle

Lighting a candle can be a subversive act. Certainly this was the view taken by my wife, Dee, during 'Desert Storm'. We lived in a closed community of houses near London's Imperial War Museum. Many of our neighbours were politicians who at the time were household names. In addition there were senior civil servants, one of whom was directly involved planning and executing the British government's commitment to the Iraq conflict.

Dee was deeply exercised by the declaration of war. Perhaps being the mother of four sons who, in other times, would have been eligible for conscription, influenced this. Like others, she felt powerless, questioning whether there was anything she could do. A woman of deep faith, she prayed for peace, and looked for a way to act upon her prayers.

Her decision was simple. Each night as dusk fell she lit a candle in the first-floor window of our mews house. As she did so she 'bargained' with God for the life of one non-combatant. Her prayer was that if she stayed faithful in lighting the candle, God would save the life of one non-combatant. Ever the realist she knew that this was profoundly a matter of faith. Who would know whether or how such a prayer could be answered? For her, it was 'better to light a candle than to curse the darkness.'

At the time I was working with some Roman Catholic sisters on a housing estate in Peckham. Together we were striving to bring our experience of small Christian communities elsewhere in the world to a desolate neighbourhood where burglary, drugs and casual violence were all too evident, and hope was in short supply.

A few evenings after Dee began her vigil, I was attending one of the Peckham community's regular meetings. We were a mixed crowd in every sense. Our host had family living in Riyadh, the largest city in Saudi Arabia. Iraq had begun a bombardment campaign using Scud rockets the night before. The first of the rockets exploded in an apartment block where the mother of our host was staying. No one was killed or injured. I could scarcely believe my ears.

I hurried home later and shared the miraculous story. Was this evidence of prayer answered? 'I believe so,' Dee replied. So did I. Whether it was or not is one of the imponderables of faith. The nightly gesture of lighting the candle and saying the prayer began to impact upon our neighbours. A former home secretary's wife came over to ask Dee the significance of the candle. Dee explained and her friend promised to do the same. Soon two candles blinked across at each other. The wife of the civil servant with responsibility for the war enquired of Dee and her friend what the candles were all about. They explained. Sensitive to her husband's position she would not light the candle, but agreed to say the prayer.

As the war progressed, there would be a regular evening phone call from our civil servant neighbour, inviting us for a drink. Our stance on the war was not a secret. He knew of my nightly vigils at the foot of Downing Street prior to the war, and gently teased me, saying, 'It's going to happen.'

When we met at his home, the discussion always turned to the war. In some sense it almost felt cathartic. Our conversations were friendly, polite and courteous. I felt privileged to have the opportunity to wrestle with the issues with someone so intimately involved, and I deeply respected the thoughtfulness with which military decisions were taken.

One night was particularly disturbing. It was 14 February 1991. A report was coming of a 'smart bomb' dropped by coalition forces, destroying a shelter in Baghdad. Several hundred women, children and men had been killed. That night as we made our way to our neighbour at his invitation, Dee said to me, 'Don't talk about the war.'

I replied, 'I won't if he won't.'

As the door was opened he said, 'We didn't do it.'

'I didn't say anything!' I replied.

It was clear that consciences were tender. This was more than collateral damage. Targeting civilians was in violation of the UN Charter on Human Rights. Suggestions circulated that there was evidence of Saddam Hussein 'hiding' among his people, and some said intelligence indicated his presence in the shelter. It is questionable, even if it had been so, whether such an attack could be justified.

It was a sombre evening, and perhaps something of a tipping point in both the conduct of the war, as well as growing concern about the nature and outcome of the conflict. During a visit to Baghdad eight years later, I was to see the remains of the Amirya shelter, and hear the full horror of the story.

Most of us feel like Dee. To seek 'things that make for peace', when the whole world seems hell-bent on war, seems futile. How could anything she do make any difference? It would have been all too easy to do nothing, to give up. Dee's faith was simple and profound. Aware of the way in which 'powers and principalities' reveal themselves in 'flesh and blood', as St Paul has it, she sought to do what she could, and leave the rest to God. Out of the simple act of lighting a candle emerged a moment of divine serendipity and encouragement, with the tale of the apartment block in Riyadh; the solidarity of neighbours in prayer, and the opportunity to talk and share with someone intimately involved in the dilemma of war. Christians are ambivalent about prayer. Some years ago I noted words from an old, and sadly now departed friend, when he wrote:

> We are not easily reduced to prayer. We who grope towards praying today are like a city gutted by fire. The struggle against injustice has exacted from us an awful cost. Albert Camus in a similar period wrote: 'There is merely bad luck in not being loved; there is tragedy in not loving. All of us today are dying of this tragedy. For violence and hatred dry up the heart itself; the long fight for justice exhausts the love that nevertheless gave birth to it. In the clamour in which we live, love is impossible and justice does not suffice.'[1]

True prayer is a response that chooses to love others because we are loved by God. Prayer is never a private act, rather it is an interior battlefield where we must achieve a victory over doubt, even reasonable questions, before realistically engaging with the outer world. Then it becomes possible to risk lighting a candle rather than cursing the darkness.

Intercession is a choice to place oneself between powerful forces. It becomes an act of spiritual defiance. Intercession visualises an alternative to that which seems inevitable. It seeks to bring about the peace that God has promised, and as Walter Wink poetically puts it: 'It breathes the air of a time yet to be into the suffocating atmosphere of present reality'.

There is something impertinent, shameless and persistent in such prayer. It is like haggling in a bazaar, rather than in the ordered liturgy of Church intercessions. The 'God incidence' of the saved lives on the night of the Scud attack on Riyadh gave impetus to the prayer and subsequent action. The sceptic can all too easily reason away the circumstances, but to the person of faith, as Wink has put it: 'The message is clear: History belongs to the intercessors, who believe the future into being.'

On a gravestone in a Donegal village church are the following words: 'It is better to light ten candles, and have nine blow out, than curse the darkness.' Perhaps that is faith.

25

Revelation

'Desert Storm' ended in February 1991 with Kuwait liberated but a decision not to invade Iraq.[1] Columns of Iraqi military vehicles and personnel had been destroyed on the road from Baghdad to Kuwait. 'It had been like shooting rats in a barrel,' commented one of the coalition troops. Politically little had changed. Saddam Hussein was still president and his Ba'ath party remained in power. The UN applied sanctions in the aftermath of the conflict. A 'No Fly Zone' was to be enforced by aircraft of the US-led coalition, to prevent an attack on the Kurds and Marsh Arabs who had supported the coalition.

Following the war, I convened a conference of sixth form students in Southwark Cathedral. I had invited a rabbi, an imam and a bishop to outline their understanding of peacemaking within the traditions of the Torah, Koran and Bible. Together we discovered how 'things that make for peace' are integral to all three 'Peoples of the Book'.

It was an inspiring and encouraging occasion. Was there now a role for young people to play in seeking peaceful ways forward? The imposition of sanctions and the 'No Fly Zone' had put a temporary lid on the bubbling cauldron of the region. Huge uncertainties remained. In Iraq opposition to the regime was brutally crushed. Large stockpiles of weapons provided by the West for Iraq's war with Iran gave cause for believing that weapons of mass destruction (WMDs) could be under construction. There was a further concern. Conscription was taking place in Iraq in order to strengthen a decimated army for potential future conflict.

In the spring of 1999, I was invited to join a delegation of church leaders to Iraq. The visit was organised by Canon Andrew White with the objective of observing the impact of sanctions, to engage with Iraqi government representatives, and offer support and encouragement to Christian communities.

There was little enthusiasm for the delegation from the Archbishop of Canterbury's office, or the British government. Reservations were expressed over the wisdom of such a visit. There was fear of adverse publicity, and the concern that we would be taken hostage. These were not unreasonable anxieties and provided valuable checks and balances, as we assessed the implications of making the trip. We went ahead based on assurances Andrew White had received from the Iraqis for our safety. Andrew had wide experience in the region which gave us increasing confidence to risk the journey.

In early May 1999 we journeyed by way of Amman in Jordan, to Baghdad.

Our delegation was put up at the Al Rasheed hotel, the remaining nominally five-star establishment in the city. It was heavily bugged. The only place we could not be monitored was by the hotel's empty swimming pool. It was empty because of bomb damage to the city's water supply. Each morning we met there for prayer and study on the Book of Revelation, which I had prepared.

Although many consider Revelation to be a treatise on the 'end times', it is more substantially a work offering strategies of resistance against hostile powers. The author, John the Divine, sought to encourage the struggling churches of Asia Minor, faced with the power and hostility of the Roman state, to trust in God who acts in history. Towards the end of Revelation, John reflects that 'the home of God is among mortals. He will dwell with them; they will be his peoples, and God himself will be with them; he will wipe away every tear from their eyes. Death will be no more; mourning and crying and pain will be no more, for the first things have passed away.'[2]

By this radical statement John sought to bring home to the churches God's intent, through his redeemed people, to bring in the kingdom of justice, love and peace. John's communities are to play an active role in the fulfilment of this vision. When he wrote about Christ's coming, John intended his hearers to understand that whenever God's people are faithful to the demands of the kingdom, Christ is present. When they face persecution for their fidelity, Christ is both present, and is coming. Revelation seeks to encourage believers to stay faithful, regardless of the cost, seeking God's saving justice for all humanity.

Reading the text each day, we were reminded of the temptations to compromise faith in the environment of an all-powerful state. Like John's readers and hearers we were being called to remember what had brought us to Christ in the first place. Surrounded by hostility in an alien land, we understood something of the temptation to compromise on our mission. Our prayer and worship around the empty pool was an act of defiance and resistance. There would be people we would meet more courageous and vulnerable than us, and our fellowship with them would be an act of solidarity and comfort.

As we sat in silence one morning, the words of Nikos Kazantzakis in *Report to Greco* came to mind: 'I believe in a world that does not exist, but by believing in it, I create. We call "non existent" whatever we have not desired with sufficient strength.'[3]

Our visit had risks. The anxieties expressed back in Britain were well-founded. These times of prayer and reflection encouraged us. We recovered our faith and belief in the world that does not exist, but by believing we could participate in creating it. Our belief in Christ as the Lord of history was renewed. Jesus' words, 'And remember, I am with you always, to the end of the age'[4] strengthened our faith and hope in Christ who had come, was present, and would come again. So we prayed: 'Amen. Come Lord Jesus. The grace of the Lord Jesus be with all the saints. Amen.'[5]

Sitting under the vine and fig tree

Peacemaking is an exercise of the spirit as much as it is of the will. Our early mornings around the dry cisterns, reflecting on the Book of Revelation, prepared us for the tasks ahead. It is easy to become disheartened, particularly when circumstances seem so intransigent.

Preparing well, assessing the obstacles ahead, acknowledging that setbacks are inevitable, and owning the truth: 'Failure is not the falling down, but the staying down' are all part of the spiritual struggle. So is the capacity to live freely in the Spirit of Christ, returning to the sources of our faith. For us in Iraq the Bible was providing both the resource and authorisation for the risks we were taking in pursuit of peace.

Our time in Iraq was short. There was much to do. Minders were ever present, reporting on what was said and done, by whom. The risks we were taking were nothing in comparison to those who met with us, welcoming us into their homes and communities. In everything we did and said we were mindful that we would be leaving, and they would be staying.

One day we were invited to the home of a Christian doctor. Inviting us to share a common meal, he took the unusual step of requesting our minders to join us. It was a brave but calculated gesture. As he welcomed all the guests to the table, the doctor took a large round unleavened loaf into his hands. Breaking it into pieces, he declared, 'Those who come under my roof come under the protection of my God, let us share bread together.' It was the closest to a grace possible, but as much, too, of a statement of true Middle East hospitality, and the pursuit of peace.

At the table, we had been carefully placed in order that the host's friends and acquaintances might take the opportunity to tell us how things really were. It fell to my lot for the duration of the meal to divert our accompaniers. Towards the end of the meal our host beckoned me to go with him. We entered a garden. 'We will be followed,' the doctor advised. For a few precious moments I was given his account of the state of things. They were not good, but he had hope.

Sitting under his vine and fig tree he said, 'Now let us talk of peace.'

The prophets Micah and Isaiah speak of 'days to come' when an arbitration will be made by God between the 'strong nations'. The outcome will be swords beaten into 'ploughshares, and ... spears into pruning hooks'; 'nation shall not lift up sword against nation, neither shall they learn war any more'. The scenario for this utopian moment was so similar to the location I was in, that the concluding words of the prophet's text seemed to ring in my ears: 'they shall sit under their own vines and under their own fig trees, and no one shall make them afraid'.[1]

Micah, whose faith was in Yahweh, the God of the Hebrews, nevertheless understood that if there was to be disarmament and peace between the nations it would be necessary 'for all ... peoples (to) walk, each in the name of its god, but we (the Hebrew people) will walk in the name of ... our God forever and ever'. Micah knew, as we do today, the capacity of religion to be divisive and even to be violent. His vision of a restored humanity, living in peace, allowed for the acceptance of difference, opening the possibility of a new order of peace.

What the doctor displayed during those brief encounters was obedience to Jesus' command: 'love your enemies'. He had practised the gospel: 'if your enemies are hungry, feed them; if they are thirsty, give them something to drink'.[2] His pursuit of peace was a day-by-day decision. He had realistically assessed the dangers inherent in such an approach. A worldly wise observer of human nature, he had faced his own fears reckoning that those who sought his life were more afraid than him. At the same time his faith led him to believe in the ever present possibility of change. As one writer has put it: '... the one who hated you yesterday and still hates you today, but maybe not tomorrow, if only you find a way to that person's heart'.[3]

Before we parted, the doctor said: 'I am building this garden for peace. One day you and I will come and sit here and there will be no more war.' It is a vision to be fulfilled. As of 2016, the doctor and his family, along with many Christians, are exiles from their homeland. Of the garden there is no record. A bomb crater once, it could have returned to a wasteland or it might have been tended in loving remembrance by others. Maybe we shall never know.

On the bookshelf above my desk lies one of those symbols of hope that emerged from the Iraq visit in 1999, that leads me to believe that nothing is wasted, and that God 'has not left himself without a witness in doing good' as St Paul puts it.[4] On the trip, I had taken a small number of draft study booklets that I had written on the Gospel of Mark.[5] I distributed them as best I could, even though they were written in English. With the final post of Christmas Eve 2000, a package arrived. Several copies of my draft publication, now translated into Arabic, fell to the floor, with a note thanking me for the resource and telling me that 5,000 copies had been dispersed amongst the Christians across Iraq. It would have been hard to imagine a better Christmas present.

My work on St Mark had been significantly influenced by a Quaker friend, Ched Myers, and his monumental study of the same gospel, *Binding the Strong Man*.[6] Myers presents us with a Jesus whose work is 'to lead the "revolt" against the powers, to bring their rule to an end'.[7] In Mark, Jesus is revealed as the 'stronger' man who 'ties up the strong man;' a thief breaking and entering.[8] Not the most usual depiction of Jesus, but one that fits his own description of himself as 'a thief in the night'.[9] This *Yeshua* – Saviour – will fulfil the dream of the prophets and 'liberate the prey of the strong'.[10] But Jesus will do so not by violence but through the theo-politics of compassion, forgiveness, healing and restoration of human-ness to humanity.

Sitting in the peace garden of my doctor friend took me deep into reflection. Both Isaiah and Jesus spoke of 'jubilee' – 'the year of the LORD's favour'. Isaiah concludes his proclamation by adding 'and the day of the vengeance of our God'.[11] Writing in 1996, Jean Vanier asked: 'What is that vengeance? Does it mean that God will punish the oppressors and evil doers? I don't think so. God's vengeance is to raise up the weak, the humble and the afflicted. This is the folly of God.'[12]

Our world does not easily accept 'the folly of God'. Isaiah continues his vision of God's 'vengeance' as: 'to comfort all who mourn … to give them a garland instead of ashes, the oil of gladness instead of mourning, the mantle of praise instead of a faint spirit' (or 'spirit of despair').[13] Then, observes Vanier, 'Isaiah speaks about how they bring life: "They will re-build the ancient ruins," which means they will renew our wounded humanity'.[14]

The 'things that make for peace' are not the bombs of the superpowers, nor the torture chambers of the oppressors. They are those values that recall us to our senses, and re-make us as human beings.

Becoming children of peace

'Hospitality is the soul of religion' observed Paul Tillich. Hospitality could equally be the core of peacemaking. The experience around the Iraqi doctor's table, and the 'talking of peace' were expressions of a profound hope that a different world is both possible and necessary.

As so often, signs of hope emerge not from great power-broking deals, but from amongst the hidden ones, the weak and those who lack influence. 'Never doubt that a small group of thoughtful, committed citizens can change the world; indeed, it's the only thing that ever has', said anthropologist Margaret Mead.

The doctor revealed many of the characteristics of peace-building by his actions. He demonstrated generosity of spirit, a welcome of the stranger and 'enemy' as brothers, a shared experience of food, a fearlessness, trust in God, and a belief in something better to come.

All this was played out against level-headed acceptance of reality. There *were* real dangers. Yet truth had to be told and stories needed to be shared. Engineering encounters without violating the principle of hospitality towards the enemy had to be arranged. Non-violent resistance was enacted through a refusal to show fear, or seeking peaceful outcomes by making threats.

'"Revolt" against the powers' was expressed through a striving to restore respect for a shared humanity, a refusal to see the 'Other' as enemy of whom to be afraid. 'Vengeance' became an act of resistance rather than retribution. Overarching all of this was a spirit of forgiveness, practised with the conviction that there is no future without forgiveness.

Micah describes this way of living as 'the walk'. Opening up a path through obstacles in order 'to do justice, and to love kindness, and to walk humbly with ... God'.[1] Walking the walk is to be done in real time, with humility and without arrogance, recognising that reaching the sacred place of justice and forgiveness is no saunter, but a hard struggle.

Prior to the second Gulf War, Hans Blix was responsible for searching out evidence of WMDs in Iraq, and said: 'Peaceful relations between states can and must be practiced both at the conference table and at the kitchen table.' That sums up all that we experienced during our time in Iraq, and indicates what must happen to resolve the wider reality of human conflict. Much prevents conflicting parties acting in the way exemplified by the doctor and his fellows. Gabrielle Rifkind offers one important reason:

> We seldom manage to extend our humanity beyond those we know and with whom we have relationships. Our compassion rarely reaches beyond family and friends. I remember that, as a young child, when seeing images of suffering in the world, the only way I could deal with this was to tell myself that those who suffered were different from me and did not have the same level of emotions and feelings. By this act of differentiation I freed myself from having to care about them, or take any responsibility.[2]

Who of us has not felt that? On the Sunday morning of our visit to Baghdad, we gathered in the vandalised Anglican church of St George, accompanied by our minders together with some twenty others. Here were Christians: Anglicans, Reformed, Catholics, Aramaic; also some Muslims and Bahais and others making no claim to religious faith. Yet they were present.

On the previous Saturday we had spent time restoring the damaged church. We carried the baptismal font from where it had been thrown in the churchyard back inside the church. We cleared, cleaned and reconsecrated the sanctuary and altar, and offered a simple prayer of rededication.

On Sunday this motley representation of humanity, made in the *imago Dei* stood around the Table of Sharing. After a short liturgy, we passed the handshake or 'kiss' of peace. It was profound and moving. An Iraqi government commissar shook hands with the UN humanitarian director. A German wept alongside a Briton as they stood beside memorials to the dead of former conflicts between their nations. And I witnessed the glistening of a tear in the eyes of at least one of our minders as we embraced each other.

The bread and wine of the Communion was shared without distinction – Catholics, Protestants and Orthodox, and maybe Muslim and agnostic too. I was reminded of words uttered by a fellow priest, now an archbishop, in his London parish one Christmas Eve when the local Muslim mayor knelt before him and asked a blessing. Pressing the wafer into his hands, the priest declared: 'Take him, he's good for you.'

This cosmic moment of transcendent unity offered a glimpse of humanity in a single moment gathered into the Eternal God, whom Christians discern as Redeemer and Sanctifier. Here it seemed to me was the true purpose of Eucharist: a location where, in thankfulness for our humanity, we can find ourselves, and seek those 'things that make for peace'.

Within the 'religions of the Book', Judaism, Islam and Christianity, there are well-worn threads of peacemaking. Sadly they have too often been hidden. Buddhism and Hinduism also seek the promotion of non-violence.

Whether agreement is found on finer points of doctrine or not, such virtues are common values if we are to share a future for humanity. Selfless love for the 'other' is paramount. 'The Christian God is a God without vengeance,' observes Jon Sobrino, 'even – if one may say so – without rights. What is most sacred to God is not himself but human beings. God loved first.'[3] Jewish writer Shaul Magid reminds us: 'reconciliation is a founding principle of Christianity … religion can or should be the vehicle for world peace.'[4]

Albert Camus was unyielding in his demand that:

> What the world expects of Christians is that Christians should speak out, loud and clear … that they should get away from abstractions and confront the blood-stained face history has taken on today. The grouping we need is a grouping of men (sic) resolved to speak out clearly and pay up personally.

A few years ago the Mennonite Church suggested what they called a 'modest proposal for peace. Let the Christians of the world agree they will not kill one another'. It would indeed be a start. Origen of Alexandria stated it more sharply: 'We will not raise arms against any other nations, we will not practice the art of war, because through Jesus Christ we have become children of peace.'

Midnight in the moral order

The smart bombs that penetrated the Amiriya shelter in Baghdad on the eve of St Valentine's Day in 1991 killed around four hundred and eight civilians: men, women and children. They were dropped by United States forces. The attack had been ordered because electronic signals and satellite observations of people moving in and out of the building indicated the likelihood that Saddam Hussein was sheltering there. 'Shelter 25' had been a public refuge during the Iran-Iraq war.

The morning was bright, sunny and peaceful when we arrived for our visit to the shelter. We were greeted by Umm Chyda, the warden, who had lost eight members of her family in the attack. She explained that the shelter was built on two levels. The lower level contained the boilers. When the bomb hit, those on the upper level were incinerated. Those in the basement were boiled to death from the scalding water of burst water tanks.

On the upper floor, the bomb's flash had acted like a camera leaving an outline of a mother and child etched into the wall where they sheltered. The image is seared into my memory, reminiscent of black and white Christmas card drawings of Mary and the Christ Child. It seemed almost blasphemous.

Throughout a sobering morning we listened as people recounted remembrances of loved ones killed and wounded in the attack. The walls bore silent DNA testimony to lives snuffed out in milliseconds. I wrote that evening some words of Martin Luther King: 'It is midnight in the moral order – there is a knock on the door of mankind.' These were civilians whose only fault was to be on the wrong side, in the wrong place, at the wrong time.

Though the official justification for the attack was a strong belief that the president, prime minister and other members of the government were sheltering among the people, nothing could justify the massacre of innocents in such a holocaust.

A day or so later we visited one of Baghdad's hospitals, and saw young people suffering from cancer. The medical staff were well-qualified and deeply caring, but the sanctions imposed by the West were impacting the supplies of intravenous (IV) delivery systems, drips, catheters and other equipment necessary to facilitate consistent treatment.[1] Bomb damage had led to intermittent electricity and water supplies of a few hours each day, which also adversely affected patient care. Repairs to the system were slow and rudimentary.

The effect of all this was to add further suffering to the children. Their treatment was interrupted, as was the air conditioning, affecting medical personnel, patients and their loved ones.

We visited a centre managed by Mother Teresa's Missionaries of Charity, and saw horribly disfigured children born after 'Desert Storm'. The number of such birth defects markedly increased following 'Desert Storm', and one report indicates that coalition forces used 320 tons of bombs containing depleted uranium. When exploded, tiny particles of irradiated dust are released. These, when ingested by pregnant women, can lead to birth defects in the unborn foetus.[2]

We were sobered by the stories we heard, and the suffering we had witnessed. They provided a stark reality to the thousands of similar horror stories that we read about and watched almost every day in the news. Indeed, as I was writing these lines, a report from Amnesty International documented 30 chemical attacks on 171 villages in Darfur, Sudan. 'Victims (were left) struggling to breathe, vomiting, covered in blood, while children have died in agony.' Another report indicated that 'A suspected US drone strike against Isis militants in Afghanistan killed at least 18 people ... reports of civilian casualties were being investigated.'[3] In this same week, barrel and blister bombs have been dropped on the besieged city of Aleppo in Syria.[4]

It is easier to be moved by the plight of 'people like us' than by those we perceive as different from us. Our visit chastened us. Everyone we met *was* like us. To paraphrase Shakespeare: 'They eat like us, get hurt by weapons created by us, get sick, need medicine, bleed, and die – like us.' And when treated badly, they too often want revenge.

If, in London, Washington or Berlin, we had experienced the violence meted out by smart weapons in Iraq, we would have risen up in protest, demanding things to be different. As Shakespeare has Shylock ask sardonically: 'What's the Christian's kind and gentle reaction?'[5]

For many in Britain and the United States, what determined the justification of the first Gulf War was the belief that it was both legal and 'just'. Legality was defined by United Nations mandate, and an appeal to six criteria, which have evolved since the fourth century of the Christian era defined it as 'just':

1. War must be fought by a legal recognised authority; for example a government.
2. The cause of the war must be just.
3. The war must be fought with the intention to establish good or correct evil.
4. There must be a reasonable chance of success.
5. The war must be the last resort (after all diplomatic negotiations have been tried and failed).
6. Only sufficient force should be used and civilians must not be involved.

Elements of these criteria emerged when Christianity was being formally adopted as the religion of the Roman state. Prior to the fourth century, evidence largely supports the view that the early Church forbade Christians to participate in war. Christians who refused to enter military service were often imprisoned or martyred.

When Christianity became the religion of the state under Constantine in the fourth century, St Augustine sought to provide a justification for war 'as a work of Christian love'. The need to justify war ethically and theologically became imperative with the spread and establishment of Christendom. By the thirteenth century, the theologian Thomas Aquinas argued that war could be justified as 'a work of justice for the common good'.

The basis of the 'Just War' was established amongst Christian princes and rulers, and increasingly used as justification for campaigns against so-called 'infidels'. Essentially, the same arguments exist today when the Christian West seeks to justify war against the rest. Less is said about the 'Christian' basis, and more about 'our values' but the distinction is too subtle for many in the world.

Despite the association of formal religion with the establishment, there is another tradition within Christianity that has sought a commitment to non-violence, and a refusal to serve in the military. Those holding this position argue that Jesus, out of unconditional love for all humanity, endured humiliation and violence, leading to his judicial execution by the Roman state. Preparing for his mission in the Judaean wilderness, Jesus faced the temptation to achieve his objectives by force and violence. He refused, believing such a choice to be an act of disobedience to God.

Jesus counselled that only the force of freely offered self-giving love was ultimately capable of overcoming evil with good. It was love with consequences, including the risk of being regarded as cowardly or disloyal or a traitor. It meant being prepared to suffer with those who suffer, being as willing to die as any soldier. 'The standard doctrine of nonviolence,' observed Thomas Merton, 'says that you can disobey a law you consider unjust but you have to accept the punishment.' In the two world wars of the twentieth century, conscientious objectors experienced such calumnies.

Movements like the Society of Friends – more colloquially known as Quakers, have long believed that as followers of Christ, they should not take up arms. Some refused even to help the war effort, believing that any assistance would be to endorse violence. Others drove ambulances or carried stretchers. In the Quaker meeting I attend from time to time, one of the former members during the First World War accompanied every hospital train returning from the Somme. In the Second World War his son, still a member of the Meeting, cared for and helped rehabilitate the child survivors of the Auschwitz concentration camp.

For those who perceive the refusal to take arms as unpatriotic, the Fellowship of Reconciliation has argued that such love is 'a basis for national loyalty'. In the heat of conflict, taking such a stance and seeking to defend it is frequently misunderstood. Phrases like the 'love of God' can be religiously threadbare, engendering distrust that can only be overcome through the most sacrificial behaviour; a virtue to which few aspire.

Throughout its history, Christianity has held the conviction that God works to overcome evil and establish good in this world through individuals and nations. One has to be as willing to die in becoming an 'instrument of peace' as one who serves in the army would be. Making the decision not to take up arms in a time of national crisis should only be done with the greatest humility. Any attempt to present oneself or one's cause as superior is contrary to the spirit of Christ, as is being intolerant towards those who disagree.

Debate has raged over 'Desert Storm'. Was it a 'Just War'? If so, how did it fulfil the criteria? We often discussed this in Iraq. Some tended towards believing it so; others, including myself, did not. Our divisions were a challenge for us. Despite our disagreements, we agreed that we could only be faithful to Christ by treating each other in love.

The nature of modern warfare means civilian casualties now outweigh military casualties. During the First World War, civilian casualties accounted for some 5 per cent; in the Second World War the figure arose to 50 per cent; in the Vietnam War to 80 per cent and in more recent conflicts, 85 to 95 per cent.[6] The idea that 'Only sufficient force must be used and *civilians must not be involved*'[7] self-evidently no longer applies.

What we witnessed in Iraq revealed a disturbing emphasis on women and children as victims, and sanctions that hurt most the poorest and vulnerable. The people with power, influence and money widely circumvented sanctions.

> From any point of view, Christian or not, the reality of war confronts human beings with two dimensions that have been present throughout the history of the human race and in all cultures: the inequality of power relationships and the human suffering associated with the multiple tensions that deny peace to persons and peoples.[8]

Witnessing the 'collateral damage' of Amirirya, the impact of bombing upon the infra-structures, and the medical consequences of nuclear-tipped shells on children and pregnant women, sharpened my concerns as to the justice and legality of the war. The United States and her allies sought to justify 'Desert Storm' as an act of 'humanitarian intervention'. Iraq's invasion of Kuwait was an unjustifiable act, and the accompanying barbarity inexcusable, deserving arrest and arraignment in an International Court of Justice.

Undoubtedly, one of the reasons for the war was the protection of oil interests. No similar intervention had occurred during the massacres in Rwanda. The devastation caused went far beyond anything 'humanitarian'. To date, the USA has refused to reveal the extent of Iraqi military and civilian casualties.

The debate we had within our delegation made clear that there was no simple solution. Some argued that where a wrong is being done and the resources are available, intervention is justifiable. Others queried whether intervention could be right if the 'Just War' principle *that civilians must not be involved* was broken, and ongoing suffering caused.

What the experience of those days in Iraq did lead us to agree upon was that if such 'is never to happen again', both 'just warriors' and advocates of non-violence needed to work together towards 'a new era when the dangers, excesses, and inevitable injustices of war are clearly seen by all'.[9] It would not be enough to be say 'no war', we had to work together to seek non-violent options, and we needed to do it now. Could we do so? Without such engagement, it would remain 'midnight in the moral order'.

Violence is breakdown – a refusal to dialogue

It was late on our final Saturday night in Baghdad when the call came to be ready to meet with the prime minister, Tariq Aziz. The cars that collected us were driven at high speed through the dimly lit city streets. Passing through the security barrier, we were confronted with a multistorey building darkened save for windows high up, where the prime minister had his offices.

It was a widely held view that to be in the elite of Saddam Hussein's government, individuals needed to have personally indicated their loyalty to the regime by demonstrating ruthlessness and cruelty. Aziz was the public face of the polity, his excellent English making him easily understood and understandable. Nevertheless, there was a sense of a dark side, and, as one of our party remarked, 'Blood on his hands.'

Whether this was true, we were unquestionably dealing with a brutally oppressive regime. Early in his presidency, the West had supported Saddam Hussein, as Iran had been seen as the greater threat. But evidence from Amnesty International and other human rights agencies showed the torture and killing of Iraqi citizens were always integral to Hussein's rule.

Ascending in the lift for our meeting with Aziz, I counselled our group not to smile as we exited. Both Lambeth Palace and the British government were anxious lest our visit was used for propaganda purposes. We well understood the risk. As we emerged from the lift, there stood a smiling Tariq Aziz, and a television crew to capture our arrival.

With serious faces we shook hands formally with the prime minister. We were ushered into a conference room. Here Aziz immediately outlined his government's grievances over the West's policies towards Iraq. Chief was the impact of sanctions, the imposition of a 'No Fly Zone', and a refusal by the West to understand the complexities of Iraqi tribal realities.

Much was standard rhetoric for visitors, and opportunities for genuine dialogue were limited. We raised the issue of Iraq's human rights record; in turn Aziz questioned the incineration and scalding of the victims of Amiriya, and the destruction of the infrastructures of sewage, water and electricity. When we challenged the alleged storage of vital medical equipment, he asked why the UN sanctions exemptions were so labyrinthine.

From a Western perspective it is all too easy to dismiss such a conversation as little more than tit for tat. That is to misunderstand how the Middle Eastern mind works. When honour is at stake, parties haggle as in a bazaar. If a bargain can be struck that does not humiliate the weaker party, progress is made. If not, it isn't. Our powers of negotiation were limited, though we did agree to seek to represent some of the concerns expressed to us.

Assessing the value of our meeting was difficult. We had steered clear of adverse publicity. Yet we had met with the prime minister. We had witnessed some of the lasting impact of 'Desert Storm' upon the infrastructure, as well as seeing the effect of the convoluted sanctions exemptions leading to a mismatch in the provision of equipment rendering much unusable. The testimony of the relatives of the dead in the Amiriya shelter had been sobering.

We faced two main difficulties: first, that our time with Aziz was limited, and second, the lack of support for our visit from Lambeth and the British government. We had to make the best of it. With hindsight, I have always wondered whether somehow we missed an opportunity with Tariq Aziz, and whether we could have achieved something more. Perhaps that is the lot of all engaged in such processes.

Our meeting brought us very close to the dark heart of things. It was rumoured that torture chambers and prison cells were situated just below Aziz's office. True or not, certainly orders were issued here. Was he a monster? The irony is, such people seem so normal, so like us.

Slavenka Drakulic, writing in *The Guardian* of those brought to trial at the International Court in The Hague for alleged war crimes during the conflict in former Yugoslavia, observed: 'The more I occupy myself with the individual cases of war criminals, the less I believe them to be monsters.'[1] Such cruelty and the extremism that accompanies it 'begins with thousands of small acts committed by ordinary people'. Any study of the Holocaust bears testimony to that reality. 'War does not come from nowhere,' observes Drakulic: neither, as Pico and Rifkind point out, do 'institutions ... decide to destroy or kill, or make peace or war: those actions are the responsibility of individuals'.

Despite real ambiguity about our meeting with Tariq Aziz, it settled for me an important question: that however unpalatable the deeds of such people might be, keeping communication open is essential. However unpalatable and monstrous the behaviour of an individual, at the other side of the table is a fellow human being. All peace processes come down in the end to making relationships. Exposing dark deeds, and seeking justice that is restorative are not necessarily mutually exclusive. Few conflicts lack antecedents, however flimsy or substantial their basis.

This view was reinforced by a story in the Marble Arch synagogue from the chief rabbi of Israel reflecting on the story of Cain and Abel, the first case of fratricide.[2] In my edition of the New Revised Standard Version of the Bible, it is preceded by a subheading that reads: 'Beginnings of the First Civilisation'.

'Do you realise that one quarter of humanity was killed in one short moment of history?' enquired the rabbi. 'Adam, Eve, Cain and Abel, this was the population. With Abel's murder – one quarter died. How do you kill if no one has taught you? ... Abel suffered many blows as mankind learned to kill. How do I know? Because the Hebrew tells us that Abel's *bloods* – plural, cried from the earth. And why did this happen? Because there was no dialogue between the two men. Violence is breakdown – a refusal to dialogue. The story of Cain and Abel lies at the heart of the scriptural version of the human story, to remind us of just this: that if we do not talk together, we cannot walk together – and we shall all perish.'

How far we are from the Divine vision of 'beating swords into ploughshares'. Yet if we have somehow 'learned to kill', as the rabbi put it, can we not also 'unlearn'? If, through our own imagination and enterprise, we have beaten the raw material of metal into swords, can we not unlearn the process? Sometimes, clues to the possibility of such un-learning come from surprising sources.

In her review of Drakulic's book, Melissa Benn suggests that we can 'un-learn' even from the most unlikely people.[3] She observed prisoners accused of war crimes, from both sides in the Bosnian-Serbian Conflict of 1991–95. They were held together in the Scheveningen Detention Centre in The Hague, Holland. Drakulic reflects that 'somehow they revived "brotherhood and unity" of the old Yugoslavia. Serbs accused of killing Muslims happily play cards with Muslims charged with the torture of Serbians'. As Drakulic said, 'They have obviously reached a compromise that enables them to live together – something that people back home can only dream about.'

But if the apparent harmony inside Scheveningen is indeed the mysterious, frustrating epilogue of this war, one cannot but echo Drakulic's final cry: 'What was it all for? ... Nor can one but cheer and weep at her single two word answer: "for nothing."' Whilst that answer is both true and depressing, however the compromise was reached enabling the prisoners to live together, it offers a glimmer of hope of a different future.

The decision to meet Aziz was risky. The establishment was hostile, and argued we came away with nothing, pawns used by Aziz for his own purposes. But being there and talking was better than not being there. We raised issues, we listened, and encountered another point of view.

As we left Iraq, and reflected on our meeting, I thought of some words of the peacemaker A.J. Muste: 'Mankind has to find a way into a radically new world. Mankind has to become "a new humanity", or perish.' Four years later, some of us who visited Aziz sat with prime minister Tony Blair, pleading again: 'Stop the War.' Sadly, the signs of 'a new humanity' were still eluding us.

Enduring freedom

In the early afternoon of 11 September 2001 during a retreat in the Surrey countryside, Colin Slee, then dean of Southwark Cathedral in London, burst into the sleepy atmosphere, declaring: 'A plane has crashed into the Twin Towers in New York; a second into the Pentagon, whilst a third has crashed in a field in Pennsylvania. The world can never be the same again.'

For a horrifying half hour or so, we crowded into the one bedroom on the premises where a small television relayed pictures from New York and Washington. The collapsing Twin Towers in Manhattan have become icons of an event that has dominated Western foreign policy ever since. The world indeed has never been the same. We returned to our meeting and held a short period of silence. Then back to business, though the images we had glimpsed kept on running in our minds.

It would be an all too brief interlude before talk of retaliatory action flooded the political agenda. Almost immediately, new coalitions were formed. The bombing of the alleged strongholds of those who planned the attacks was predictable. Those of us who had been engaged in seeking alternative strategies to war over Iraq in the couple of years since our return from Baghdad prepared ourselves for the inevitable.

Within hours of the 9/11 attacks, phone calls, conversations and reflections were being held by peacemakers and 'just warriors' alike. I talked with Jim Wallis in Washington, who I was to visit in early December. Outlining two possible 'paths' in response to the terror, Wallis declared: 'We need a path that speaks the language and spirit of justice, and (a path which) invokes the rule of law in promising to bring the perpetrators of terrorist acts to accountability.'

Peacemakers cannot be naïve about those who have violated the standards of human life and values to the degree witnessed on 9/11. Natural justice demands that the perpetrators of such acts should be brought to judgement and held accountable. What risks that justice, and loses moral high ground, is when innocent people suffer further as a consequence.

'If we do not use the first path,' Jim commented, 'then the second path uses the language of war and invokes a spirit of retribution and even vengeance, emotions we can all understand, and such language fails to provide the moral and practical boundaries for that response.'

'Mr President,' requested one woman of George W. Bush, 'don't spread our pain.' For a brief while in the uncertain days after the shock of 9/11, there was a question whether the true test of the West's character would be the terrorists being denied their victory, by a refusal to mimic a world created in their image.

Such a sentiment was expressed by some two thousand five hundred church leaders in the United States. 'We must not allow this terror to drive us away from being the people God called us to be,' they declared, while demanding 'those responsible for these utterly evil acts be found and brought to justice ... we must not, out of anger and vengeance, indiscriminately retaliate in ways that bring on even more loss of innocent life.'[1]

It was not a universal Christian response. In November 2001, the Roman Catholic bishops officially sanctioned 'the war against terror'. They argued that military intervention in the light of 9/11 qualified as 'Just War'. Elsewhere, advocates of non-violence found strength in the words of César Chavez: 'Nonviolence is not inaction. It is not discussion. It is not for the timid or the weak. Nonviolence is hard work. It is the willingness to sacrifice. It is the patience to win.'

On 7 October 2001, President Bush launched 'Operation Enduring Freedom'. I had begun a period of sabbatical leave and had been for a couple of weeks in a cottage on the west coast of Ireland. Conscious of the gathering clouds of a potential military storm, I had committed myself to pray three times each day for peace and justice.[2] On each occasion I lit a candle, conscious of some words of Jim Wallis that this could only be a part response: 'We must not just light candles now; we must make a new commitment.' It was the commitment to non-violence: 'the willingness to sacrifice ... the patience to win' that was needed.

On our return from Iraq in 1999, the challenge of building a movement that was not simply anti-war, but that brought the possibility of 'thinking different' about how to prevent future conflicts, seemed imperative. If 9/11 had not happened, perhaps the successive conflicts in Afghanistan, Iraq and the more contemporary war in Syria and the rise of Isis or Daesh might too have been avoided. But happen it did. And, as so often is the case, the failure of governments to respond differently was only matched by the failure of peace groups to seek more effective and articulate dialogue, untarnished by rhetoric.

War and violence have something absolute about them. They appear to offer answers that the subtlety of the conviction 'there must be a better way' do not. As peacemakers faced the seeming inevitability of 'Operation Enduring Freedom', a few voices ventured alternatives. One was David Batstone, an ethics professor at the University of San Francisco, and an executive editor of *Sojourners* who sought to offer an alternative agenda in 'A Platform for a Movement'.

Batstone began his thesis with the assertion that 'the intentional murder of innocents must never be justified, morally, legally or for some strategic end'. Terrorist acts are intentional murder. They are not, as Osama Bin Laden and his ilk sought to preach, the actions of freedom fighters in pursuit of 'holy war'. They are distortions of religious ideology, and seek the destruction of the social fabric that makes up human community. As 'agents of terrorism', said Batstone,

> they are guilty and responsible for their crimes.
> Governments including the US and Britain through their security forces are justified in pursuing those who have committed crimes against humanity ... The safety of innocent people demands the apprehension of those who have committed crimes against humanity; and justice demands due punishment.

But he warned those legitimately pursuing the guilty not to use pursuit as an excuse or opportunity to serve their own interests' increase in a region. This risked further instability. Reflecting on the experience of the people of Afghanistan and Iraq, Batstone argued that they 'have suffered under violent conflict and oppressive regimes for decades. Like the accountant sitting at her desk on 110th floor of the World Trade Center, they are no more responsible for terrorist cells or their activities'.

In the immediate aftermath of 9/11, Batstone believed that 'World opinion supports the rightful pursuit of justice by governments' but it would be a support that would dissipate if such pursuit appeared to engage in vengeful retribution that imitated the acts of terrorists. He warned President Bush that it was unwise and provocative to say to potential allies facing problems of fundamentalism in their own countries that 'Either you collaborate with us, or you are our enemies'.

Batstone called for the Abrahamic faiths – Jewish, Christian and Muslim – to 'dig down deep into their own wells and stretch out far to their distant cousins to lock arms in peace and civic unity' because of their shared 'spiritual practices of reconciliation and forgiveness'.

Addressing the government of the United States, he said it 'must do everything to practice reconciliation between itself and the Arab States, and between the Israelis and Palestinians. In both cases a great deal of forgiveness must be asked for and granted'. He warned of the dangers of a 'One sided allegiance to Israel' by the United States, an allegiance 'that has been deaf to the justifiable demands for Arab justice. Reconciliation requires each side – and the United States – to recognise that both Israelis and Palestinians have valid historical, cultural and religious reasons for their existence'.

Finally, he warned that citizens who have been violated through the 9/11 (and subsequently the Madrid, London, and in more recent times, Paris and Nice) attacks experience genuine vulnerability. People have a heightened sensitivity for better security, yet instinctively they do not want essential constitutional rights forfeited out of fear. 'We must be willing to gamble on freedom rather than be captive to our fears,' he concluded.

Batstone sought for a 'platform' upon which peace-builders could build, by cultivating political and religious allies, and giving space for the development of Chavez's principles, 'a willingness to sacrifice' and a 'patience to win'. Such a 'platform 'and principles remain a necessity today.[3] Peace-building requires strategies that anticipate conflict. It is not enough to wait for the possibility of conflict to appear, and then seek to resolve it.

Governments ceaselessly plan for war. It is a routine activity. Military personnel train for war every day. Scientists give their minds to the invention of weapons that will kill ever more effectively. By comparison, the resources and determination of peace-builders are tiny. Yet as Christians we claim allegiance to the God of peace, the values of reconciliation and forgiveness that lie in the 'deep wells' of the Movement that Jesus Christ founded. To these we must rededicate our lives. These are the 'paths to peace'. Only such a commitment can truly produce 'enduring freedom'.

Carving a compassion

The site of the Twin Towers of the World Trade Center in New York was renamed Ground Zero, following their destruction on 9/11. I left Ireland in early November that year to complete my sabbatical in the United States, and visited the Church of St Paul, which previously stood in the shadow of the Towers. Here the ongoing task of documenting and forensically clearing the site was being monitored; and tireless groups of people were ministering to the rescue workers and bereavement teams. Dee and I were accompanied over the 'Do not cross' police lines to visit Fire Station 10. In the churchyard we had prayed for the victims from the Diocese of Southwark who had been killed. At the fire station we thanked and conversed with the survivors of the crews who had struggled to save others.

It was a moment of extreme poignancy. As we prayed the words, 'Our Father ... your kingdom come ... forgive ... as we forgive ... do not bring us to the time of trial,' the crane above us continued to demolish the remains of once seemingly impregnable towers.

The police officer accompanying us that morning was responsible for logging and supervising of the disposal of the human remains uncovered in the excavation. With a catch in his throat, he told us that morning he had been given a woman's hand holding that of a baby.

This shocking image stayed with me. These fragmentary remains of those whom the psalmist describes 'fearfully and wonderfully made'[1] symbolised the dehumanising power of violence. Those fragile, butchered hands represented all of the world's crimes against the living.

We visited Ground Zero in fulfilling a promise made back in London to those who had lost loved ones. Many relatives would not have even the most fragmentary remains to bury. More than a fulfilment of a promise, it was also an act of pilgrimage. Somehow amidst the horror this had become a holy place. When pilgrims visit holy places, they do so in the hope of being changed in some way.

A couple of evenings previously I'd had dinner with a school friend of one of our sons. He had seen the towers fall from his own office. He spoke of how the event had affected him. 'I am not a person of faith … What September 11th did for me was to make me sure about two things: first there must be no revenge; and second, I need to do something useful with my life. If I had a faith I wouldn't want it based on need. I am not needy; I am successful and I love life. Any faith that I would want to embrace would be one that commanded me to do something for others.'

I found myself asking would the awfulness of 11 September change me? If so, how? Were there new possibilities, or would we return to the same old, same old? The move from peace to war had been quick. Yes, evil was loosed on 11 September; and justice required that its perpetrators be punished. But could we learn not just to look after ourselves, but 'to do something for others', as my friend said?

The events of 9/11 raised once again the urgency of a comprehensive road map leading to a Middle East peace settlement. The sanctions against Iraq were hurting the poorest and killing children, but not its leaders. It was a time to address the realities of Western hegemony and self-interest in the region, and to explore a different kind of economic relationship with countries such as Afghanistan. A new outlook was needed that would 'win more hearts and minds away from terrorism, than endless bombing campaigns', said Jim Wallis.

Amongst the challenges facing all parties was that of fundamentalism. On 17 November 17 2001, in mid-town Manhattan, I accompanied Jim Wallis to a dialogue with Karen Armstrong, Susannah Heschel and Feisel Abdul Rauf, in the Cathedral of St John the Divine. They represented the Abrahamic traditions, Christianity, Judaism and Islam. Together they sought to address the theme: 'Fundamentalism and the Modern World.' Opening the conversation, Karen Armstrong pointed out:

> Fundamentalism represents a kind of revolt or rebellion against the secular hegemony of the modern world … Fundamentalists typically want to see God, or religion, reflected more centrally in public life. They want to drag religion from the sidelines, to which it has been relegated in a secular culture, and back to centre stage.

Very few people who call themselves fundamentalists, she argued, actually take part in acts of terror or violence. Armstrong observed that what is common to 'every fundamentalist movement I've studied in Judaism, Christianity, and Islam – is that it is rooted in profound fear'.

Susannah Heschel identified herself with liberal Judaism, but she nevertheless argued that it 'betrayed some of the central religious principles of Jewish life'. Such 'betrayal' contributed to the rigidity, nostalgia, and even bigotry of Jewish ultra-orthodoxy. Liberal Jews, she argued, had to find ways of experiencing religiosity as fully as the ultra-orthodox. Yet entering such dialogue is never easy. 'Too often,' she concluded, 'they want to missionise me.'

Faisal Abdul Rauf reflected: 'Much of what we call fundamentalism today in the Muslim world is more a psychology, a reaction to a perceived attack.' As with Judaism and the ultra-orthodox, so for many Muslims, there is a revolt against secularism. This in turn has produced a reaction from a militant secularism, resulting in Muslim paranoia and fear. He warned against the oversimplification that 'religions contribute to conflict … The source of all conflict is always an identity differentiation between the "I" and the "you", however we may define it. It could be Arab against Jew. It could be black against white, it could be Hutu against Tutsi, it could be Harvard against Yale, it could be man against woman'.

Rauf expressed caution over the phrase, 'clash of civilisations' because it led to the misperception of the West against Islam. 'We've been demonised in that way,' he said. What was needed was a *dialogue* amongst civilisations. 'How we frame the dialogue will frame the future. If we frame the dialectic in terms of dialogue among civilisations, we will create harmony. But if we foster the dialectic as a clash of civilisations, we will actually perpetuate the clash.'

Neither Armstrong, Heschel or Rauf sought to be apologists for any form of 'fundamentalist terrorism'. Each offered an explanation of how fundamentalism is a reaction to secularism, and a perceived rejection of God in public life. Armstrong illustrated this referring to one of Osama bin Laden's mentors, an Egyptian Sunni Muslim, Sayyid Qutb. During the early 1950s, President Gamel Abdel Nasser, president of Egypt, sought to secularise the Egyptian state. In the process he incarcerated thousands of members of the Muslim Brotherhood, many without a trial. One was Sayyid Qutb who had entered the movement as a moderate. Over the next 15 years of hard labour and witnessing the torture and execution of many of his brothers, he concluded that 'secularism was a great evil'. In 1966 he was executed by Nasser. None of this, argued Armstrong, justifies the truth enunciated by W.H. Auden, 'Those to whom evil is done do evil in return.' But it does give a reason.

Jim Wallis opened his contribution that evening by referring to his own conservative, if not fundamentalist background. He told of how as a teenager he had tried to take a girl from his church to see *The Sound of Music*, but the girl's father had blocked their way, saying: 'If you go to this film, you'll be trampling on everything we've taught you to believe.'

His observation raised a smile. 'The man knew his religion was to make him different from the world, which is a fair point,' Wallis continued. 'I wished he would have chosen to break with America at the point of its materialism, racism, poverty or violence. But he chose Julie Andrews.'

We live in an age when a widely held view is that more secularism is the counter to fundamentalism in religion. To such an outlook Jim declared: 'That's a very big mistake. The best response to bad religion is better religion, not secularism.' And if fundamentalism is said to take religion too seriously, 'the best answer … is to take faith *more* seriously than fundamentalism sometimes does … The question is not whether religious and spiritual values should inform public discussion, but how? Separation of church and state does not require the removal of religious values from the public square.'

Each contributor warned against secularist disdain for religion, increasingly prevalent in the media, governments and other opinion formers. Religion is a fact. It is important for people to gain intelligence about it, and not think that some crash course in fundamentalism, whether in Islam, Judaism or Christianity, is sufficient.

Fundamentalism represents something of a paradox. On the one hand it demands religion play a greater part in public life. On the other, said Karen Armstrong, it 'represents a defeat, because when people are so fearful, so threatened they accentuate those aggressive aspects of their faith and their scriptures, and downplay those texts that speak of compassion and justice'.

'What we must all be striving for,' she reflected, 'whether we are religious or secularist, is the compassion that our religions teach us and that our own Western society prizes so highly. We regard ourselves as a compassionate, tolerant society that respects the rights of others. We got this from the Abrahamic religions, from all three of these faiths.'

'The future of politics' said Jim Wallis, 'is more and more about what kind of people we want to be, what kind of community, what kind of world. It's going to be a conversation about values – religious values, moral values, spiritual values … The one thing religions need to change their neighbourhoods is the dynamic, power and promise of hope.'[2]

The night after visiting Ground Zero its sights, sounds and smells from the still smouldering ruins lingered in my mind. The policeman's account of the discovery of the mother and child's hands haunted me. How could compassion be carved, harmony through dialogue? How do we acknowledge each other's fears and sense of exclusion? How do we disagree creatively and respond honestly over the thing we cannot accept?

The word 'compassion' comes from two Latin words, *pati* and *cum*. Literally translated it means 'to suffer with'. True compassion enters into places where people hurt. It means being prepared to 'suffer with' others. What I had witnessed and heard throughout the day had led me emotionally and intellectually to a renewing of a spirit of compassion. I could not simply be a bystander whilst others hurt, nor allow the future to be left to chance.

To wage war ... or reconciliation?

In the immediate aftermath of 9/11, America, and much of the rest of the world, was in corporate shock. Despite the evidence of the twisted and smoking ruins of the Twin Towers, a sense of disbelief permeated the international psyche. Although it was to be only a few short weeks before the bombing of Afghanistan would begin, there was a confusion of voices as to the appropriateness of such a response.

The bishops of the Episcopal Church of the United States issued a call to 'wage reconciliation'. Boldly, given the numbers of US citizens who had died on the 11 September 2001, they said: '... we in the United States now join the company of nations in which ideology disguised as true religion ... wreaks havoc and sudden death'. They spoke of compassion, of entering into 'a new solidarity with those in other parts of the world for whom the forces of terrorism are a continuing fear and reality'.

Offering their sympathy and a shared grief for the bereaved and injured, the bishops invited prayer for the president and other world leaders, 'that they may be given wisdom and prudence for their deliberations and measured patience in their actions'. They invited prayer for 'our enemies and all who wish us harm; and for all who have injured or offended'.

Giving thanks for the rescue workers, the bishops acknowledged those 'who are reaching out to our Muslim brothers and sisters and others who are rendered vulnerable at this time of fear and recrimination'. Reflecting on the teaching of St Paul in his second letter to the Church at Corinth, they set their remarks in the context of Christ's reconciling activity: 'God was pleased to reconcile to himself ... whether on earth or in heaven, by making peace through the blood of his cross.'[1]

The bishops then commented:

> This radical act of peacemaking is nothing less than the right ordering of all things according to God's passionate desire for justness, for the full flourishing of humankind and all creation.
>
> The peace has already been achieved in Christ, but it has yet to be realised in our relationships with one another and the world around us.

However disparate and dysfunctional Christians are, we belong to each other in a worldwide Church. Ours is a common vocation to 'bear one another's burdens across the divides of culture, religion and differing views of the world'. The events of 9/11, the bishops concluded, demanded a commitment to 'self-examination and repentance.' They wrote:

> We are called to self-examination and repentance: the willingness to change direction, to open our hearts and give room to God's compassion as it seeks to bind up, to heal, and to make things new and whole. God's project in which we participate by virtue of our baptism, is the ongoing work of reordering and transforming the patterns of our common life so they may reveal God's justness – not as an abstraction but in bread for the hungry and clothing for the naked. The mission of God is to participate in God's work in the world. We claim that mission ... Let us wage reconciliation. Let us offer our gifts for the carrying out of God's ongoing work of reconciliation, healing and making all things new. To this we pledge and call our church.

The alternative stance taken by the Catholic bishops of the United States, caused Daniel Berrigan to critically observe: 'So doing (they) ignored two resources: the Gospel and recent history.' Of the Gospel, he observed:

> the bishops reduced the Sermon on the Mount to a dead letter. Other words and instructions of Christ – 'Love your enemies,' 'Put up the sword,' and the sublime legacy of the Eucharist,

'My body given for you,' 'My blood poured out for you' – these may as well never have been spoken or enacted.

The 'recent history' Berrigan was referring to was noted in the Italian Jesuit journal *Civitá Cattolica* following the first Gulf War – 'weapons of indiscriminate killing and destruction show beyond doubt that modern wars cannot be or be called just'.[2]

A few months after the Catholic bishops statement, a 'smart bomb' destroyed an entire wedding party of some fifty-five people in a small Afghan village. This event the authorities described as 'collateral damage'. Berrigan remarked of this: 'I said to my soul, "The Catholic bishops have blood on their hands."' Harsh though such a remark may seem to those of us who have become used to cultural Christianity's pact with power, it is sobering to set the arguments for 'Just War' as a 'lesser evil,' against the radical demands of a Christ who calls us to a 'ministry of reconciliation'.[3]

To my mind, the Episcopalian bishops were calling humanity, and Christians in particular, to 'drink from their own wells'. This 'well' is centred in the person of Christ, not as 'just warrior', but as truth teller, peacemaker and reconciler. When Jesus stood before Pilate accused of stirring up the people, of challenging the Faustian bargain between religious elites and the occupying power, he knew the consequences. He said; 'My kingdom is not from this world. If my kingdom were from this world, my followers would be fighting to keep me from being handed over to the *Ioudaioi*.'[4]

Throughout history, Christians have been tempted to interpret this passage as Jesus referring to the afterlife or 'heaven', when he declares: 'My kingdom is not of this world.' The late Walter Wink translated Jesus' use of the term 'world' as meaning 'system', in modern parlance. Jesus was in effect saying to Pilate: 'I am not of your *system*. If my *system* were like yours, then my followers would act as those of systems that repress and make war.'

Berrigan understood Jesus' dialogue with Pilate as offering an opportunity to salvage his humanity. 'Renounce your illegitimate power,' he pleads. 'Join those whose noblest credential is that they "bear witness to the truth."'[5] It is an offer that Pilate would refuse, but biblical evidence suggests that dis-ease surrounded his decision. St Luke indicates that Pilate said to the religious elites, 'I find no basis for an accusation against this man.'[6] More domestically, St

Matthew records Pilate's wife sending a message to him as he is in the very act of making judgement, saying: 'Have nothing to do with that innocent man, for today I have suffered a great deal because of a dream about him.'[7]

The dilemma that faced the Christian community in the light of 9/11 was epitomised in the apparent contradiction of the stance taken by the two sets of bishops. Was it justifiable to go to war in retaliation for the attacks on the Twin Towers and other targets? Or was this a moment for a different kind of response, one that sought to 'wage reconciliation' rather than 'wage war'? In the end the West, perceived by many in the East as 'the Christian West', opted for war, one in which the 'collateral damage' in terms of lost and ruined lives of innocent citizens, combatants and those perceived as terrorists, would outstrip by many thousands those killed and injured in the 9/11 attacks.

The years since 9/11 have been marked by increasingly brutal and brutalising conflicts across the world. Such an outcome raises once again the question: 'Can weapons of indiscriminate killing ever make modern warfare just?' To my mind the answer to that question is a resounding, 'No!'

The call by the Episcopalian bishops for 'self-examination and repentance, the willingness to change direction' was no easy alternative. So ingrained in our corporate psyche is the notion of retaliation; of 'giving them a taste of their own medicine', that Christ-like alternatives such as loving our enemies or praying for them get short shrift. It is always harder to commit to love that is the foolishness of humanity and yet the wisdom of God.

It is sobering that the Episcopalian bishops' call still remains unanswered. In the First World War, Welsh nonconformists and Quakers conscientiously objected to fighting. But perhaps for the first time in the American Episcopalian and the Church of England the question, 'What *would* Jesus do?' was being faced. Is it possible that we have reached a tipping point in rediscovering the true values of the Prince of Peace? What had become clear was that to refuse to take sides would by default mean accepting the decision to go to war.

Organise and speak out

The year 2002 was to prove long and complex for war-makers and peace-builders alike. The decision to attack Afghanistan through a Western military alliance with 'boots on the ground' was to be the prelude to a long and costly conflict, still unresolved at the time of writing.

The source of the 9/11 attacks had been narrowed down to a small terrorist group known as Al-Qaeda, based in Afghanistan and Pakistan. Saddam Hussein too presented an ongoing cause for concern to the West. Western intelligence sources suspected that Iraq had WMDs – possibly including nuclear bombs. In 2002, no evidence existed of Al-Qaeda cells in Iraq. Yet, a mood was growing that whilst dealing with Afghanistan, unfinished business leading to the possible overthrow of Saddam Hussein could be completed.

A former head of the International Atomic Energy Agency, Hans Blix, was dispatched with a team to inspect 700 possible nuclear weapon sites. Before the inspections were completed, Blix's team were summarily pulled out of Iraq. He stated that 'In no case did we find weapons of mass destruction.' But his conclusion was out of sync with the increasingly bellicose mood of both President Bush and Prime Minister Blair, and ignored. Subsequently Blix was to indicate that he believed Bush and Blair acted 'not in bad faith, but with a severe lack of critical thinking.'

During December 2001, I spent some days in Washington with Jim Wallis, seeking realistic alternatives to war. This was a prelude to 15 months of concerted effort seeking to prevent war. The scale of the 9/11 attacks had left the peace movements reeling. Demonstrations were organised against the possibility of a war in Afghanistan, and the prospect of a further war in Iraq. It was this latter possibility that galvanised public opinion in late 2002 and early 2003. In 2001, Jim and I both concluded that it would take something more than protest if there was any realistic chance of stopping the war.

In the USA David Cortright[1] proposed ten reasons why an attack against Iraq would be 'monumental folly'.[2] In 1999 the UN published a report stating that the 'bulk of Iraq's proscribed weapons programme has been eliminated'. Those 'proscribed weapons' included long-range ballistic missiles and chemical weapons. Cortright argued that the United States had no grounds to seek to topple the Hussein regime, because Iraq had complied with the United Nations requirement to dismantle its weapons.

However, to ensure the continued fulfilment of the UN's disarmament's efforts in Iraq, Cortright recommended the return of inspectors[3] to complete their work. Subject to satisfactory confirmation of compliance, Cortright proposed that the UN agree to lift the sanctions previously imposed upon Iraq. Such a gesture, he suggested, could encourage Iraq to be compliant and potentially the leader in the Middle East as a 'zone free of weapons of mass destruction'. This would not only fulfil the specification in the original Gulf War cease-fire resolution, but could turn Iraq into an ally, as distinct from an enemy.

In summary, Cortright's 'ten reasons' for not attacking Iraq were:

1. No act that justified the use of force – *casus belli* – had been committed by Iraq against the United States.
2. A military campaign would kill thousands of innocent victims, and impact further on a civilian population already suffering from sanctions.
3. The cost of war would be in tens of billions of dollars.
4. Military overthrow of Saddam Hussein would require occupation of Iraq by the US and other coalition forces for many years.
5. War would provoke Saddam Hussein to use whatever weapons he has against attackable targets notably Israel, or US and coalition troops.
6. Any ground war in the region would threaten further to destabilise the Gulf region, and fuel the conflict between Israel and Palestine.

7. Anti-American hatred would be further stirred and the forces of extremism lead to wider use of suicide bombings against the US and its allies.

8. Any attack would undermine international cooperation in blocking funding and support for Al-Qaeda and other terrorist networks. The war against Iraq might be won, but the war against terror, lost.

9. An unprovoked attack against Iraq would set a dangerous precedent of pre-emptive war and undermine the foundations of international security.

10. The effect of such war would be a violation of the UN Charter and the principles of international law, and lead to a further weakening of the effectiveness of the United Nations.

Cortright was offering some of that essential 'critical thinking' which Hans Blix believed to be so lacking. Sadly, of course much of what he predicted came to pass.

Cortright was convinced that if Christians, together with peoples of other faiths and none, 'organise and speak out, we can prevent the coming disaster and begin to build support for a more peaceful and cooperative approach to preventing terrorism and reducing threats from weapons of mass destruction'.

'Organising' and 'speaking out' occupied the time for many of us in the ensuing months of 2002. In Britain, Church of England bishops took an unprecedented line in opposing the waging of war on Iraq. Downing Street was alleged to be angry at their stance, a report in the *Daily Express* commenting from an inside source: 'The bishops really annoy us. Some are coming out as if Saddam is a reasonable guy. They do not know what they are talking about.'

Our response to this was widely reported in the media. We said we 'do genuinely believe that the difficulties we face are huge. But having been to Iraq, we cannot see how any military action cannot involve us in attacking innocent civilians'.

Tony Blair had expressed his hatred of war, but said that in 'certain circumstances ... it is the right thing to do', though he indicated that he had not yet closed the door to alternatives. It was in that spirit I commented: 'If we support the US in an attack,

Mr Blair's moral authority would go, whereas if he were able to be seen as a statesman who recognises the complexity of this problem and can lead the nations to a solution that includes the ending of the threat of weapons of mass destruction and the repression of the people of Iraq, but without going to war, then I think he will go down in history ... The United Kingdom is listened to by the United States and our voice is a significant voice. Mr. Blair's voice is particularly powerful.'

These remarks, and others by bishops, were reported in Iraq. Canon Andrew White, then Vicar of Baghdad, reported that amongst the Iraqis he had met there was gratitude 'for the position taken by the leaders in the Church of England. They knew exactly what the Bishop of Coventry had said, what the Archbishop of Canterbury had said, what the Bishop of Bath and Wells had said. They said it had done a huge amount to reassure the Iraqi public'.

A few days later, I spoke at the September anti-war rally in Hyde Park, where the estimated attendance was between 150–400,000 people. It was a formidable experience. I acknowledged I was speaking to people who believed there were times war could be justified, and those who believed war always to be wrong. 'But what unites us now is a sense that preparations for war could begin with a unilateral, pre-emptive strike that would be illegal, immoral and unwise. True peacemaking demands that we recognise that a bomb dropped on an Iraqi, Palestinian or Jew as a bomb dropped on any of us; peacemaking demands no more unilateral actions by powerful nations; peacemaking demands the dismantling of all weapons of mass destruction.'

Michael Langrish, then Bishop of Exeter, argued in his Synod that any war would be 'against the criteria of classic "Just War" principles. The moral case for military intervention against Iraq, at the present time, remains clearly unproved'. The Bishop of Chichester took a similar line, and was criticised by the former conservative MP Sir Andrew Bowden.

We did not expect our stance against armed intervention in Iraq would find universal support. However, we were pleasantly surprised by the support we received, not only from within the churches, but also from former senior military personnel. Although some of us participated in demonstrations, much of the work in striving for an alternative to war was undertaken through lobbying, meetings, emails, correspondence, vigils and prayer.

Throughout, we sought to be respectful of the genuine difficulties faced by political leaders. We reminded ourselves of the injunction of St Paul to 'be subject to the governing authorities; for there is no authority except from God, and those authorities that exist are instituted by God'.[4] But we knew that too that there was a 'higher law', which St Paul enunciated later in the same chapter: 'Owe no one anything, except to love one another; for the one who loves another has fulfilled the law. The commandments … are summed up in this word, "Love your neighbor as yourself." Love does no wrong to a neighbor; therefore, love is the fulfilling of the law'.[5] Ultimately, we had to be faithful to this law.

At the close of my speech in Hyde Park I sought to give a reason why as a bishop I was taking the stand I did. I explained that Jesus entered the human story as 'Prince of Peace' and that key to that 'peace' was commitment and practise of the 'higher law', one that does 'no wrong to a neighbor', and regards all fellow humans as neighbours, to be nurtured and loved as oneself. To make peace is the primary charge placed upon all, and any, who would strive to follow Christ.

34

A knock on the door of humankind

'Do not have your child baptised if you do not want them to get into hot water. Look what happened to Jesus.' This notice was posted over the simple tin font inside the door of a church building I visited in one of the *favelas* that cling to the hillside below the statue of Christ in Rio de Janiero, Brazil.

Peacemaking demands a similar warning. By the end of 2002, matters were hotting up. *The Church Times* headed its lead on 6 September: 'Iraq: rift widens between Blair and bishops.' The Archbishop of York, David Hope, inaugurated special prayers during Epiphany 2003 against war with Iraq. The General Synod, not noted for its radicalism, debated a motion that 'To undertake a preventative war against Iraq would be to lower the threshold for war unacceptably'. The motion was passed by a substantial majority, voting, 'Hold your fire.'

In October 2002, Jim Wallis and I met to discuss the possibility of a joint American and British church leaders delegation to meet with President Bush and Prime Minister Blair in the New Year. Along with other church leaders, we wrote appealing to both men to 'step back' from their calls for war. We reminded them: 'It is a long held Christian principle that all governments and citizens are obliged to work for the avoidance of war … To pursue alternative means to disarm Iraq of its destructive weapons including diplomatic cooperation with the United States in effective weapons inspections and the gradual lifting of sanctions.' We warned of our concern that any such war would be illegal, unwise and immoral.

By January 2003, plans for a meeting with Prime Minister Blair were well advanced. Whether President Bush would agree was less certain. Our delegation of American and British church leaders was to meet in London in February. On the 5 January, the eve of

Epiphany I contributed an op ed piece to the *Independent* on *Sunday* newspaper. Entitled, 'We must answer the Midnight Call on Iraq', it began with words from Martin Luther King: 'It is midnight in the moral order. There is a knock on the door of mankind.'
I went on to reflect:

> It is a strangely apt observation as we enter 2003, and the Prime Minister has issued notably jeremiad warnings in his New Year message, with its continued litany of despair over war with Iraq, the continuing threat of global terrorism, and the stark realities of a stalled peace process in the Middle East and the systemic crisis in Africa.

Conscious of the implications of a bishop in the Established Church being openly critical of the government, I observed:

> Throughout history, relationships between the Christian faith tradition and governments have often been at their most vulnerable at times of moral crisis. Yet vulnerability offers to all parties the possibility of being exposed to alternative options, different responses, other solutions. Today we live in such a time.

In the United States, polling revealed only 15 per cent of the population in favour of war with Iraq. 'The poor are off the agenda' remarked one religious leader. Aid agencies expressed concern over risks to crisis relief and development programmes that they believed would result from renewed conflict in the Middle East. Apocalyptic predictions were made indicating the possibility of further holocausts throughout Africa, the Indian subcontinent, and elsewhere.

Throughout Christmas 2002, church leaders used the birth of the Prince of Peace to reaffirm their opposition to war. At the same time they recognised that this was no occasion to be ostrich-like over the dangers of heightened terrorist activity. We acknowledged that whatever the veracity of the "intelligence chatter", there were plenty of highly motivated terrorist groups able to wreak havoc.

In the light of this I asked in my article whether war, in Iraq or elsewhere, would remove or heighten this threat. One of my correspondents observed:

> 'I have long held the belief that we must fight extremists, evil and terrorism with massive aid programmes, unrelenting positive discourse and education – regimes led by despots would eventually crumble if the populations in such countries were bombarded with the above rather than with bombs.'

This simple, yet profound view, lies at the heart of the present dilemma.

In my Christmas address I sought to inject vision of hope for a better, kinder future. I reminded hearers of Isaiah's great proclamation: 'For a child has been born for us, a son given to us; authority rests upon *his* shoulders; and he is named Wonderful Counselor, Mighty God, Everlasting Father, Prince of Peace. *His authority* shall grow continually, and there shall be *endless peace*'.[1]

George Frederick Handel's wonderful oratorio *Messiah* renders this text with majestic triumphalism and hope. It is an *authority* and *peace* to be established within the human story. Its *signs* are to be seen wherever human beings seek for a more just society, a fairer world, the ending of war. One such sign was found in the campaign for global economic justice, Jubilee 2000. This movement, begun in the mid 1990s, sought to highlight the plight of poor nations caught up in the spiral of unrepayable debt. By the end of the 1990s, millions of people were rallying to a different drum, demanding, 'Drop the Debt now.'

In my *Independent on Sunday* article I reminded readers:

> A nerve was touched about the fundamental inequality that exists within humanity. For a while a movement gathered which resolved to make a difference and to offer hope. There is little doubt that the investment of billions of dollars that it will take to support one day's fighting, could, if re-directed solve many of the causes of discontent, and eradicate the breeding grounds of terror without resort to war ... The stark question we face is: will our world be one in which humanity lives in constant fear, promoting a spirit of cynicism and despair? Or is it possible that this moment of 'midnight in the moral

order' offers the possibility for a different 'knock on the door of mankind' – other than the grim reaper?

Christianity, I continued,

> has always taught respect for the civil power, but it has always argued that there are limits to that obedience. At the heart of Christian faith lies the task of reconciliation. When we pray for peace we need to do so with a degree of realism for what is at stake: a willingness to give up elements of long held ideals, to accept 'loss of face', and to receive the opponent as 'brother' or 'sister,' as well as dealing with the memories of past evils.

The article was published on the Feast of the Epiphany, when the Magi, mystics from the East, in all probability Persia, modern-day Iran, came to seek the Christ child. We had celebrated Christmas. Believer, unbeliever and the simply curious had sung carols and listened to stories about a child bringing 'peace on earth, goodwill to all people'.[2] I reminded readers that St Paul 'speaks of "God being in Christ, reconciling the world to himself." This is the new moral order. It is the task of people of goodwill to work for justice, to seek truth and pursue it, to live peaceably and in a spirit of freedom. That demands of us participation in society, among those close to us as well as those distant from us. The peace of the world is as much in our neighbourhood as it is elsewhere. The knock on the door needs an answer.' I concluded: 'The task is to prevent the war. The ultimate goal: a world of just and equal sharing.'

Needless to say, neither this article, nor the sermons and homilies offered by clergy over the Christmas season warning of the consequences of war, were universally applauded. There was some voluble criticism in the media, government, as well as amongst fellow Christians. But there was a growing disease, expressed in large anti-war demonstrations held in cities across the globe.

The opening weeks of 2003 witnessed frenetic activity amongst politician, peacemakers and military alike. A visit to Britain by President George W. Bush was scheduled for February. Protests and vigils continued to be held. One that drew media attention was the scaling of Buckingham Palace gates by a Quaker activist, Lindis Percy. She hung a sign saying, 'Elizabeth Windsor and Company. He is not welcome here.' Arrested on some one hundred occasions for such protests, she said that she had 'searched her conscience before breaking the law'.

Other Christians held vigils. There was an ecumenical and interfaith mass prayer and witness in central London prior to what turned out to be the largest ever 'Stop the War' demonstration. The Church of Scotland challenged President Bush to offer 'a convincing explanation of the circumstances for war against Iraq' and to accept that a 'peaceful future could only be reached by a truthful confrontation and acknowledgment of the past'.

Meanwhile, behind the scenes, frantic efforts were continuing for meetings between church leaders from the United States, Britain and elsewhere with Tony Blair and George Bush. Dates had been pencilled into diaries, venues booked for meetings. The American church leaders had provisional flight plans. Much now hung on whether either or both of the leaders of the Western world would meet us. Indications began to emerge from Downing Street, and indeed certain quarters within the Church that some of us were in hot water. It seemed that the 'knock on the door of mankind' was getting louder.

35

A Six Point Plan

One afternoon in February 2003 my phone rang. It was Jim Wallis. 'Peter, we have a problem,' growled his deep American accent. 'It seems that Tony Blair will not see the delegation if you are a part of it.' I was aware of press reports on Downing Street's frustration over the bishops' stance but had not realised it was personal. I had been a supporter of the prime minister, particularly over the Good Friday Agreement in Northern Ireland, over which we had corresponded. I was puzzled. 'OK,' I said to Jim. 'What do you want to do about it?'

'Well,' he replied, 'I don't want to go ahead with it if you are not there.'

'This thing has to be bigger than any individual, Jim,' I replied. He agreed, but insisted that I support him in going back to the sources who had contacted him to pursue reasons. I agreed.

During the next hour or so, I reflected on my own actions. I had been scrupulous in not making the issue personal. I had acknowledged that Iraq was complex, the risk of international terrorism significant, and respected that governments have to make difficult and at times unpalatable decisions. I recognised too that a bishop in the Established Church should only take such a public position in opposition to the government for the most profound of reasons.

Yet I also understood how easily war shunts the Gospel aside, holds it to scorn and buries it. Jesus' strange command to 'love your enemies' is, as Daniel Berrigan has put it:

> a self-cancelling act ... *Love* and then *enemies*. The two cannot coexist, they are like fire and ice in the hand. The fire melts the ice, or the ice extinguishes the fire. The fire wins out (at

least in the gospel text)! The verb *love* transforms the noun *enemies*. The enemy is re-born by the power of love.[1]

In the hour between Jim's phone calls that winter afternoon, I experienced my own 'Here I stand. I can do no other' moment. Allegiance had to be first and foremost to the God whom I was committed to serve and had devoted my life. God's demands won out over all others. If I was to be excluded, so be it, that was the cost, and the decision of others.

When Jim's second call came, I was at ease. 'You are back with us,' he rumbled, 'but it's conditional.'

'OK,' I replied, 'and what are the conditions?'

'That you don't speak to the prime minister during the meeting, and you leave it to others.'

'Interesting,' I responded. 'How did you achieve this?'

'Well, Rowan's being made Archbishop of Canterbury next week... and they wouldn't' want an international incident, now, would they?' he chuckled.

The next few days were busy. British ecumenical leaders were due to meet with their American counterparts in London on the Monday. On Tuesday afternoon a 15-minute meeting was scheduled with Tony Blair. Despite the silence imposed upon me for the meeting, I was to coordinate the discussion amongst the Brits and other international church leaders at Inter Church-House in London on the Monday.

Driving into London on Sunday night, my mobile phone rang. It was Jim. He and the American delegation were snowbound in Washington and all flights cancelled. They were unsure whether they would make the meeting. 'You'll just have to do it,' said Jim.

Irony of ironies. Were things too advanced for the meeting to be cancelled in such circumstances? Without the Americans, and Jim's personal standing with the prime minister, would a delegation of Brits do it – especially with someone present who had been silenced? We decided to play it long. The following morning the British delegation met, and agreed that Tuesday afternoon was more than 24 hours away, and snowstorms rarely close airports in the US for any length of time. Meanwhile, we should plan.

We began our time together with prayers and the sharing of experience. Given that most of us knew *of* each other was helpful, even if we did not actually *know* each other. Accompanying us were two Iraqi Christians whose insights were to prove particularly useful. For the next half day or so we began sharing our thinking.

We were aware that several ideas for alternatives to war had been floated. One that had some traction, was of a UN protectorate-style government in Iraq with oversight by military from Arab and Muslim states, rather than Western coalition forces. Those of us who had been to Iraq had spoken with military personnel in Britain, and some thought the idea worth considering. Our Iraqi friends believed Saddam Hussein was willing to do a deal. 'He likes fishing. Let Saddam go fish!' they said. One possible interim solution was Saddam going into internal exile.

We were unanimous that the Iraqi army and the civil police should be maintained. We wanted to see the dismantling of the security police and release of political detainees. We proposed prosecution and trial before the International Court at The Hague of those involved in torture and killing. A further idea tested in dialogue with military folks, was to position Western forces in a nearby friendly nation, to ensure the Iraqi army did not violate the terms of any UN protectorate.

The morning and the early afternoon of the Monday passed quite busily, and we were beginning to shape up some recommendations of what was ultimately to become a 'Six Point Plan'. In mid-afternoon, the Americans arrived, having escaped the blizzards. The ensuing hours led us to sharpen up our thinking, and by mid-morning on Tuesday we had a clear set of proposals to present to the prime minister.

In summary our aims were:

1. Remove Hussein and the Ba'ath Party from power. Target Hussein but protect the Iraqi people. Establish an international tribunal to indict Hussein and his top officials for crimes against humanity.
2. Pursue coercive disarmament. Intensify inspections. Deploy an international military force with a UN Mandate to support and enforce inspections.
3. Foster a democratic Iraq. Put in place an internationally directed post – Hussein administration that could assist

Iraqis in initiating a constitutional process leading to democratic elections.

4. Organise a massive humanitarian effort for Iraq, by focusing on the suffering of the people of Iraq and immediately trying to relieve it.

5. Recommit to the 'road map' to peace in the Middle East. Address the root causes of the Middle East conflicts with a peace plan including a two state solution to the conflict between Israel and Palestine by 2005.

6. Refocus the world's energies on networks of suicidal terrorists. By focusing on Iraq, attention has been distracted from this objective. Unless an alternative to war is found, a military conflagration will be unleashed. Many people of faith and others who seek alternatives to war, perceive these six aims as providing a radical, and yet real alternative.[2]

Our delegation[3] and agenda were now complete and as clear as possible. We prayed and set off for Whitehall. On the afternoon of 18 February 2003, we were to meet first with Clare Short, then secretary of state for International Development, and then with Prime Minister Blair at 10, Downing Street.

Vow of silence

'You present the Six Point Plan to Clare Short,' Jim invited me as we prepared to meet her at the Department for International Affairs. The meeting was lively and challenging. At the same time, Ms Short seemed to accept the wisdom of what was being proposed. Surprisingly, however, as we left for Downing Street, she asked us not to outline the plan to Tony Blair. As Jim and I sat in the ministerial limo before she joined us, I argued that we should seek to persuade her to rescind this stricture as we made our way to Downing Street. Jim, who had been very reliant on her good offices for access to the prime minister, felt that as a guest it would be impolite to push it.

I said I understood, but that we shouldn't forget that she was a politician and, however helpful, would have her own agenda. I argued we had not been through all that we had been to lose the opportunity presented by our meeting with the prime minister. Given the vow of silence I was under at the Downing Street meeting, however, unless Jim decided otherwise, we would remain under Ms Short's stricture.

In Downing Street each of us was introduced to Tony Blair. The meeting was scheduled for 15 minutes, but in the end lasted for 45. We told the prime minister that as church leaders we had sought this meeting, in part, because of Mr Blair's declared commitment as a practising Christian. We believed that the issue of war was both a spiritual and moral concern.

As we sat down, all parties agreed that there were real issues in respect of terrorism, and that WMD were deeply moral matters. We re-emphasised our belief that Saddam Hussein was a real threat to his own people, and potentially to the wider world.[1] We explained that our delegation was unique in bringing together American, international and UK church leaders, all unanimously opposed to a fresh war over Iraq. We reiterated concerns widely expressed in the media that 'the unintended and unpredictable consequences of war make it a too dangerous and destructive option'. We spoke of our concerns of the effects such a campaign would have on innocent women, men and children, some members of the group speaking from direct experience of witnessing the after-effects of 'Desert Storm'.

The Americans were anxious to point out to Tony Blair that both he and the British people were in a position, more than any others in the world, to influence a decision over war in Iraq. We advised of the danger of a decision to go to war being simply the result of American power. We urged the prime minister to let Britain lead the way in persevering in seeking other ways to resolve the current crisis. The role and place of the United Nations and the possibility of a mandate or protectorate were hinted at, along with renewed efforts by inspection teams, and the presence of an international force from non-Western nations.

Bishop Riah of Jerusalem told the prime minister, 'The road to Baghdad lies through Jerusalem.' We acknowledged the role of the British government in making the critical connection between the various elements of concern in the Middle East, including terrorism, Iraq and the Palestinian/Israeli issue. Being more used to protocols than some present, I broke my vow of silence before the end of the meeting, thanking the prime minister for the time and attention that he had given to us. We believed at the time that we had witnessed a Christian leader genuinely wrestling with the complex political issues before him, with reflection on theology and ethics.

As the meeting broke up, and Tony Blair worked the room shaking hands, he paused with me and said, 'Thank you for being so kind to me.' It was totally unexpected, and I could not quite see how my remarks should have elicited such a response, unless officials had painted a somewhat less than rosy picture of me beforehand.

We left Downing Street to face the media where I reported that the prime minister had 'listened carefully', but could offer no indication as to whether our visit had influenced him in any way to pursue other than the increasingly pressing war option.

That evening Jim and I dined together and reviewed the events of the past few days, and our wider engagement with the issue of war in Iraq. Again I expressed my frustration that we had not shared the Six Point Plan in any detail with Tony Blair. The following day I encouraged Jim to talk again with Clare Short, and she gave her assurance that she would outline the plan to the prime minister.

As we went our separate ways, there seemed to be sort of calm before the storm. Jim's wife, Joy Carroll, was expecting their second son. During the course of her delivery, a senior cabinet minister phoned Jim to ask for details of the Six Point Plan. Jim recalls how Joy shouted across the labour room, 'Take the calls! Stop the war! I'm not pushing yet!'.[2]

Alas, it was too late. Despite international protest, almost unanimous opposition from the international Christian leadership, and even the words of Pope John Paul II, 'It is a crime against peace that cries out with vengeance before God. Let us pray so that the Pharaoh's heart will not be hardened and the biblical plagues of a terrible war will not fall on humanity' – war was declared on 20 March 2003.

A year or so later, I was sitting at a dinner in a London club next to a government minister who was to address us. He had left his briefing notes unguarded on the table. These included reference to all attending the dinner. I happened to glance at them and noted alongside my name were remarks about my opposition to the Iraq war. I have reflected on that chance glance, and much else that surrounded the campaign to 'Stop the War'. Of course I expected that the government would hold information on me. I accepted the biblical reality 'whoever resists authority resists what God has appointed'.[3] I had 'resisted authority' solely on the principle of the 'higher law' – that 'Love does no wrong to a neighbor; therefore, love is the fulfilling of the law'.[4]

Whilst that might be argued as holding the moral high ground, it would not protect me from the weight of government authority. In many other countries, opposition such as mine would have been met by the full force of the state. It speaks much of democracy within Britain that freedom of speech remains widely respected. It is something to be strongly guarded.

Some words from the American preacher Howard Thurman perhaps best summed up my stance. He said:

Too often the price exacted by society for security and respectability is that the Christian movement in its formal expression must be on the side of the strong against the weak. This is of tremendous significance, for it reveals to what extent a religion born of a people acquainted with persecution and suffering has become the cornerstone of a civilisation and of nations whose very position in modern life too often has been secured by a ruthless use of power applied to defenceless peoples.[5]

Countering terror

War was declared on 20 March 2003. All attempts to prevent further conflict had failed. Circumstances changed for the military, and for peacemakers alike. During the lead-up, I had been surprised at the number of both former and serving military personnel who had privately supported the position I had taken. Now, for the serving personnel things would be different, and as a pastor to widely diverse communities including military and their families, for me too.

I decided to write to a number of military commanders outlining the position I had taken prior to war being declared. I indicated that the decision to go to war was a political one, and that I understood their duty was to do the government's bidding within internationally agreed terms of war. I assured my correspondents that as a church we would offer our support, care and prayer for combatants and their families.

I received a surprising number of appreciative responses, and was told that my 'thoughtful' letter had been read to the service personnel on naval vessels sailing to the Gulf. In the ensuing conflict, I had a number of informal conversations with individuals responsible for the outcome of the conflict, and its aftermath. I considered these confidences a great privilege.

Whatever the war's outcome, we were where we were. Having sought an alternative to war did not give me the right to wash my hands of responsibility for its consequences. Equally, the commitment to support, care and pray for military personnel and their families did not remove the belief in a Christian Gospel that held that the only thing you should owe anyone is love for one another, for to love the other is to fulfil the law.[1] Nor could I escape my duty to live out the injunction of Jesus to 'love your enemy'.

Casualties are an inevitable consequence of war. During our 1999 visit to Iraq, we had seen the damage caused to infrastructures and utilities. We had witnessed the lasting impact of weapons of war on children, women and non-combatant men, and the attendant suffering from psychological and physical injuries and sickness. We had seen the devastation caused by 'smart bombs' that had taken the lives of those sheltering from them. These were the 'neighbours' and the 'enemies' whom we were commanded to love.

As the war progressed, casualties amongst coalition personnel increased. At the same time there appeared to be a conspiracy of silence over the repatriation of the dead. I contacted all the Members of Parliament in my diocese saying: 'I am concerned at the lack of honour and respect being given to fallen service personnel, and the cloak of secrecy that seems to cover the return of remains to these shores, and the lack of public recognition.'

I expressed the hope that senior government ministers would follow the example of the former American president, Ronald Reagan, and be present when the dead and injured were repatriated. I continued, 'When personnel are killed and their remains are returned we do not hear about them. When you ask men and women to take on the responsibility for the lives of their fellow citizens by laying down their own, we need to acknowledge that.'

I suggested that, on repatriation, 'There should be a colour party and chaplains present, and the event should be televised so that the public can see what is happening. We need to know the reality. This would demonstrate to the British public the government's support for those who have fallen.' Whilst my intention here was genuinely one of respect, at the same time, I hoped that such public awareness might raise a spirit of caution for future engagement in such conflicts.

What eventually emerged was action taken by the Royal British Legion at Wootton Bassett in Wiltshire, near to the repatriation airbase at Lyneham. Here members of the Legion and increasing crowds of respectful citizens lined the streets as the bodies of the fallen passed in a funeral cortège.[2]

On the first anniversary of 9/11 in 2002, President George W. Bush quoted two lines from the Gospel of St John, as he sought to affirm America's role in policing the world: 'This ideal of America is the hope of all mankind. That hope lights our way. "And the light shines in the darkness. And the darkness has not overcome it."'

There is danger in misapplying Scripture in such circumstances. The words from St John directly refer to Christ as the Word of God. They are not about America. There is little doubt that much of what lay behind American foreign policy at the time was bad theology. Unsurprisingly, many Christians in Iraq faced persecution from others because, as one put it to me, 'America and Britain are Christian countries, they blame us for the war. We are terrified. We really don't know what the future will hold.'

The task of 'stopping the war' became secondary once conflict began. War has its own momentum. The questions now beginning to face us were how to counter terrorism, and how to handle the aftermath of war. I was invited to join a group[3] headed by Bishop Richard Harries of Oxford, to produce a report that would address these matters. It was entitled 'Countering Terrorism: Power, violence and democracy post-9/11' and was published in 2005.

Introducing it, Harries said, 'The real purpose of the report was about winning the hearts and minds of Muslim communities.' He said many churches were already doing this, and we indicated a number of 'joint meetings and peace marches of Christians and Muslims, sometimes involving Jews' had taken place throughout Britain.

The report examined 'international order and the ambiguity of American power'. In his preface, Harries commented that 'it is not terrorism, but American foreign policy and what they perceive as American expansionism, which constitutes the major threat to peace'. We reflected that one of the influences promoting war came from the 'Christian Right' in the United States. It did so out of a strong sense of what it believed to be moral righteousness. We expressed concern at its pre-millenialist[4] interpretation of biblical texts to back such a stance, describing it as 'worrying' and a 'dangerous illusion'. We argued, 'There is no uniquely righteous nation. No country should see itself as the redeemer, singled out by God as part of his providential plan.'

In the report we identified some principles for application in peace-building. We concluded:

1. The whole political sphere, including the pursuit of international order, lies open before God. Those who make decisions and act within it are ultimately accountable to a power higher than any human assembly.

2. All human beings of whatever nationality or religion, share a basic human dignity. Respect for this dignity is the underlying moral principle for relationships between states as well as individuals. So international order is to be built, not on brute power and fear, but on law that is ultimately grounded in the divine wisdom.

3. States pursue their own interests. They are right to do so on the understanding that their interest is the pursuit of 'The good', that is, the condition of well-being and flourishing proper to human beings. This includes taking the interests of other states into account.

4. Politics is too important to be seen in purely political categories. It has a theological underpinning and an ethical imperative. Winning hearts and minds is fundamental to the process of countering terrorism.

5. While the pacifist witness remains an essential strand in the Christian approach to war, for most Christians the criteria of the 'Just War' tradition appropriately applied to the conditions of modern warfare, including counter-terrorism, remain an indispensable tool of moral analysis.

6. Morally permissible pre-emptive military action is that which is directed against a threat whose seriousness and emergence are sufficiently clear, and where no effective non-military alternatives are available; morally impermissible military action is that which is directed against the threat whose seriousness and emergence are not sufficiently clear, or where effective non-military alternatives are available.

7. Democracy, with all the corresponding rights of freedom of expression, freedom of assembly, and freedom of worship is a desirable, universal goal. But it certainly cannot be imposed upon any other country by force. Furthermore, it needs to be appropriated in culturally appropriate ways.

8. Religion can exacerbate or mitigate conflict. It is important to take into account the tendency of religious views of the world to absolutise issues and divisions that might otherwise be the subject of political negotiation and compromise.

9. The Church has a Gospel of peace to proclaim. It impels the followers of Jesus to act as peacemakers (Matthew 5:9), by prayer for the world and its leaders, by working for reconciliation between contending parties, and by seeking to establish that justice whose fruit is peace.

10. Churches have a particular role to play in articulating the faults, wrongs and inconsistencies of all parties to a dispute, including those of the country to which the Church belongs.

11. Christians will be alert to the politics of fear. (They are) to set these threats within a biblical perspective of trust in God.

12. The tendency of some religious groups both Christian and Muslim, to give an oversimplistic reading of current events is harmful. To read human history with a confidence that one knows precisely what God is doing through current events is an illegitimate extension of our limited, creaturely status and viewpoint.

13. The debate on nuclear weapons needs to be conducted with much greater honesty and consistency. If certain countries retain their nuclear weapons on the basis of the uncertainty and potential violent volatility of international relations, on what basis are the same weapons denied to other states?[5]

Our report was published in the midst of continuing conflicts in Iraq and Afghanistan. We hoped that it might assist in addressing future potential conflict areas, such as Iran. In recent years, conflicts in Syria and Iraq have been fuelled by Iranian involvement. However, in July 2015 under President Obama, the United States concluded a deal with Iran over its nuclear programme. Iran agreed to discontinue it, and the US agreed not to go to war against Iran.

This signified in 2015 a radical change in US foreign policy. As the international peace-building organisation Ploughshares reflected:

> Civil society played a critical role in this historic victory. Ploughshares Fund pulled together a diverse and dynamic network – scientists, diplomats, military leaders, arms control experts, nonproliferation advocates, nuclear weapons analysts, faith-based groups, Middle East specialists, and many more – all working together for the same goal.

Those in our small working party hoped that we too had made some small contribution to this outcome.

One controversial aspect of our report was the suggestion that the Church should lead the way in apologising for 'the West's handling of Iraq'. We recalled a 'long litany of errors' that marked recent history. It was something of a fond hope, given the rawness and inconclusiveness of both recent and current conflicts – governments were unlikely 'to publicly acknowledge such factors, let alone express remorse for them' in the immediate future.

Although it had been a long time coming, the Vatican's expression of sorrow for the persecution of the Jews through the centuries offered a template for an apology. Whilst acknowledging the risk of such being perceived as a cheap gesture, we argued that, in time, such an approach would be significant for the Iraqi people, as the beginning of a process of healing memories.

Much water has flowed under the bridge of human affairs since then. Establishing effective government in Iraq remains to be fully achieved. Ending the conflict in Syria, and establishing paths to peace that enable the war ravaged communities to rediscover what it is to be human, remains to be achieved. Defeating hydra-headed terror groups and restoring a common sense of humanity is an ambition yet to be addressed by the international community. The migration crisis caused by tribalism, war and poverty shows no sign of abating. The seeping wound of divisions between Palestinians and Israelis remains to be healed.

All of these issues affect and impact upon 'people like us', yet the wider political uncertainties in Western political leadership mean that reinvigorating peace processes, and 'road maps' for a better future are largely neglected. Peoples of faith, and particularly Christians, need to re-engage with what Pope Francis has called 'the active witness of non-violence as a "weapon" to achieve peace'. It is a task that has never been more pressing.

Suffer ... little children

During the past 30 years I have visited the Holy Land a number of times. I have witnessed tensions between Israelis and Palestinians first hand, and have crossed and recrossed the border between Israel, Gaza and the West Bank. On both sides I have listened to stories of hurt, fear and violence.

On an early visit to Jerusalem I was near the entrance to Hezekiah's Tunnel. In the eighth century BC, the city was defending itself from the Assyrians. Recognising the imminence of a siege, King Hezekiah set about protecting the city's water supply. He ordered the construction of a 1,750 metre tunnel that would allow water to flow deep into the city.[1] As I ruminated on this, I became aware of two boys, aged about eight years. They were hissing, shouting and throwing stones at each other. The incident was over almost before it had begun. What shocked was the mutual hatred, and deeply ingrained mutual fear and suspicion in ones so young.

I felt tears welling up. Both lads were the age then of our youngest son, John. The name John means 'God is gracious'. I thought about him, comparing how secure and safe his life was, unaware of the realities under which these two anonymous boys lived. Yet they too were children of a gracious God: and for all the semantics of theologians – the same God!

> There is indeed a sign which is sovereign among the signs that humankind makes: the sign of tears. There is also a speech which is privileged and takes precedence over other speech, even speech in the words of scripture: the cries of the wronged.[2]

It is not difficult to see both 'the sign of tears' nor hear 'the cries of the wronged' in the Middle East. Of all the regions of the world upon which to reflect, this is the most perilous. The ease with which offence is taken, the mildest criticism distorted, and accusations of prejudice made where none was intended, makes objective commentary profoundly difficult. Knowing this, I too risk being misunderstood.

Yet it is children, whether Arab, Israeli or Palestinian, who face the long-term impact of fear, prejudice, persecution and conflict. As Bishop Riah said in Downing Street, 'The road to Baghdad lies through Jerusalem.' 'Baghdad' here represents all of the conflict zones of the Middle East

In Gaza City, following an outbreak of violence between Israelis and the forces of the Hamas government, I visited a group of ten- or eleven-year-old girls who were in a post-trauma therapy group. Some had experienced their homes being destroyed and witnessed loved ones killed. All had sleep disorders, bouts of uncontrolled anger and panic attacks. Some children, too traumatised to communicate, were deeply withdrawn. Poverty worsened stress disorders in many. Parents too were depressed and helpless, unable to provide for their children's basic needs.

After one visit to Gaza, I recounted our experience to an Israeli government minister. The minister pointed out that Israeli children also suffered from rocket attacks fired by the Hamas government. I had not witnessed any children in Israel who had been victims, but was aware of the reality. I did make the argument that the superior nature of Israeli firepower brought greater destructive capacity. This was, and is, a fact.

Yet it is also true, as a report in *The Daily Telegraph* stated:

> In Israel, children in the south who have been subjected to ongoing rocket fire from Gaza since 2001 also experience severe Post Traumatic Stress Disorder (PTSD) symptoms and long-term effects of exposure to rocket sirens, the need to scramble to bomb shelters, sometimes in the middle of the night, and, most recently, the threats posed by Hamas-dug tunnels between Israel and the Gaza Strip In the southern Israeli city of Sderot, a study by NATAL, the Israel Trauma Center for Victims of Terror and War, estimates that between

75 percent and 94 percent of all the children aged 4 to 18 demonstrate symptoms of PTSD[3].

Both realities are unacceptable. It is more horrible when a large number of individuals, particularly children, suffer. However, to imply that because more suffer, the suffering of the individual is somehow lessened, is nonsense. As Søren Kierkegaard once reflected: 'a single event of inexplicable horror has the power to make everything inexplicable, including the most explicable of events.'

Being a child of the Second World War, I grew up disturbingly aware of the Nazi extermination policy against the Jews. My father was at Belsen shortly after its liberation. It is impossible to view the conflict in Israel/Palestine without some reckoning of that destruction which Jews refer to as *Shoah*. History. Whenever I am in Jerusalem I return to *Yad Vashem*, the Holocaust memorial. Meaning, 'A place and a name', *Yad Vashem* commemorates and bears witness to all those without the dignity of a grave.

Established in 1953, *Yad Vashem* has been in a process of continuous development since. During my early visits, many of the photographic displays had a familiarity borne of school textbooks, and the story board accounts I had read in memoirs, or seen in documentaries. Because of a certain 'familiarity' with the exhibits, I was not unduly moved, though my mind was full of questions, and remains so as I wonder at the depth of human depravity.

What did touch me with the 'sign of tears' was walking out of the sunshine into the darkness of the Children's Memorial. This building, carved out of an underground cavern, bears testimony to the nearly 1.5 million murdered children. Entering the building, memorial candles reflect infinitely in mirrors like myriad stars in a dark and sombre space. In the background voices intone the names, ages, background and countries of origin of each child.

In his novel *The Song of Names*, Norman Lebrecht[4] spoke of the writing of 'the book of souls'. He tells the story of one called 'the young Rebbe' whose father 'the Alte Rebbe, who never lived to grow old' died in the Treblinka death camp of typhus shortly before the camp was liberated. The father gave to the son the task of preserving the names of all those who died in the camp. This 'book of souls' was to be kept in memory 'of those who died in the sanctification of God's name'.[3]

The suffering and death of children through violence of war, or the industrialised destruction of the camps, bear witness to the same thing: the death of hope. 'The sign of tears', whether of a single traumatised child whose name is known, or one of a nameless number on a list that has conveniently been lost, is the same sign.

In 1989, governments across the world committed themselves to the UN Convention on the Rights of the Child, and since then all countries, except the United States of America, have ratified the convention. The Convention is composed of some 54 Articles. The foundation of all the other articles is that which states: 'Every child has a right to life. Governments must do all they can to make sure children survive and develop their full potential.' (Article 7).

Upon this foundation of child's 'right to life' the following is to be built : 'Every child has a right to a name' (Article 8); 'No child shall be tortured or suffer other cruel treatment or punishment' (Article 37); 'Governments must do everything they can to protect and care for children affected by war' (Article 38) and 'Children neglected, abused, exploited, tortured or who are victims of war must receive special help to help them recover their health, dignity and self-respect' (Article 39).

In all I have witnessed in Europe, Africa, Latin America, Iraq, Israel and Palestine there is no more pressing reason for pursuing the 'things that make for peace', than the future of children and young people. Unless we learn quickly how to resolve even the most intransigent of conflicts, we shall never prevent the endless cycle that consumes untold future generations.

What makes the focus of children within the Israeli/Palestinian context so poignant is the location of the three great religions of the book, Judaism, Christianity and Islam in Jerusalem.

Each of these faiths claim that all human beings bear the *imago Dei* – the image of God. The repetition of the 'song of names' in the children's memorial in *Yad Vashem* is to sanctify the memory of each life destroyed. To name them, says Lebrecht, is to 'sanctify God's name'; to recall that in the killing of souls, God is also killed. By remembering souls, God is also remembered.

If all humanity bears the *imago Dei* then those who teach and adhere to the truths taught by the great religions have a responsibility to return to the founding principles of such faith and reclaim them. During a visit to the D-Day Memorial Museum at Caen in Northern France, I came across a copy of a German Jewish Prayer Book published in 1893. In it I read the following: 'Judaism teaches: 1. The unity of mankind. It commands us therefore – 2. to love our neighbour. 3. to protect our neighbour and his rights, 4. to be aware of his honour, 5. to honour his beliefs, 6. to assuage his sorrows.'

Such teaching encapsulates the essence of the Hebrew concept of *shalom*. Though roughly translated *shalom* means 'peace', it represents more than the absence, or ending of conflict. *Shalom* 'means primarily an integral wholeness, the antithesis of all schizophrenia and division'.[5] 'According to the rabbis,' says Lapide, '"all commandments are to be fulfilled when the right opportunity arrives. But not peace. Peace you must seek out and pursue!"' There is precious little, if anything, in this that either Christians, Muslims or humanists could not embrace.

When Jesus said 'Let the little children come to me'[6] it was not for some quasi-papal blessing. Children then, as so often now, were of little consequence. Jesus used extreme hyperbole to describe what would happen to anyone who caused a child to suffer: 'It would be better for you if a millstone were hung around your neck and you were thrown into the sea than for you to cause any one of these little ones to stumble.'[7]

Whatever the rights and wrongs of the Israeli-Palestinian conflict – the statement of Jesus, himself a Jew, a citizen of occupied territory, stands as judgement on all conflicts that cause 'little ones to stumble'. Jesus sought to enlarge the scope of the Abrahamic blessings beyond his own people, in reaching out to the Samaritan woman.[8] As one commentator has observed:

> If John's Jesus preached today, he would claim that no Israeli Jews can be children of Abraham until they act like Abraham and stand with oppressed Palestinian refugees. Similarly, John's Jesus would challenge that no Palestinian can be true followers of Jesus unless they identify and empathise with the survivors and victims of the Holocaust. God's design includes both Palestinians and Israeli Jews. The Jesus of John makes this a reality we dare not ignore.[9]

'The ultimate question for a man to ask,' wrote Dietrich Bonhoeffer from his prison cell in Hitler's Germany, 'is not how he is to extricate himself heroically from the affair, but how the coming generation is to live.' It was such a question that many Jews who had survived the *Shoah* raised in its aftermath. Irving Greenberg said that Auschwitz was 'a call to all humans to stop the holocaust'. It was 'a call to the people of Israel to rise to a new level of unprecedented covenantal responsibility'. He continued, 'Jews today, in Israel and elsewhere, have a special responsibility to those who perished, to work for the abolition of that matrix of values that supported genocide.'[10]

Children in the Middle East and across the world remain victims of values that support genocide in an infinite variety of expression. There is a paradox here. Never before in history have 'The Rights of the Child' been laid out as they are in the UN Convention. At the same time, never have children been so universally victims as in today's world. Both Greenberg and Bonhoeffer understood the need for 'a new level of unprecedented covenantal responsibility' towards future generations. Together Jews, Christians and Muslims have a shared responsibility under God to address the question: 'How is the coming generation to live?'

A house divided: A Church in conflict

'Religious societies are not havens of peace and serene joy, never mind kenotic self giving', observed Sara Maitland in her *A Book of Silence*.[1] Towards the end of 2008, Archbishop Rowan Williams asked me to chair the newly convened Anglican Communion Pastoral Visitors facilitation. An unholy row with threats of division, had visited the worldwide Anglican Church over issues of human sexuality and interpretations of orthodoxy. Our particular religious society was certainly not a haven of peace.

A few weeks before this invitation, I had visited the site of the plane crash in Ndola, Zambia where the secretary general of the United Nations, Dag Hammarskjöld died in 1961. I was seventeen years old when he was killed, and his death had felt like a personal bereavement. As I stood by the simple memorial, I recalled some of the things I had vowed when I became a Christian in my teens. To use Hammarskjöld's words from his only published work, *Markings*, I too had committed myself to offer 'selfless service to humanity'; to be prepared to 'sacrifice all personal interests', and seek 'the courage to stand up unflinchingly for your convictions'.[2]

In choosing to follow Christ in my teens, I had found something both to live, and if necessary, to die for. Under the paling African sun, I reflected then just how the challenge of conflict resolution and peace-building, however inadequately met, has occupied my life. For me it has been at the heart of the Gospel of Christ.

'How beautiful on the mountains are the feet of those announcing the gospel of peace'[3] writes Isaiah, and how spine-tinglingly George Frederick Handel interprets these words in his oratorio, *Messiah*. And it is Jesus who promises to peacemakers that they shall be called 'children of God'.[4] Yet, inexplicably given Scripture's emphasis on God as a God of peace, peacemaking has largely been overlooked as a core value of Christian discipleship.

Conflict in the Church is nothing new. It seems to have been there from the start. Nor should we be surprised. It is full of people like you and me. Because people like me, and possibly you, dear reader, are involved in it. However we come, and whatever we bring to both our faith and to the Church, is tangled up with our stories, our insecurities, prejudices and egos. In my early idealistic days I sought the perfect church. One day a wise friend advised: 'Peter, if you find the perfect church, don't join it, you'll only ruin it.' Jean Vanier warns of the 'risk of wanting to have a perfect community which is better than others'.

Given such a *potpourri* of people, conflicting elements, disagreement and division are inevitable. Given that fact, what is the gospel approach to resolving difference? Equally, it is naïve to assume that being charged up with a vision that offers the potential for the practice of courage, self-sacrifice and discipline, it will not also be attended by egoism and potential self-righteousness. And if induction into the Christian faith came with some kind of inoculation against selfishness, arrogance, conflict and violence, how could it offer hope to a world wracked with the consequences of such realities? St. Paul understood this when he remarked: 'For our struggle is not against enemies of blood and flesh, but against ... the authorities, against the cosmic powers of this present darkness, against the spiritual forces of evil in the heavenly places.'[5]

Just as the world faces what Willard Swartley has called 'vexing questions', so does the Church:

> Why are certain specific people our enemies? Why do they want what we also want? What does it mean to overcome evil with good? Is peace something that we can achieve, or does it have a gift and grace dimension, both in personal and sociopolitical dimensions?[6]

Questions like these are accompanied by wider ones: What would be the impact on conflicts if all Christians refused to use violence? Can evil really be overcome with good? Do we live by faith, or fate? Is justice and prosperity for all, or just for people 'like us'?[7] Or as Martin Luther King has put it: 'It is not enough to say, "We must not wage war." It is necessary to love peace and sacrifice for it.'

Paradoxical as it may seem, it is precisely this raft of questions that undergirds much of the conflict in the Anglican Communion today. These were to occupy the international team of conciliators selected by Archbishop Rowan, for the next five years.

Arriving in the United States for the first of what we called 'hearings', our task was to listen to the voices of difference and dissent, and subsequently strive to represent these in a non-partisan way to the conflicting parties. To begin with, we met with a measure of resistance and suspicion. The first 24 hours were key to demonstrate our commitment to impartiality. At the same time the inclusion of the term 'pastoral' in our brief required us to listen sympathetically and empathetically. We wanted to demonstrate, too, that despite the divergence of views being expressed, and irrespective of our own opinions, we believed that on all sides were good people whose convictions were held with integrity.

If there was to be any healing of division, any true reconciliation, it would be up to the parties themselves to determine how such a process was to begin. Reconciliation could not be demanded. No outsider could insist on peace. Nor could anyone force their will on another. Neither could parties seek to wear down their opponents claiming 'peace when there is no peace'.[8]

Despite much suspicion and apathy, all parties agreed, in principle, that Gospel values required a willingness to seek reconciliation. The difficulty lay in the semantics of interpretation. Building confidence and trust took time. When it came, it was during informal times of 'breaking bread together', in refreshment breaks and quiet conversations.

Quite what we achieved over three years remains difficult to evaluate. Our encounters across the Communion seemed to me to reflect an insight offered me at the beginning of my ministry: 'I am so glad you are going into the church, you'll meet such lovely people.'[9] True. But equally true was the fact they could also be intransigent and in a state of armed neutrality with their opponents.

All attempts at rapprochement, let alone reconciliation, eventually met the proverbial brick wall. Conflicting parties largely continued to hold their ground believing their particular interpretation of Scripture and tradition was 'right'. If 'two wrongs don't make a right' certainly 'two rights' don't make a right either.

Ideological difference, whether theological, philosophical or political, requires the application of a degree of humility, if progress is to be made towards resolving conflict. Some years ago I came across one of those *bon mots* that occasionally sums up the dilemma:

> The only religions worthy of respect
> Are those commencing
> With following essential text
>
> 'brothers and sisters
> believe me when I say
> we have, at least, a fifty-fifty chance
> of being wrong;
>
> now... let us pray.'[10]

For three years members of the Pastoral Visitation team travelled around the Communion, mostly in pairs, to listen, take note, and strive to represent what they heard and saw to the archbishop. I am not sure that it could be confidently said that we reached either the point of acceptance, or the 'fifty-fifty chance of being wrong', and thus nor the point of being able to say, 'now... let us pray.' But I think the Churchillian principle of 'Jaw jaw' was better than 'war, war' – however little changed.

I have reflected long and hard on 'rivalries over identity'. Here arguments so often turn on issues of authenticity, competing claims to being possessors of the truth, and true heirs of God's ancient promises – as Robert Beck has pointed out.[11] In a sense there was nothing new here; rivalry within religious communities is as old as tea. The problem with such rivalry is that it draws participants away from their true vocation to be witnesses to grace, truth, love and peace. Or, as one of the co-founders of the *Catholic Worker*, Peter Maurin put it: 'The task of the church is to work for the kind of society where it would be easier for people to be good.'

What became evident during the Pastoral Visitation, even if unacknowledged before, was that rebuilding broken relationships in the Church is no soft option, neither does it lack contention. We can be glib when we speak of reconciliation as a core goal and value of our faith. It is neither easy, nor gentle. But we are a 'religious society', to use Sara Maitland's phrase, that depends for its authenticity on a continuous commitment to the process of reconciliation.

Our liturgical discipline of repentance and confession requires us to examine past relations and behaviours. This we do, not simply to be shriven from our sins, but in order to seek to come to terms with the past; build new relationships, and work towards an agreed future. If we do not, then not only does our 'religious society' not function properly, but we have no coherent message of hope for our increasingly fractured world.

'War ... to disappear from history'

Saturday's post dropped a single letter on the mat. Its contents revealed a brochure of the International Prayer for Peace held in October each year. Founded in 1974 by the dean of Westminster Abbey, Edward Carpenter, as a Christian initiative, it was soon to become an event in which, 'The peace of the world must be prayed for by the faiths of the world.'

The reminder was timely. As I concluded editing the previous chapter, I was conscious of the dilemma that has dogged me through all the years of striving for the 'things that make for peace'. How can the Church's Gospel be credible, when it is so evidently unable to practise what it preaches?

This is a serious question. Sobrino is right when he observes:

> The church does not find it easy to be the historical embodiment of Jesus and of his God, or to be an effective, not just routine dispenser of the ministry of reconciliation. To be these it must do two things. The first is to show conviction in faith that reconciliation (with its requirements of truth and conversion) is good and possible. The second is to do this with credibility.[1]

To show such conviction means acknowledging aspects of our Christian story that are profoundly uncomfortable. Sadly the Christian world has not been noted for its peaceableness. In the past century Christians killed Christians, as well as others of countless different faiths and none in two world wars. The atomic bomb was dropped by a Christian nation. Today arms made by so called Christian countries are sold to nations whose peoples are often in need of food, medicines, and basic human rights. Christian nations continue to possess military might that threatens the very future of humanity on the planet.

Owning up to such a legacy and facing its truth is an *a priori* task if credibility is to be restored to witness. This is difficult and costly. Yet, if we who claim the unmerited grace and unqualified forgiveness of God for our transgressions, cannot put an end to our conflicts by reliance on God's grace and the Holy Spirit, the future for humanity is bleak. We have nothing to offer it. Simply, we cannot do nothing and leave everything as it is.

The uniqueness of Christianity is its rootedness in reconciliation. 'God was in Christ reconciling the world to himself, and he has given to us the ministry of reconciliation,' says St. Paul.[2] Here is the vision – reconciliation; the means of enabling it – the person of Christ; and the vocation for Christ's followers – the ministry of reconciliation. There is a deep paradox here. Few Christians would disagree with that all too brief summary of what lies at the foundation of our faith. Yet our divisions remain a scandal. Our obsession with our own 'stuff' whether on sexuality, orthodoxy, or any number of other disagreements, blinds us to the wider concerns that threaten humanity's future.

More scandalously is our participation in wars where Christians have killed Christians; where the supply of weapons has outstripped humanitarian resources in countries whose peoples are poor; as well as our complicity in the production of, and tacit reliance on, weapons of indiscriminate mass murder.

If Christianity is to be credible in our time, it needs to recover the 'historical embodiment of Jesus and his God'. Achieving such credibility, as Sobrino reminds us, comes 'through major gestures of truth, justice and forgiveness'.[3] In its liturgies, the Church dispenses forgiveness through acts of confession, penance and absolution. These are significant gestures in the disciple's search for truth, justice and a more faithful adherence to Christ.

In the Church's story there have been 'major gestures of truth, justice and forgiveness', acknowledging its complicity in the transatlantic slave trade, racism, anti-Semitism – and most notably the *Shoah*. To admit complicity in the arms trade and tacit acceptance of nuclear deterrence requires humility of a different order. Part of the reason for this has been the Church's need for security and respectability guaranteed in the era known as Christendom. This allowed it to justify war, when the Gospel imperative demanded otherwise. This, suggests Sobrino, makes the task of 'full reconciliation' difficult. At best such justification may produce 'partial reconciliation', but this is scarcely adequate in today's torn and broken world.

These are post-Christendom times. Christianity that once belonged to everybody exists no longer. Being Christian today demands a more radical discipleship, one committed to recovering the 'historical embodiment of Jesus and his God'. It requires an urgent new commitment to the peace of the world that Christ came to save, and a re-engagement with the God revealed in Christ's coming. 'A God without vengeance, even ... without rights' as Jon Sobrino has put it. It is to stand with a God who is on the side of the oppressed; who brings an end to death, and ushers in the age of peace; a God of unlimited and unlimiting love and compassion.

To imagine a world of disarmed humanity, in which 'peaceful kindness will be the law', as Martin Luther King envisaged, seems like utopia. Yet is it? Remember that the prophets Micah and Isaiah spoke of weapons of war being converted into tools for the provision of food. They also spoke of people of different faith traditions living side by side in harmony; and prophesied a time when nations would not 'learn war any more'.[4] This vision of hope, together with the practice of jubilee, was not only the manifesto of Jesus,[5] but provides us with a template for a truly new world order today.

Whilst writing this chapter I was in London, listening to a young female professor from North Africa speaking on future hope for her people. She spoke powerfully of her experience of the 'Arab Spring' and the continuing dangers she and her people felt from unresolved conflict. As she spoke I thought, 'My God, is *this* the enemy?'

Travelling home later on the train, I was joined by young soldiers returning from a day selling poppies for Remembrance Day on station platforms. They were boisterous, slightly drunk, but friendly; none older than twenty-five. During the journey we talked. All of them had joined the army in their teens, and were disappointed not to have gone to war.

Later in the journey their corporal joined us. I asked him about the campaign medals on his tunic; two for service in Northern

Ireland, and one in Iraq. He spoke of how he had lost mates 'senselessly' in Iraq, and witnessed the most terrible injuries to Iraqi women and children. 'I never want to go into conflict again,' he said. Then looking at his charges he reflected, 'They all want to go, but they have no idea what it is really like.' He talked of the futility, the mindlessness, and the lack of realism people had about war. 'Yet,' he concluded, 'I know if we had to go to war again, I'd do my bit.'

Undoubtedly we are a long way from turning 'swords into ploughshares, and ... spears into pruning hooks' and even further from not 'learning war any more'. We are a long way too from ending the various internecine quarrels that mar the unity required of us as Christians. Yet both are incumbent upon us, because as St. Paul reminded us, 'We have been entrusted with the ministry (the task!) of reconciliation.'

Reconciliation is the breaking down of all barriers that divide, and striving together to create new relationships built on love, justice and peace. Such a task is both lengthy and costly. When wars end with armistices and treaties, this is but the beginning of a process that might lead to combatants being reconciled. To begin with at least, former enemies behave towards each other with caution, suspicion and fear. Often there is a long period of coexistence when very little can put at risk the fragile peace. There may be an end to fighting, but this is not reconciliation.

True reconciliation takes us beyond the minimalist and the utilitarian. 'Reconciliation is not some peace-and-love state of paradise where all are one. It is an awkward, difficult process where former enemies find painful ways to begin cooperating for a better future,' observes David Bloomfield.[6] For Christians in conflict with each other it means facing up to hard truths, that my fellow believer is my 'enemy'. Because the default position as Christians is the language of 'love', it is hard to own that, in the words of Henri Nouwen, 'behind the smooth word, the smiling face, and the polite handshake ... is a frozen anger ... which ... paralyses a generous heart.'[7] To love the enemy, as Jesus directed, is 'an awkward, difficult process', continues Nouwen, and there are no short cuts.

In the past few years I have learned a great deal about reconciliation working with peace-builders in the secular arena. Many of the people I have learned with have been people of faith,

Christian, Muslim, Jewish: and many have not. What I found striking is how the language of peacemakers echoes that of my faith tradition: forgiveness, perseverance, collaboration, peacemaking, mediation, sacrifice, and of course, reconciliation.

Bodies like Conciliation Resources, Safer World, International Alert and others, work from a non-sectarian perspective. Their commitment to the transformation of broken relationships across the globe is impressive. I have witnessed sharpness of focus, urgency and the refusal to give up. The individuals undertaking this do so from both humanitarian and religious motives, to stop violence and build peace. This is the task of humanity.

Such activity is both risky and costly. As Daniel Berrigan once observed: 'There are no makers of peace because the making of peace is at least as costly as the making of war, at least as exigent, at least as disruptive, at least as likely to bring disgrace and prison and death in its wake.' My colleagues working in diverse theatres of conflict around the world would agree. Like Berrigan, they would say: 'Peace-making is tough, unfinished, blood-ridden. Everything is worse now than when I started.'

Recently I listened to two presentations by individuals who had been working in separate conflict areas, one in the Pacific, the other in Africa. Both had been engaged in these situations for many years. Progress in each situation had been painfully slow, and the toll on the teams engaged in peace-building was enormous. How, I asked, do you keep going? The answer in each case was the same: because of the alternative to peace. More fear, more destruction, more lives lost, more children orphaned and killed, more corruption.

Throughout my journeying in peace-building what has sustained me has largely been my faith and commitment to Jesus Christ. It was he who called peacemakers 'children of God'. Inside a small garden house where I meditate, there is a plaque which reads: 'Bidden or Not God is Present.' Whether God is owned or not, peacemaking is a divine calling. I see in those with whom I work, believers or not, common ground.

In the opening chapter of this book, I recalled the Italian surgeon, Gino Strada, who stated war must 'disappear from history. Same as slavery had to disappear from human history … and today the concept of slavery is disturbing. War should disturb us equally. It makes absolutely no sense. It's very particular to the human race and it's crazy because it is destroying humanity'. This we know.

We know too that in March 2014 the Pope, Archbishop of Canterbury and the Grand Imam joined in a commitment against human trafficking and modern-day slavery. They have been joined subsequently by leaders from other Christian and multifaith traditions. Slavery does exist today. It did not disappear from history with the ending of the slave trade. Significant change has happened in the past 200 years. Peoples of faith, notably Christians, understood slavery to be dehumanising and immoral. They followed their consciences, against enormous opposition, much of it from people within their own faith tradition. They took their fight against its evil into the bastions of parliament and the establishment.

Today both Pope Francis and Justin Welby, Archbishop of Canterbury, are seeking to engage parishes and communities in the fight against people trafficking. Herein lies a call to a quality of discipleship and commitment that will demand of ordinary people a willingness to 'comfort the afflicted, and afflict the comfortable'.

Undoubtedly slavery is a great evil to be combatted, and it is good that peoples of faith are being engaged once again in achieving its abolition. But war is a greater evil. If the Christian community is to participate in the ending of slavery, then it must commit itself to making 'war disappear from history'. Only then can Christ's peaceable kingdom being revealed. We simply cannot put making an end to war on the 'too hard' list. Like slavery, we have to see this as an evil that must be stopped 'because it is destroying humanity'.

It is not enough to appeal for the Church, or the 'faiths of the world', to strive to put an end to war. We need a vision of the future that binds us together as a human race, committed to each other, to the environment and well-being of the planet, and an end to all those evils that divide us. We need to reimagine the future in the spirit of what the Old Testament calls 'Jubilee', and what Jesus referred to as 'the year of the Lord's favour'.[8]

There will be no quick fix. We must do as the Scriptures do, and take the long view, accepting that the ultimate outcome of such a reimagining of humanity's future will be in other hands than ours. That does not, however, give us the get out. All movements for radical change take pioneers who set the vision. Edward Carpenter called for 'The peace of the world to be prayed for by the faiths of the world'. Indeed it must, but prayer demands action, and it is those who are peacemakers who become the children of God, and that is a task for all created in the *imago Dei.*

Jubilee: The hidden agenda

Peace is always more than the absence of war and violent conflict. It is also about the presence of justice. Justice begins with a recognition of our common humanity, our equal worth and value, regardless of gender, ethnicity, disability and economic circumstance. 'I believe in a world that does not exist, but by believing in it, I create. We call "non existent" whatever we have not desired with sufficient strength' – so wrote Nikos Kazantzakis in his novel, *Report to Greco*.[1] To believe in a world where humanity lives in peace is a utopian ideal. Yet not to strive for it is to fail to live up to our human potential, and Christians to their Gospel.

In his novel, *The Shoes of the Fisherman*, Morris West observed: 'It takes so very much to be a full human being that there are very few who have the enlightenment or the courage to pay the price.'[2] To desire a world of peace and harmony, is to desire something good. To work for it and to tackle the causes of disharmony and violence is an obligation and a responsibility.

In the spring of 1993, Bill Peters, a former diplomat and ambassador, came into my office in London. At the time, I was the chief executive[3] of one of the Anglican world mission agencies. We had been going through difficult financial times, and budgets were tight. Bill was chair of the society's council, and well aware of our problems.

Bill was direct. 'Peter,' he said, 'would you consider giving me a thousand pounds?' Clearly the remark was not aimed at me personally, but rather at the grant funding programmes of the mission society. I gulped. We were making cutbacks. Bill knew this, but pursued his request. 'We will be celebrating the year 2000 soon, and I want to make it a significant occasion for the world's poorest. It should be a year of jubilee. I want to see an end to Third World debt. Will you help?'

In such moments you wonder whether you are in the presence of prophet or a nutter. Bill told me of his partnership with Martin Dent of Keele University, and of their plans for Jubilee 2000. I began to sense a prophetic possibility.

Bill got his thousand pounds, the first of many grants from charities, churches, faith groups, development organisations and trade unions. Jubilee 2000 became one of the most successful public awareness campaigns of all time. It influenced for good bodies such as the World Bank, the International Monetary Fund (IMF), and governments. Although it did not bring about the end of unrepayable debt, it raised consciousness and set in train mechanisms that brought debt relief and hope for many nations.

Momentum gathered quickly. During 1998, the G8 Economic Summit of the world's richest countries was held in Birmingham, England. I was among thousands of demonstrators calling on governments for action. The IMF and the World Bank were beginning to put into place schemes that would enable debt relief to be available to the world's most Highly Indebted Poor Countries (HIPC).

In succeeding decades, Jubilee 2000 spawned other campaigns including Make Poverty History and the Jubilee Debt Campaign. It was influential in the setting of the Millennium Development Goals (MDGs) which that committed the 191 UN member states to time-bound, quantified targets for addressing extreme poverty. The target date for achieving this was to be 2015.

In 2005 I saw for myself the impact of Jubilee 2000, and the benefits that the granting of HIPC status to an indebted poor country could bring. During a visit to Zambia, I gave a key note address in the Anglican cathedral in Lusaka, the capital. I drew attention to the dangers of unremitted debt on the wider welfare of people, education and health, and the risks such debt brought of corruption.

During this time, Zambia was accorded HIPC status which it had been seeking for some time. There was much rejoicing and relief. Yet HIPC status placed strict conditions on benefitting countries. This included acknowledgement by funders and beneficiaries that previous debt relief programmes had failed to create economic sustainability. Beneficiaries now needed to keep records of reform, and to present reports on progress to the IMF and the World Bank.

My address in Lusaka Cathedral provoked media attention. With the granting of HIPC status to Zambia, various broadcasting outlets, including the BBC, sought my reaction. I expressed delight that a fresh opportunity was being given to the people of Zambia. I responsed to questions about corruption amongst government officials and others by saying this must now stop. Under the debt relief terms obligation was laid to pay the wages of public officials, lack of which had been the cause of much corruption.

The celebrations that accompanied HIPC status were understandable, but it offered no easy option. It did not guarantee an improved economy. Whilst there was initial improvement, severe drought and famine in 2005 jeopardised progress. Far from decreasing, Zambia's debt burden increased in successive years.

In 2015 the Jubilee Debt Campaign reported that in 2010 the IMF had predicted that 'Zambia's debt payments would triple from $60 million in 2010 to $180 million by 2015'.[4] And in 2015 the campaign drew attention to a 'set of new loans of $60 million from the UK government, via the World Bank, for Zambia to adapt to the impacts of climate change'. The Jesuit Centre for Theological Reflection said of the loans:

> Instead of reparations, the UK is pushing for loans for climate change through the World Bank. Climate loans will only lock our countries into further debt, and further impoverish our people. This will not provide the compensation required to enable people to cope with the impacts we are facing. Loans for climate change are not acceptable.

Both Action on Trade Injustice and Jubilee Debt Campaign have sought to achieve fair trade, along with international government policies that would assist in the struggle to eradicate extreme poverty. The purpose of the MDGs was to facilitate the well-being of the whole human race. Given the realities of free trade and open markets, achieving such ambitious altruistic aims would prove challenging for all participants. Vested interest in keeping the status quo remains strong. Debt and trade injustice continue to discriminate and exclude socially, culturally and politically. We are still a long way from the practice of jubilee.

The gospels reveal how Jesus exposed the extent to which wealth and power were in the hands of a tiny elite. He criticised them for their lack of compassion and solidarity with the poor. His focus on the poor and their pain and suffering was his riposte to the elite. His 'salvation' was to be expressed in love and compassion on those for whom his guts literally ached.[5] Jesus's 'judgement' was upon those systems, structures and persons which prevented liberation, love and compassion.

'The Gospels tell us,' says Felix Wilfred,

> that Jesus was concerned about human suffering and privations rather than sin. Unfortunately, Christian soteriology[6] came to be constructed around sin and not on the most important aspects of Jesus's praxis for the wellbeing (*salus*) of human beings and of communities. His vision of liberation was anchored in the experience of the divine as a compassionate God in solidarity with suffering humanity.[7]

Jesus' announcement of 'jubilee' in the Nazareth synagogue demonstrated the practicality of his 'good news'. It would offer hope by addressing the failings of the past. To begin with, Jesus gained the admiration of his hearers.[8] But they wanted more, and admiration turned to anger. Rumours abounded of his 'miracles' elsewhere, as he was a hometown boy. 'Why listen to him,' they questioned, 'unless he can do some wonders here?'

Jesus refuses. Telling his fellow citizens that no prophet is accepted in his own town, he challenged them by saying outsiders can judge a prophet better. Feeling insulted, they tried to throw him off a cliff.[9] Suggesting that salvation comes when humanity faces the suffering of its most vulnerable, freeing them to become fully human, irritates more than the few gathered in the Nazareth synagogue. Jesus' stance for the dignity of every human being as the indwelling place of God infuriates all who perceive themselves to be special in the eyes of God. When the emphasis in salvation is placed on 'sin' as against 'suffering', it all too easily leads to judgement of others, deprivation, discrimination and division: all potential igniters of conflict.

The 'hidden agenda' of jubilee lies at the heart of 'things that make for peace'. 'Jesus' confrontation in the Nazareth synagogue laid bare the degree of resistance to the 'other' as being of equal value as a human being. Peace, as I have remarked often, is not the absence of conflict *per se*, but the management of conflict in such a way that it prevents violence, and opens up the real possibility of equal sharing.

Practising jubilee today remains as difficult as for the Nazareth community. Underestimating the power of productive forces, capital and the market economy, let alone privatisation of goods, selfishness, and individualism to resist jubilee, is to be naïve in the extreme. The prophet Isaiah's cry remains true: only 'when the veil shrouding all the peoples is destroyed', and tears are 'wiped from every face and throughout the world', will the 'indignities' of division, discrimination and inequality be removed from all God's people.[10]

Archbishop Oscar Romero wrote:

> I do not tire of telling everyone, especially young people who long for their people's liberation, that I admire their social and political sensitivity, but it saddens me when they waste it by going on ways that are false. Let us, too, all take notice that the great leader of our liberation is the Lord's Anointed One, who comes to announce good news to the poor, to give freedom to the captives, to give news of the missing, to give joy to so many homes in mourning, so that society may be renewed as in the sabbatical years of Israel.

Jubilee is a theme that resonates in the Jewish, Christian and Muslim traditions. It is also a concept that many who have no particular religious allegiance find attractive, and reasonable if we are to create a fairer, just and peaceful world. The question, as Morris West put it is: 'Do we have the courage and vision to pay the price?'

Bread not stones

Unsurprisingly perhaps, the year 2000 did not bring the utopia of a debt-free, reconciled humanity. However, Jubilee 2000 spawned other campaigns. The struggle for a more just world remains far from won. Some campaigns were quite short-lived. I participated in one entitled, 'Bread not Stones'. This was inspired by Jesus' question: 'Is there anyone among you who, if your child asks for bread, will give a stone? If you then, who are evil, know how to give good gifts to your children, how much more will your Father in heaven give good things to those who ask him!'[1]

Debt remission and peace-building are serious issues, but there are occasionally light, even comic moments in addressing them. One such occurred during the launch of Bread not Stones in 2002. A group of church leaders had been invited to ride in a donkey cart through the City of London. The cart was to be festooned with banners proclaiming 'Give bread not stones'. The occupants of the cart would randomly give out bread or stones to passers-by. There would be a relay of clerical passengers riding in the cart, whilst others handed out explanatory leaflets.

However a breakdown in communication meant that neither the banners, leaflets, nor the bread and stones arrived. Neither did most of the church leaders. Standing in the drizzle a few hundred yards from the Bank of England, were two young women with a donkey and cart. I spoke to them and asked if other church leaders had arrived. 'No,' they replied.

Nearby were two City of London policemen on large horses who had been detailed to accompany our motley procession through the city. Friendly enough, like all good policemen, they eventually advised us to 'move on'.

No one else had arrived. I bargained for a few more minutes before contemplating a lonely and pointless gesture. The donkey cart still had no visible signs of the campaign's intent.

In the nick of time, Roberta Romanger from the United Reformed Church arrived. Together we climbed into the cart and made our slow, embarrassed way through the streets looking like prisoners in a tumbril being taken to the Tower. People looked on bemused. I studiously avoided eye contact. As we passed the London Stock Exchange, one of the policemen leaned down and asked: 'What's this all about, then?" I remained silent. Roberta cheerily responded, 'It's all about justice.' 'Justice?!' questioned the policeman incredulously. It was clear that his ideas and ours were some distance apart.

For half an hour or so our humiliation continued, until we arrived at one of the City churches to hollow cheers. Here were bishops and other church leaders, as well as banners, bread and stones in abundance, along with photographers and reporters. As Roberta and I left the cart, it was filled with assembled prelates and dignitaries, all posing for photographs.

There is something of a parable about this episode. Debt brings humiliation and suffering. Our short period of embarrassment, the failure of the organisers to provide resources, as well as the misunderstanding over the nature of justice we sought to convey, were petty hurts by comparison. Passing anonymously through the streets in a donkey cart, we caused curiosity and even amusement. It did not change anyone's perspective. The struggle 'for a just and equal sharing of the things this earth affords' was not made any clearer. The posing in the church courtyard by well-meaning non-participants added a final touch of irony.

I have visited many slums around the world. Many were like those described by Tiniyko Maluleka, as 'an organised rubble of tin cans, with its squalor and pretentious contrasts inspires not only revulsion: it inexplicably invokes admiration and a weird sense of belonging'. One illustration must suffice for the whole world. It was in the Banayapi township on the edge of the South African city of Durban. A community of some thirty tents, none of which were waterproof, provided shelter for around twenty families. The informal settlement overlooked the site of Mahatma Gandhi's former *ashram*. During my visit, gunfire broke out from there, evidence, said my hosts, of continuing feuds between rival liberation groups.

A thirteen-year-old girl with excellent English, deprived of schooling because her parents could not afford the obligatory uniform, interpreted for me. She recounted accounts of the abuse of women and girls; of daily incidences of rape and violence. Many of the young men standing around bore the marks of bullets and beatings. One young man was very disturbed by his ill treatment, and his mind had gone.

Around the tent encampment were small areas of cultivation. Portaloos provided the only sanitation. Basic supplementary food rations were provided by teams from local churches. With the ever present risk of violence the location had become too dangerous for aid agencies, all of whom now had withdrawn. Situations like this continue to be endlessly repeated across the world. Yet, such places always fill me with a mixture of despair and hope in almost equal measure.

Despair, because the problems seem so insurmountable. Hope, because everywhere good people are working for change. With scant resources, community land is developed, crèches, clinics, block-making factories, sewing circles are formed. Mostly these are initiated by 'little people'; anonymous nurses, teachers, development workers, clergy of all faith traditions, as well as folks who just see a need and set out to meet it in whatever way they can.

For many years in the Vlakfontein township of Johannesburg, an Anglican priest, Jeremy Pratt, sought to live a contemplative life amongst the poor. He did so in a spirit of solidarity and shared poverty. He set up workshops for the community, offering training in simple skills so women in particular could begin to earn small sums of money. Each afternoon children returning from school would be offered bread and peanut butter. Politically it was a time a time of great tension, and frequent bouts of violence broke out between rivals.

When Jeremy Pratt died, his funeral took place first in the township, and later more formally elsewhere. The night he died there had been violence in the neighbourhood. The following morning at the township service, one of the protagonists stood up and declared: 'I am not a Christian, but Father Jeremy led us as a community. He didn't live and die here for people to fight each other.' That speech, evidence of the respect in which Jeremy was held, brought a sustained period of peace between rival groups.

It is often such quiet, anonymous heroes of humanity, who provide the answer 'Yes' to Morris West's question: 'Do we have the courage and vision to pay the price?' Such people are living signs of jubilee. They demonstrate that 'In our era the road to holiness necessarily passes through the world of action', as Dag Hammarsjköld[2] observed.

'Holiness' smacks of a kind of pietism. But rightly understood, it is the conscious choice to practice jubilee, through healing, restoring, forgiving, reconciling and redistributing resources. Jesus maddened the religious elite because he exposed their failure to offer joy and hope through concrete action to the confused majority of humanity. Hammarskjöld sought to 'grow firmer, simpler, quieter, stronger'. It is an ambition for any who seek to live jubilee, and build peace.

'Whatever is given can always be re-imagined', observed Seamus Heaney. Jesus' vision of a world in which there is a perpetual spirit of jubilee remains a dream first to be imagined, then fulfilled. We can stop giving stones, and begin sharing bread. As the Indian Christian poet and reformer Pandita Ramabai observed: 'People must not only hear about the kingdom of God, but must see it in actual operation, on a small scale perhaps and in imperfect form, but a real demonstration nevertheless.'

Whilst individually, and as communities, we can practise jubilee, we cannot stop there. Jubilee is a political act. It is about changing systems, 'engaging the powers' as Walter Wink once put it, adding, 'God's will is the transformation of people *and* society.'[3] Following Jesus means being prepared to challenge the political, religious and economic systems that refuse to practise jubilee.

When Jesus spoke to power he said, 'You are of this world (or *system*); I am not of this world (*system*).'[4] For a Church that often emphasises the 'other worldliness' of Jesus, it is easy to think that when he said, 'I am not of this world,' he was talking about heaven, as I mentioned earlier. However, this does not fit in with the context. Jesus is not offering 'pie in the sky when you die by and by' here. He is calling on his disciples to believe and act in radical obedience to the law of God, so that life-giving change can happen.

Albert Camus, the existentialist philosopher who rejected Christianity yet sought to remain in dialogue with it, believed strongly that evil had to be resisted. His critique of Christians lay in what he believed was 'their inability to render complete resistance (as being) restricted by their hope in another world. Their belief in an omnipotent God makes them more acquiescent to their fate, no matter how unjust'. By lacking sufficient passion to resist, concluded Camus, Christians have become implicit collaborators with the forces of death.

Jubilee is both an act of resistance and hope. It is a strategy for bringing people together, of overcoming divisions of race, religion and gender; one that goes beyond the narrowing bands of nationalism, and its attendant defensiveness and barely controlled violence. It is a strategy for overcoming the evil that dehumanises, causing the 'other' to suffer, and one offering the possibility of reclaiming our humanity, and making possible a future for humankind.

Jubilee 2000 did not bring the utopia of a debt-free world. Too many still receive 'stones instead of bread', but the vocation of humanity, and in particular people of faith, is to practise jubilee, and bring in the kingdom. Without it there can be no viable future for humanity.

The struggle to be human

The second decade of the twenty-first century has been marked by a shaking of the political, economic, ecological and military foundations. The gap between the world's richest and its poorest continues to grow. Attempts at convincing of the dangers of climate change and seeking to control it show limited signs of success. Humanity's chance of long-term survival is in the balance.

Of course, there have been signs of hope. The breaking down of the Berlin Wall, the ending of apartheid, and the Kyoto climate agreements are examples. Yet the arms race continues apace, and the risk of nuclear warfare increases. Wars and rumours of wars continue to bring untold human suffering. Cyber attacks and 'Star Wars', once the stuff of fantasy, are now present realities. Fear stalks the earth exposed in xenophobia, nationalism and protectionism. All this contributes to a growing sense of impending cataclysm.

From my earliest days as a Christian I have been certain of one thing: Jesus Christ entered our world as a human being, and offered himself as a model for humanity. In his life, death and resurrection, Jesus offers us hope, peace and salvation. His exemplary life and witness should settle for all time the question of humanity's future, but it hasn't. Sadly, too often Christians, instead of being those whose 'feet have brought the good news of the gospel of peace' have worn 'boots of the tramping warriors'[1] – that are the very antithesis of humanness.

For some years, I had the privilege of working with the late Walter Wink, an American theologian and advocate of non-violence. He reiterated a powerful truth about the nature of God, as revealed in the person of Jesus Christ: 'God is human.' In Jesus, God was taking on a human face, and because of Jesus, God would never be the same.

Jesus revealed in human form God as 'love' – and that love is the central reality of the universe. It was a love revealed in a life of compassion for loss, a passion for justice, and a commitment to sacrifice all for the healing of humanity. It was to prove a love that non-violently confronted inhumanity in all its forms, and through the formation of a small intentional community, sought to model a society of justice, love and truth.

A number of years ago, I found some words that gave this 'love' a contemporary focus, and with which many people have identified:

> Jesus says in his society there is a new way for people to live.
>
> You show wisdom by trusting people
> You handle leadership, by serving
> You handle offenders, by forgiving
> You handle money, by sharing.
> You handle enemies, by loving,
> And you handle violence, by suffering.
>
> In fact you have a new attitude toward everything, toward everybody. Toward nature, toward the state in which you happen to live, toward women, toward slaves, toward all and every single thing. Because this is a Jesus society and you repent, not by feeling bad, but by *thinking different*.[2]

It is simple, yet profound and provides a basis for a way of living that is life-giving and hopeful. Yet, humanity's story has been bedevilled by suffering. The overwhelming evidence of the New Testament is of a God who in Jesus comes to make a new society possible, in which there is an end to sadness and death. This same Jesus, however, has too often been transmogrified into a vengeful divinity, siding with the self-appointed and self-righteous. Too many soldiers' belts have declared *Gott mit uns* – 'God with us' – offering a justification for intermediate acts of judgement, until Jesus returns.

It is argued that this 'return' will occur when God's patience has finally run out. Consequentially God will use all necessary force to coerce humanity into submission, regardless of the cost. But can this *really* be so? If it is, we could only conclude that a religion of love had been turned into one of fear and hate. And, 'Jesus would

do all the things he resolutely refused to do the first time around.'[3]
As the Human One he would no longer be the Galilean teacher
renouncing violence in the name of the God of love at the centre
of the universe. What then of the 'Jesus society' and the 'new way
for people to live'? What then of trust, service, forgiveness, sharing,
suffering and new attitudes to create a world of equality? What then
of the 'evening up' that Mary's Magnificat speaks of – 'the mighty
brought down from their heights, and the humble lifted up'?

Such inconsistency lacks credibility. With Wink, 'I believe that
Jesus did look for the final triumph of God in history. He did
await an actual realm of justice and peace', and he lived as if it was
dawning. His was a vision of 'unveiling' – exposing the violence and
oppression of the dominating owers, and meeting it with self-giving
love. This love was expressed in Jesus's words, 'Whoever welcomes
you, welcomes me, and whoever welcomes me, welcomes the one
who sent me.'[4]

Throughout history this radical energy and consistency has
too easily been exchanged for a faith defined by respectability.
Too often churches have become refuges for the comfortable and
morally upright, rather than communities where the Christ of the
poor is welcomed. Instead of being in solidarity with such folk, we
have become fearful of the stranger. We fear anything that does not
come from people 'like us'. Thus we have become defensive, fearful
of other religions, unwilling or unable to accept or people who
may not embrace our faith, but 'we don't know how to recognise
as friends, and we create enemies for no good reason'.[5]

Fear in religion is often a more dominant emotion than love.
When fear dominates, love dies, we become defensive, aggressive
possessive, selfish and violent. 'It is the greatest error of humanity,'
says Wink, 'to believe that it is human. We are only fragmentarily
human, fleetingly human, brokenly human. We see glimpses of our
humanness, we can dream of what a more human existence and
political order would be like, but we have not yet arrived at true
humanness.' Provocative as he may appear, Wink spoke out of a
deep theological tradition within Christianity.

'Only God is human,' he reiterates, 'and we are made in God's
image and likeness which is to say we are capable of becoming
human.' The record of humanity's inhumanity, all too immediately

present to us, through the media, and in our history, exposes our fragmentary, fleeting and broken humanness.

Few who have studied Jesus' life and witness can deny its efficacy and exemplary humanity. Gandhi once observed: 'If I have read the Bible correctly, I know many ... who have never heard of the name of Jesus Christ, or have even rejected the official interpretation of Christianity who will, probably, if Jesus came in our midst today in the flesh be owned by him more than many of us.' It is said that Gandhi read the Sermon on the Mount every day convinced that it contained a truth 'more powerful than the empire that occupied his native India, or the enmity that divided Hindus and Muslims'.

'We are incapable of becoming human by ourselves,' declared Walter Wink. 'We scarcely know what humanness is. We have only the merest intuitions and general guidelines.' Just so. Rightly understood, Jesus reveals our humanity, and seeks to enable us to become fully human. Christians believe that Jesus is both Son of Man – the Human One, and Son of God. Because God is 'true humanness', asserts Wink, 'then divinity inverts. Divinity is not a qualitatively different reality; quite the reverse, divinity is fully realised humanity.' He reasserts, 'Only God is HUMAN. The goal of life, then, is not to become something that we are not – divine – but to become what we truly are – human.'

Like Gandhi, Jews, Muslims, Hindus and others can revere Jesus in his exemplary humanity. On Christmas Eve 2016, I received a seasonal greeting from a Jewish friend who commented: 'For only the third time in the past hundred years Christmas and the first day of Hanukkah are coinciding – and it does seem like a moment when different faith traditions, not to mention ideological perspectives, need to find common ground in the multiplicity of our spiritual and intellectual guiding lights.'

Another friend spoke of her son's Hindu mother-in-law who was to spend Christmas with them. Explaining that as a family they would go to church, but she should not feel obliged to come, the woman replied: 'Oh! No, I want to come and meet your God.'

After Christmas Midnight Service in Bath Abbey one year, I was greeted by a group of Muslim men who had attended the service. They told me that they wanted to come to church to honour Christ and his mother. It was itself the very act of 'Islam' – which translated, means peace, purity, submission and obedience.

This book is about 'things that make for peace'. It has been subtitled 'A Christian peacemaker in a world of war'. In a sense that is all it has been about, seeking what it means both to be a Christian in such a world, but also what it is to 'make peace'.

As a follower of Jesus Christ, I know my own humanity can only be enlarged through relationship. Jesus understood that he too needed relationship to complete his humanity. He spoke of God as *Abba* which we loosely translate, 'Father'. The sense of the title is profoundly intimate, the closest of relationships is conveyed: 'I am in *Abba* and *Abba* is in me'[6], Jesus repeats in several places.

Richard Rohr sums it up: 'God is absolute relatedness. I would name salvation as simply the readiness, the willingness, the capacity to stay in that relationship.'[7] It is because of that loving intimacy and commitment to humanity's well-being that Jesus becomes Saviour: Saviour of our humanity – Saviour from our inhumanity – Saviour to enable our full humanity. It is a commitment that costs everything.

To save humanity, paradoxically Christ both 'gives' and 'loses' his life. He 'gives' it, because if truth and love are ultimately to win out, God as the source of that love has to be seen. He 'loses' it, because his judicial crucifixion is a political act, carried out through an alliance of the religious elite and the Roman state.

Throughout his ministry Jesus knew that his interaction with the poor, sick and unclean threatened the political and religious status quo. As Ched Myers has reflected: 'Ours is not a hospitable world for visionaries – and not without good reason, for charlatans abound. Gospel radicalism is still dismissed in the metropolises of the West by dominant ideologies of Christian realism.' A realism which, he reflects, has 'demonstrably failed us. In its name the four apocalyptic horsemen of empire, militarism economic exploitation and environmental revolt ride freely over the earth'.

There is no greater challenge for Christians today than to 'seek the things that make for peace'. Humanity needs a new vision, of a world in which there is 'a new attitude toward everything, toward everybody … toward all and every single thing'. It is an attitude that stems from our understanding that if Christ is the Human One, the model and template for our humanity, then we must live towards all others as if they were the Christ. Leonardo Boff observed:

Once Christianity affirms that a man is at the same time God, it stands alone in the world ... We Christians learn the meaning of human persons, their roots and their humanity, by meditating on the human life of Jesus Christ ... It was in a man that the primitive church discovered God, and it was in God that we come to know the true nature and destiny of human beings.[8]

The early decades of this century have not been marked by a spirit of hope. Apocalypse and cataclysm have all too evidently revealed 'the greatest error of humanity ... to believe that it is human'. By re-engaging with the humanity of God discerned in Jesus, Christians can truly offer Christ's society to the world, by living in the spirit of Peter Claver's dictum: 'Deeds come first, then words.'

When we live in a spirit of love, rather than fear, like Jesus we can live as if the realm of justice and peace is dawning. We can cease being defensive, fearful of people who do not necessarily embrace our faith, but whom we can refuse to create as enemies and instead recognise as friends. We can acknowledge both in us and them that 'we are made in God's image and likeness, which is to say we are capable of becoming human'. For 'the goal of life is to become what we truly are – human', reminds Walter Wink.

Jesus called his new society the 'kingdom of God'. Pope Paul VI described it as 'the absolute good' – a good to which everything else must defer. The 'absolute good' which Jesus announced was for the whole of humanity to possess. A good that goes beyond the ties of religion, or the exclusive possession of any single group. As Jim O'Halloran, a Catholic priest comments: 'The church is part of the kingdom. It is not the whole of it ... *wherever we find goodness* or *wherever there is harmony rooted in justice* the kingdom of God is there.'[9]

The work of peace is justice

Shortly after Christmas in 2013, I parked my car in one of the back streets of Protestant Sandy Row in Belfast. The area had changed in the nearly fifty years since I first walked there in the early days of the Troubles. Then, back-to-back houses had occupied row upon row. Now, traffic on a four-lane motorway speeds around the city.

Yet there was a familiarity. For a few moments I wondered why. Then it dawned. This was the street, now rebuilt with modern houses, where I had visited the boarded-up buildings during the riot torn 1970s. Here, unbeknownst to me nearly half a century ago, was both the 'beginning', continuing and 'end' of a striving to understand and engage in the 'things that make for peace'.

Throughout those years I have witnessed in many strife-ridden places and communities, a search for peace and reconciliation. Those processes like the Peace Bridge that spans the river Foyle in Derry/Londonderry were complex. Tensions were frequent, often critical, and the tiniest miscalculation capable of bringing down the whole edifice, and destroying years of work.

I recalled too the numerous small groups I have participated in, each struggling to meet Pope Paul VI's challenge, 'If you want peace, work for justice.' I thought about how we sought to move from pasts where suspicion, fear and violence had divided, towards new relationships that made possible a shared future.

I remembered how we learned to engage 'in practices overtly labelled as reconciliation activities: meetings, dialogues and joint projects to focus on our differences and divisions, our hurts, our misdeeds, our history, our needs, our identities, our cultures', as David Bloomfield reminds us. 'These activities help us to get to know and begin to understand our former enemies who are now new partners, as they begin to understand us.'[1]

I remembered just how slow and demanding such activities are: what patience and ongoing commitment they require. I was encouraged too. During Advent 2016, we were privileged to help fund[2] a Youth Initiatives project in Belfast. This was inspired by a sixteen-year-old woman, with the aim of bringing together young people across sectarian and ethnic divides. It is the dream of a 'shared future' born out of historic division, with a commitment to dialogue and the creation of joint projects that begin the process of reconciling those formerly divided.

My epiphany moment in Belfast's Sandy Row in 2013 was both an end and a beginning. I had been here before and I would be here again. Uncertainty still threatens the very peace processes begun so long ago. Here is the potential for further beginnings for all who 'seek the things that make for peace.' For many who read this book there will be a sense of: 'That's fine for him, but I don't have his breaks, or influence.' Possibly, but it was not always so. I have lived longer in the anonymity of working with small groups of people than in the corridors of power and influence. The words of the anthropologist Margaret Mead quoted earlier remain a much more reliable dictum: 'Never doubt that a small group of thoughtful, committed citizens can change the world; indeed, it's the only thing that ever has.'

Today I live in a small English country town on a busy road with neighbours who have become friends. Together we share each other's joys and sorrows. I have been struck by how much innate goodness there is hidden among us: the couple who have fostered seventy or so children through nearly forty years; those who take into their care children with special needs. Others quietly raise money for rescue services, or unobtrusively look after elderly but very independent neighbours. Others carry the burdens of loved ones suffering from disability and memory loss, serve in the Food Bank, or visit those in prison. Of course there are prejudices, sometimes tensions, but somehow there is an unspoken feeling of belonging, of community.

My contemporary experience of neighbourliness reminds me of working on a south London housing estate with Catholics and Methodists in the 1980s, with people whose lives were blighted by poverty and violence. We had been inspired by work that some of us had engaged with in Latin America, in 'base' Christian communities. Together we sought to enculturate what we had learned into our own circumstances.

For some thirty years, groups of lay people and clergy have explored what had become known as A New Way of Being Church[3] in the life of the wider Christian community. On his appointment, Pope Francis was to speak of the need for such a way of being Church: 'Structural change to the government of the church is vital but it must follow from a new way of being church, in which we get out of the sacristy, engage with people, know their suffering and their puzzlement from within.'

Such activity has met with varying degrees of success. I believe that if we are to become 'truly human' and have a 'shared future' in which 'peaceful kindness will be the law', then we cannot do it alone. 'If you want peace, work for justice,' said Pope Paul VI, I want to modify that by saying, 'The work of peace *is* justice.'

To achieve and sustain a society in which people are to live together in *shalom* – peace, harmony – we must bring together insights and experience from both religious and secular sources, on what it means to love, forgive, and be reconciled. We need, as the poet Rumi invites us, to discover:

Out beyond ideas of wrong doing and right there is a field.
I'll meet you there.

One of the images of salvation in the Hebrew Scriptures is that of entering into a wide open space. In such a 'space' there is room 'to think about compassion for loss, anger at injustice, and the limiting of disgust in favour of inclusive sympathy,' as the philosopher Martha Nussbaum[4] has put it. But such 'space' is not only to reflect on 'ain't it awful' – but to generate 'Love (which) is what gives respect for humanity its life and aspires to justice and equal opportunity for all and inspires individuals to sacrifice for the common good'.

All the great faiths teach us that we are each other's keepers. Behind every face, there are hopes and aspirations but above all, potential for humanness. For the Christian, Jesus is that person who is hungry; that woman who is confused and naked; the child that is the victim of war. It is such with whom Jesus identifies, because they are truly his fellow human brothers and sisters.

Salvation is the entering of a wide open space; a space where the seeking of 'absolute good', the work of the kingdom can flourish, and where justice which is the work of peace (*shalom*)[5] can be found. Jesus' invitation to his followers, to 'Set your hearts on his (God's) kingdom first, and on God's *saving justice*[6] is an invitation to find in God the origin of 'absolute good'. In the Hebrew the term for this is *sedekah* – a concept often translated as 'righteousness'.

God's justice is to be found in the kindness God shows towards humans. By seeking humanity's 'absolute good' God exemplifies how we, made in God's image, should act kindly and fairly towards each other. Because God is good to us, we have an obligation to be good to others. But it is more than that. Just as God is our keeper, so are we each other's keepers. When we seek well-being and fairness, we have to be sure that in pursuing our rights, we do not deny those of our neighbour. As one writer, Pinchas Lapide,[7] has put it: 'God is the Righteous – who practices *sedekah* and sets it as an existential task for us as bearers of the divine image.'

When we practise 'saving justice' whether by almsgiving, visiting the sick, sacrificing self for others, building peace, we are doing so because we have an obligation under God. It is not something we do on our own, and in Jewish thought, it is not something that is ever complete. We practise 'saving justice' as a 'germ cell of holy discontent, an active leaven in human society',[8] and indicator of the longed for reign of God on earth.

Biblical justice is about right relationships: being right with God, self, neighbour and the environment. What prevents us from being 'germ cells of holy discontent' or 'active leaven' is fear. Fear is a dominating reality in our world. In the affluent West we fear poverty. In a world of changing values, we fear losing our moral compass. In a multicultural community we fear losing our identity; in a multifaith society, our certainties. We are anxious that if we get too close to others whose faith or values differ from our own we will be compromised. We fear loss of control of our affairs, the respect of others, and being dependent on those we perceive as different from us.

In the political arena we look for leadership that is ever more uncertain and fragmentary. We sense a loss of control, insecurity and economic uncertainty. Instead of striving to build a society with others, we crave protection from those not like us. We fear the future.

Such fear counters the Gospel command, 'Fear not.' Certainly there are things to be afraid of, and truth can be frightening. But ultimately, as St. John tells us, only 'the truth will make you free'.[9] The desire to be 'safe' is both natural and essential for human flourishing. But, says Erik Borgman,[10] 'One cannot reach safety by excluding everything that is potentially threatening. We can only reach others by approaching others as people who need protection just as we do and will want to give protection to those who protect them.'

Our vocation as humans, and in particular people of faith, is the creation of a genuinely caring society that demonstrates compassion as one humanity under God. Shortly before I wrote these lines, I heard an account of members of a Jewish synagogue in south London who were converting part of their building into a flat to house Muslim Syrian refugees. They were working on this, as Jews, with Christians and Muslims. By caring for others, and taking responsibility for them, they were also taking care of themselves.

'Each aspect of peacemaking moves towards the inclusion of the outsider, the overcoming of enmity, and the extension of the kingdom of God to all people,' observes Willard Swartley.[11] Peacemaking is the primary goal of the kingdom of God, and if we wish to be called 'children of God' and be blessed by God, we must dedicate ourselves to this task. In all I have witnessed amongst people seeking 'the things that make for peace', it is the dedicated small community of ordinary people doing extraordinary things that remains the most effective.

Peacemaking is not simply about ending wars and conflicts on the macro scale. It is recognising those places in our common life where fear becomes the dominant emotion; moments and places where we risk excluding, dominating or otherwise violating the 'other', and reducing our common humanity. It is to recognise that peacemaking is a moral commitment. When we seek the establishment of peace, we do so because as Kant wrote, 'it is the ultimate duty of political action, the highest expression of reason against irrationality.' We seek peace because the most fundamental human right is to life and it is our moral duty, as Gandhi insisted 'to struggle against injustice ... through the weapon of non violence'.[12]

Today few can doubt that today our world is a perilous place. Wars, mass migration, uncertainty in international affairs, growing protectionism, the building of dividing walls, whether virtual or real, military threats and political fragmentation, leave us vulnerable to divisions that threaten the very future of humanity.

Against such a background to seek the renewal of humanity through the building of small communities seems almost futile. It reminds me of the story of the little bird lying on its back with its feet in the air. Asked by a passing stranger why it was doing that, the bird replied: 'I heard today that the sky was falling in.' 'Well,' scoffed the stranger, 'how do you think you can change that?' 'One does what one can,' replied the bird.

I talked recently with an old friend, Jim O'Halloran who some forty years ago went to Africa, where together with others he set up the first of what we came to call 'Small Christian communities'. In the course of our conversation, he told me that today there are some fifteen thousand communities. These groups are based around meeting together, sharing, reading the Bible, dialogue and activities, and, to use Jim's words, they do 'anything constructive to build a better world'.

Key to such groups were their relationships. I too experienced this in groups meeting on housing estates in south London, Dublin and Belfast, as well as being a privileged guest in other such groups in Brazil, El Salvador, Nicaragua, Costa Rica and Guyana. Like Jim, I too discovered that such group formations were not limited to Christians. In our small group on the Gloucester Grove Estate in Peckham, London back in the 1980s and nineties, word got around of our meeting. All sorts of folks came, individuals who in their own right tried to make a difference, but were ground down by isolation and resistance. With us they found support and encouragement, despite our prayers and biblical reflection. Together we made changes in the community.

At different times Jim and I visited India, and here we came across 'Small Human Communities' open to people of all religions and no professed faith. Jim reminded me that these were formed largely of women who sought to do practical peace in their communities. One such group living on the street in Bangalore touched me deeply. They had come to identify themselves as a community through partnership with local Christian students who had helped them fund a water supply, by provision of a standpipe. This simple gesture, apparently inconsequential, had opened the door to health care for families, education for children, and recognition that, in their own words, 'we are now a people'.

One example of a 'small human community' I experienced in Britain was during the 1980s in the Yorkshire Dales, where a vibrant group of former military personnel, Quakers, and others committed to the pursuit of peace met regularly to 'Think Peace, Pray Peace, Speak Peace, Act Peace'.

For many years I have sought, with others, to encourage the formation of 'Small Christian communities' as a starting point for building a better world. Like Jim O'Halloran, who has taught and written widely on this theme, I believe if one is to reach out successfully, one must be sure of one's own identity. 'Beyond it', says Jim, 'I would encourage groups of all kinds, whether religious or civic that are doing anything to build a better world, or the kingdom. And I would have them ALL support one another in any way they can without neglecting their own work in so doing. This,' he concludes, 'is a template for building up creation, motivated by a small community and group together with the spirituality that inspires them.'[13]

I believe that the task of building small groups of thoughtful committed citizens of the kingdom of God is a priority for changing the world, and pursuing the things that make for peace. Many people in our churches, and many who have left them but still hold on tenuously to their faith, are looking for a vision to build a better world. Most know that it will be costly.

Ours is a faith that has always held together two apparent opposites: resistance and healing. It is hard to stand against the prevailing mood and culture; to refuse to be fearful when fear is all around us. It is hard to be self-giving, when all around us are self-seeking. It is hard to see others as 'our concern', when all around us 'others' are a threat and a problem. It is hard to 'seek peace and pursue it', when all around defences and weaponry are being built up and stockpiled. But that is the call of the Christ, the Prince of Peace.

We are called to resist all the things that do not make for peace and justice. Our vocation is to stand with all those who are poor, vulnerable and under attack. This means being prepared to defend those from different faiths, backgrounds and cultures from our own. It will mean reminding governments of their duty to 'establish peace' by building up community, and refusing to play on fear, and seeking to justify the use of state-sponsored violence.

The communities in which I have found the greatest strength to 'keep on, keeping on' have been those most aware of their own need of healing, as much as they have been aware of the need for the healing of the nations. As they have studied Scripture and sought discernment, they have prayed for faith, courage and hope to stand up, speak and act in solidarity for those most in need.

On Advent Sunday in 2016, I listened to the moving testimony of a Syrian priest who had been taken from his monastery by ISIS and tortured. Subsequently, in another prison he was confronted by his 100-strong congregation who had been taken hostage. All expected the worst. To their surprise their captors released them, 'Because,' they said, 'you Christians did not take up arms to fight us.' Of course such a story does not answer nor solve the deep and complex issues that face us, but it does exemplify.

My journey of possibilities from bystander to peacemaker grew out of a commitment 'guided by ethical principles, chastened by the lessons of history, and embodied in the experience of practical peacemaking'.[14] It has been enriched because of those whom I have met on the 'common ground in the multiplicity of our spiritual and guiding lights'. I have been humbled and encouraged by people of many faiths and none who have 'fought the long defeat'.

When I have asked myself why I keep on keeping on, I find A.J. Muste's answer to a similar question is mine too: 'I don't do this to change the world. I do it to keep the world from changing me.' When I am asked what kind of Church can meet the challenges of the future, I want to reply in the words of the second century Church Father, Justin Martyr: 'We who formerly treasured money and possessions more than anything else now hand over everything to a treasury and share it with everyone who needs it. We who formerly hated and murdered one another … now live together and share the same table. Now we pray for our enemies and try to win those who hate us.'

Because somewhere in the recesses of my memory stirs the story of the coming of the Prince of Peace, whose Presentation in the Temple I celebrated on the completion of this book. Like the old man Simeon who waited for 'a light for revelation'[15] – I too wait in hope.

Notes

Introduction

1. 'Meet Gino Strada', *The Guardian*, 14 July 2013.
2. Luke 19:42, italics mine.
3. I outline the arguments for Just War in chapter 28.
4. Matthew 5:9.
5. *Daniel Berrigan: Essential Writings* (Maryknoll, Orbis, 2009).
6. Psalm 34:14.

Chapter one

1. Isaiah 52:7.
2. Numbers 25:2.
3. Psalm 34:14.
4. Psalm 122:6.
5. Proverbs 16:7.
6. Isaiah 9:6.
7. Isaiah 2:4; Micah 4:1–3.
8. Matthew 25:31–45.
9. Philippians 4:7.
10. *Shoah* means 'catastrophe, great calamity'. It is used by Jews to define the European Holocaust. The word derives from a Greek word meaning 'burnt sacrifice'.
11. Pinchas Lapide, *The Sermon on the Mount: Utopia or Program for Action?* (Maryknoll, Orbis, 1986), pp. 34–35.
12. David Bloomfield, 'Rehabilitating Reconciliation', Accord Insight 3, *Transforming Broken Relationships* – (Conciliation Resources) 2016.
13. Mark 5:14–15.
14. Pinchas Lapide, *The Sermon on the Mount: Utopia or Program for Action?* (Maryknoll, Orbis, 1986), p. 36.

Chapter two

1. Allan G. Johnson, *The Forest and the Trees: Sociology as Life, Practice, and Promise* (Philadelphia, Temple University Press, 1997).

Chapter four

1. Matthew 5:9.

Chapter five

1. Ecclesiastes 3:1, KJV.
2. Ecclesiastes 3:8.

Chapter six

1. Will Hutton, *The Guardian*, 31 January 1994.

2. 'Sectarianism – A Discussion Document' (The Department of Social Issues of the Irish Inter Church Meeting, 1993), p. 29.
3. *Sectarianism,* p. 36.
4. Romans 5:10.
5. *Sectarianism,* p. 38.
6. Lapide, *The Sermon on the Mount,* p. 34.

Chapter seven

1. Martin McGuinness was chief negotiator for Sînn Feîn, and a former Provisional IRA commander.

Chapter eight

1. Mark 9:7.
2. Thomas Merton, *Seeds of Contemplation* (Wheathampstead, Anthony Clarke, 1972), pp. 46 and 94.
3. Matthew 5:38–39.
4. John 1:14.
5. A speech by Earl Mountbatten of Burma on 11 May 1979 published by the World Disarmament Movement in association with the United Nations Association.
6. Reported in *Sojourners,* August 1979.
7. *Sojourners* Nuclear Pack: A Call to Faithfulness, 1979.
8. Readers might wish to look at the text in Mark, Chapters 8 and 9.
9. Mark 8:31, 38.
10. Mark 9:2–3.
11. Mark 9:7.
12. For the whole story read Daniel, Chapter 7.
13. See Matthew 16:24.
14. See 2 Corinthians 13:7.

Chapter nine

1. Quoted in Paul Elie, *The Life You Save May Be Your Own: An American Pilgrimage* (New York, Farrar, Strauss and Giraud, 2003), p. 411.
2. Ibid. pp. 410–11.
3. *A Year with Thomas Merton: Daily Meditations from His Journals,* selected and edited by Jonathan Montaldo (San Francisco, HarperSanFrancisco, 2004), p. 275.
4. Jim Wallis, *Agenda for a Biblical People* (New York, Harper & Row, 1976), p. 17.
5. Hebrews 5:8.
6. Wallis, *Agenda,* p. 9.

Chapter ten

1. I cannot vouch for the authenticity of this story, but its source was good.
2. Jim Forest, *Praying with Icons* (Maryknoll, Orbis, 1997), pp. 127–28.
3. Jim Wallis, *Call to Conversion* (New York, Harper & Row, 1981), p. 88.
4. Wallis, *Call to Conversion,* p. 89.
5. See Matthew 6:24. Many translations offer 'wealth' or 'money' as the translation of 'mammon', but it has as much to do with 'power exercised against the will of God' – and this is my understanding here.

6. Thomas Merton, *Peace in the Post-Christian Era* (Maryknoll, Orbis, 2004), p. 157.
7. Wallis, *Call to Conversion*, p. 101.

Chapter eleven

1. These 'grassroots churches' were also known as 'base Christian communities'. The word 'base' meant in both the Spanish and Portuguese 'from the bottom', or 'from among the poor'.
2. These groups known as 'base' – meaning from the 'grassroots'; 'Christian' or 'ecclesial' Church communities – were the foundation of new models of Church.
3. For readers interested in discovering more, the most accessible book is that of Phillip Berryman, *Stubborn Hope: Religion, Politics and Revolution in Central America* (Maryknoll, Orbis, 1994).
4. Ibid. p. 9.
5. Frente Sandinista de Liberación Nacional – Sandinista National Liberation Front.
6. The Farabundo Martí National Liberation Front.
7. Berryman, *Stubborn Hope*, p. 10.

Chapter twelve

1. The Contras were US-backed and funded rebel groups that were active in Nicaragua from 1979 through to the early 1990s. They sought the overthrow of the Sandinista government, and were responsible for the massacres of many *campesinos* – agricultural workers.
2. Quoted by Ron Sider in Morris H. Morley, *Washington, Somoza and the Sandinistas: State and Regime in the U.S. Policy Towards Nicaragua, 1969–1981* (Cambridge, Cambridge University Press, 1994), p. 36.
3. Observed by Paul Theroux, *Deep South* (London, Penguin, 2015).
4. Berryman, *Stubborn Hope*, p. 48.
5. Ronald J. Sider, *Nonviolent Action: What Christian Ethics Demands But Most Christians Have Never Really Tried* (Grand Rapids, Brazos Press, 2015), p. 51.

Chapter thirteen

1. Known elsewhere in Latin America as *favelas*, these were informal settlements of poorly constructed housing very often built on land that had been 'occupied' by those made landless as a consequence of beef, banana or other crop production.
2. The *Campesina* Mass.
3. Sider, *Nonviolent Action*, p. xv.
4. Ibid. xv.

Chapter fourteen

1. CEPAD: Evangelical Committee for Aid and Development.
2. *Populorum Progressio* (*The Development of the Peoples*), see parts 30 and 31.
3. Fernando Cardenal, Faith & Joy: Memoirs of a Revolutionary Priest (Maryknoll, Orbis, 2015), p. 45. Fernando Cardenal observed of this extract that this was 'the point that made me think'. That point was the exception clause because 'This sounded like a portrait of the Nicaragua I witnessed every day.' p. 46.
4. Berryman, *Stubborn Hope*, p. 23.

Chapter fifteen

1. Raymond McAfee Brown, *Saying Yes and Saying No: On Rendering to God and Caesar* (Louisville, Westminster John Knox Press, 1986), p. 95.
2. Ephesians 6:12.
3. Romans 12:19.
4. Fernando Cardenal, *Faith & Joy*, pp. 234–5.
5. *Amnesty* magazine, December 2011.
6. Hebrews 12:4.

Chapter sixteen

1. *Farabundo Marti* National Liberation Front. The governing party was ARENA, the National Republican Alliance.
2. Teresa Whitfield, *Paying the Price: Ignacio Ellacuria and the Murdered Jesuits of El Salvador* (Philadelphia, Temple, 1994), p. 67.
3. Benjamin C. Schwarz, *American Counterinsurgency Doctrine and El Salvador: The Frustrations of Reform and the Illusions of Nation Building*, quoted by Whitfield, ibid. p. 239.
4. Miguel de la Torre, *Trails of Hope and Terror: Testimonies on Immigration* (Maryknoll, Orbis, 2009), p.50.
5. *Concilium* 1990/6 1492–1992, The Voice of the Victims. Editorial by Leonardo Boff and Virgil Elizondo (London, SCM Press).
6. Father Carlos Cabarrus SJ quoted by Whitfield, *Paying the Price*, p. 64.
7. The Underground Railway was a euphemism for US church groups seeking to rescue people at particular risk by their opposition to the Salvadoran authorities.

Chapter seventeen

1. Besides Bill Cook, these included Mark Gornik, now founder and dean of City Seminary New York (Mark and I were to return together to El Salvador in 2011); John Smith – known as the 'Biker Evangelist' from Australia; Howard Snyder from Fuller Seminary; Bill Leslie and Ted Schroeder from Chicago working with the Sanctuary Movement.
2. Ellsberg, *Blessed Among Us*, p. 695.
3. See 1 Corinthians 12:26.
4. 1 Peter 2:21.

Chapter eighteen

1. See Matthew 25:40.
2. Whitfield, *Paying the Price*, p. 39 with references to *Los Textos de Medellin*.
3. Isaiah 35:3–4.
4. Matthew 26:39.
5. Luke 14:28, RSV.

Chapter nineteen

1. Robert Ellsberg, *All Saints: Daily Reflections on Saints, Prophets and Witnesses of Our Time* (New York: Crossroad, 1997), p. 132.
2. The phrase 'to be with my brothers' is gender neutral, and capable of being both male and female.
3. Oscar A. Romero, *The Violence of Love* (Farmington, Plough Books, 1998).

Chapter twenty

1. The six murdered priests were Armando Lopez, Ignaçio Ellacuria, Ignaçio Martin-Baro, a psychologist and vice rector of the university, Juan Ramon Moreno, a theologian, Segundo Montes, superior of the Jesuit community, and Joaquin Lopez y Lopez, director of the Faith and Joy catechetical movement.
2. Jürgen Moltmann, *A Broad Place* (London, SCM Press, 2007), p. 196.
3. *Concilium* 1990/6 1492–1992, p. 78.
4. 'Killers on a Shoestring: Inside the Gangs of El Salvador, *New York Times*, 20 November 2016.
5. Jeanne Kirkpatrick, *Dictatorships and Double Standards*, Commentary 68, No. 5, pp. 34–5: source Whitfield, *Paying the Price*, p. 148.
6. Jon Sobrino, 'Fifty Years for a Future that is Christian and Human', *Concilium* 2016/1, Journeys of Liberation: Joys and Hopes for the Future, p. 75.

Chapter twenty one

1. Known variously as Holy Communion, the Eucharist and the Mass.
2. *Midrash* is an interpretation of, or commentary on, Hebrew text.
3. John 17:21.
4. For the full discussion, see Jürgen Moltmann and Hans Küng, 'Ecumenical Spirituality as we already know it.' *Concilium* 2011/3, pp. 107–113.
5. Ibid. p. 86.

Chapter twenty two

1. Felix Wilfred, *Concilium* 2016/1, Journeys of Liberation: Joys and Hopes for the Future, pp.13–23.
2. The full Statement can be read on http://www.oikoumene.org/en/resources/documents/wcc-programmes/public-witness-addressing-power-affirming-peace/middle-east-p
3. Paul Farmer quoted in Tracey Kidder, *Mountains Beyond Mountains: The Quest of Dr Paul Farmer, A Man Who Would Cure the World* (New York: Random House, 2003), p. 288.

Chapter Twenty three

1. A full account of the delegation's conversations and proposals can be found in *Sojourners*, February–March 1991.
2. Statement of the Delegation to the Middle East, 'War is not the Answer – A Message to the American People', December 1990.
3. Vietnam was a French colonial territory, which the Americans policed from 1955 through to 1973. It was a divided country, the North being largely Communist, the South, democratic. The major offensives took place in the 1960s between US forces and the Communist Viet Cong guerillas. America finally withdrew in 1973 when the southern capital, Saigon, fell to the Viet Cong forces. Widely perceived as defeat in the USA, the conflict took some fifty-three thousand American lives, whilst some two hundred thousand Cambodians and a conservative estimate of some eight hundred thousand Vietnamese lives.
4. Daniel Berrigan, *All Shall Be Well* (Maryknoll, Orbis, 2015), pp. 171 – 180.
5. For example, St Paul in Romans 13, says: 'Let every person be subject to the governing authorities' (v. 1). But having outlined both the responsibilities to, as well as the consequences of resisting the authorities, he nevertheless argues

that the whole law 'is summed up as 'Love your neighbor as yourself'. Love does not wrong a neighbour: 'love is the fulfilling of the law' (see vv. 8–10). By this means he places love of neighbour among any contrary demands of the State. Equally, he makes clear that the State may and can exact penalties for infractions of laws that seek to countermand the 'higher law'.

6. Hebrews 12:4.

Chapter twenty four

1. Walter Wink, 'History Belongs to the Incessors', *Sojourners*, October 1990.

Chapter twenty Five

1. The formal ending of the 'Desert Storm' campaign was 30 November 1995. But hostilities ceased in February 1991.
2. Revelation 21:3–4.
3. Nikos Kazantzakis, *Report to Greco* (London, Faber & Faber, 2001).
4. Matthew 28.20.
5. Revelation 22.21.

Chapter twenty Six

1. Micah 4:1–5.
2. Romans 12:20.
3. Lapide, *The Sermon on the Mount*, p. 97.
4. Acts 14:17.
5. Peter B. Price, *Mark Today – Reflections on St. Mark's Gospel for Small Christian Communities* (New Way Publications, 2002) – published in 1999 as *Mark 2000*.
6. Ched Myers, *Binding the Strong Man: A Political Reading of Mark's Story of Jesus* (Maryknoll, Orbis, 1988/2008). I was invited to contribute to the Introduction to the 2008 Revised Edition.
7. Ibid. p. 166.
8. Mark 3:27.
9. Matthew 24:43; Revelation 3:3.
10. See Isaiah 49:24f.
11. Isaiah 61:1–2.
12. Jean Vanier, *Our Life Together* (London, Darton, Longman and Todd, 2008), p. 417.
13. NIV.
14. Vanier, *Our Life Together*, p. 417.

Chapter twenty seven

1. Micah 6:8.
2. Gabrielle Rifkind and Gandomenico Picco, *The Fog of Peace: The Human Face of Conflict Resolution* (London, I.B. Tauris, 2014), p. 32.
3. Jon Sobrino, *Concilium* 2003/5, p. 84.
4. Shaul Magid, *Concilium*, 2003/5, pp.70–1.

Chapter twenty eight

1. Whilst medical supplies were exempt from the sanctions regime, they nevertheless had to be ordered through a complex system of administration, which frequently meant that the saline and other drips were not delivered at the same time as intravenous delivery systems. Because the former were

perishable, and often required consistent refrigeration to preserve their effectiveness, and electricity supply was intermittent, the effect was to render much medication ineffective.

2. Centre for Global Research: 'Congenital Birth Defects in Iraq: Concealing War Crimes against Iraqi Children, Twisting and Distorting the Evidence.' Prof. Souad N. Al-Azzawi. Global Research, 9 October 2013.
3. The quotes were from 'The essential daily briefing'. 29 September 2016.
4. Accusations have been levelled by the UN at both the Syrian and Russian military for these attacks, but at the time of writing both accused parties have denied their participation.
5. *The Merchant of Venice*, Act III, Scene I.
6. Caritas Internationalis, *Working for Reconciliation: A Caritas Handbook* (Vatican City, 1999), p.1.
7. Italics mine.
8. Maria Pilar Aquino, 'Justice Upholds Peace: A Feminist Approach', *Concilium* 2001/2, The Return of the Just War, p. 102.
9. Lisa Sowle Cahill, 'Christian Just War Tradition: Tensions and Development', *Concilium* 2001/2, p. 82.

Chapter twenty nine

1. Slavenka Drakulic, *They Would Never Hurt a Fly: War Criminals on Trial* in *The Hague* (London, Abacus, 2004).
2. Genesis 4:1–16.
3. Melissa Benn reviewed *They Would Never Hurt a Fly* in *The Guardian*, 3 April 2004.

Chapter thirty

1. The religious response to terrorism, 'Deny Them Their Victory' was the document quoted from signed by Jewish, Muslim and Christian clergy and originated by a caucus of multifaith leaders, including Jim Wallis.
2. For a full account, see Peter B. Price, *Playing the Blue Note* (London, DLT, 2002).
3. Batstone's full document is in *Sojourners*, November–December 2001, entitled, 'Platform for a Movement'.

Chapter thirty one

1. Psalm 139:14.
2. Whilst I made notes during this dialogue, the full text of it can be found in *Sojourners*, March–April 2002, 'Fundamentalism and the Modern World', pp. 20–6.

Chapter thirty two

1. Colossians 1:20.
2. Daniel Berrigan, *Testimony: The Word Made Fresh* (Maryknoll, Orbis, 2004), pp. 65–6.
3. 2 Corinthians 5:18.
4. John 18:36 – *Ioudaioi* is often translated 'Jews' – but this is misrepresentative; the term 'Judeans' is more accurate and reflects the political alliances of those who opposed Jesus.
5. Berrigan, *Testimony*, p. 82.
6. Luke 23:4.
7. Matthew 27:19.

Chapter thirty three

1. David Cortright is president of the Fourth Freedom Forum and research fellow at the Joan B. Kroc Institute for International Peace Studies at Notre Dame. In 2002 he was also a contributing writer to *Sojourners*.
2. *Sojourners*, July–August 2002. '"Commentary" – Why Not Attack Iraq', p. 15.
3. These were subsequently conducted by Hans Blix and his team as referred to earlier.
4. Romans 13:1.
5. Romans 13.8–10.

Chapter thirty four

1. Isaiah 9:6–7, italics mine.
2. See Luke 2:14.

Chapter thirty five

1. Berrigan, *Testimony*, p. 59.
2. The full Six Point Plan was published in the *Washington Post* in 2003, and is outlined in its entirety in Jim Wallis' *God's Politics* (San Francisco, HarperSanFrancisco, 2005), pp 50–2. I have offered a summary because in many ways the detail now is somewhat secondary to the overall purpose of this book, which is to observe some of the 'things that make for peace.'
3. The full delegation was: From the USA – Bishop Chayne of Washington DC, Bishop Melvin Talbert, Council of United Methodists, Clifton Kirkpatrick, Presbyterian Church USA, Revd Dan Weiss, American Baptists, Jim Wallis, Sojourners: And from the wider international Church: Archbishop Ndungane of Cape Town, Bishop Clive Handford, Cyprus and the Gulf, Bishop Riah Abu El-Assal, Jerusalem, Jordan, Lebanon and Syria; Revd Dr. Keith Clements, Conference of European Churches. From the UK: Bishop John Gladwin, Revd David Coffey, Baptist Union, Revd John Waller, United Reformed Church, Revd David Goodbourn Churches Together in Britain and Ireland (CTBI), Paul Renshaw, coordinating secretary CTBI, and, myself, Bishop Peter B. Price.

Chapter thirty six

1. The Chilcot Report published in the summer of 2016 concluded that the UK chose to join the invasion before the peaceful options for disarmament had been exhausted and noted that military action was not a last resort. Also judgements about the severity of the threat posed by WMDs was not justified, and plans and preparations for a post-Saddam Iraq were 'wholly inadequate'.
2. For a full account of the attempts to prevent the war in Iraq, as well as an American perspective, see Wallis, *God's Politics*.
3. Romans 13:2.
4. Romans 13:10.
5. Quoted in Shane Claiborne, *Common Prayer: A Liturgy for Ordinary Radicals* (Grand Rapids, Zondervan, 2010), p. 322.

Chapter thirty seven

1. See Romans 13:8.
2. Now 'Royal Wootton Bassett', a dignity endowed upon the town by Her Majesty Queen Elizabeth the Second, in recognition of the honour its people had offered to the dead and their bereaved loved ones.

3. The working group, set up in October 2004, was comprised of: The Rt Revd Richard Harries, Bishop of Oxford (chair); The Rt Revd Colin Bennetts, Bishop of Coventry; The Rt Revd Peter Selby, Bishop of Worcester; The Rt Revd Peter B. Price, Bishop of Bath and Wells.

4. Pre-millennialism takes a literal view of the Book of Revelation, arguing that Christ will return, and subsequently reign for 1,000 years. During this time 'believers' will rule with Christ.

5. This is an edited extract from 'Countering Terrorism: Power, violence and democracy post 9/11'. Church of England, September 2005.

Chapter thirty eight

1. 2 Chronicles 32:30.
2. W. Dow Edgerton, *The Passion of Interpretation* (Louisville, Westminster John Knox Press, 1992), p. 62.
3. *The Daily Telegraph*, 24 June 2016.
4. Norman Lebrecht, *The Song of Names* (New York, Anchor Books, 2004).
5. Lapide, *The Sermon on the Mount*.
6. Mark 10:14.
7. Luke 17:2.
8. John 4.
9. Yohanna Katancho, 'Reading the Gospel of John through Palestinian Eyes', in Gene L. Green, Stephen T. Pardue, K.K. Yeo (eds.), *Jesus Without Borders: Christology in the Majority World* (Eerdmans 2014).
10. These remarks from Irving Greenberg appeared in an article in *The Way*, Vol. 37, July 1997 by Norman Solomon, 'Theological Trends: Jewish Holocaust Theology', pp. 242–52.

Chapter thirty nine

1. Sara Maitland, *A Book of Silence* (London, Granta Books, 2009).
2. Dag Hammarskjöld, *Markings* (New York, Random House, 1993).
3. Isaiah 52:7, paraphrase.
4. Matthew 5:9.
5. Ephesians 6:12.
6. Willard Swartley, *Covenant of Peace: The Missing Peace in New Testament Theology and Ethics* (Eerdmans), p.2.
7. Swartley expressed these questions more fully (see pp. 2–3). His work *Covenant of Peace* offers a theological treatise par excellence in addressing these questions from a New Testament perspective.
8. Jeremiah 6:14; 8:11.
9. A quote from Earl Brill.
10. 'Towards Peace – 2006 – The Courageous Ape', *The Guardian*, 3 January 2016.
11. Robert Beck, *Banished Messiah: Violence and Nonviolence in Matthew's Story of Jesus* (Eugene, Wipf and Stock, 2016).

Chapter forty

1. *Concilium 2003/5, Jon Sobrino, Christianity and Reconciliation: The Way to Utopia*, pp 80–90.
2. 2 Corinthians 5:18–19. When restoring the chapel in the Bishop's Palace in Wells, we had this text engraved on to the floor around the base of the altar designed and made by David John.
3. Sobrino, *Concilium 2003/5*, pp. 80–90.
4. Micah 4:1–5; Isaiah 2:4; Psalm 27:7.

5.	Luke 4:18–19.
6.	Bloomfield, 'Rehabilitating Reconciliation', Accord Insight 3, *Transforming Broken Relationships*.
7.	Henri Nouwen, *The Way of the Heart: Desert Spirituality and Contemporary Ministry* (London, Darton Longman and Todd, 1981). p. 24.
8.	Hidden away in various texts in the Old and New Testaments (e.g. Leviticus 25:9–10,31; 27:17; Ezekiel 22:4; 46:17; Luke 4:18–19) lies a vision for human beings striving for fullness of humanity. It is the concept of 'jubilee'. Like all emerging, and indeed established nations, the Hebrew people found themselves defending their borders, as well as inheriting ideas from other cultures and nations, on how they should live. As former victims of slavery, the Hebrew people sought an ethic that would make provision for the release of slaves, or bonded labourers; as well as the return of land and property acquired in remission of debt. Further, they sought the renewal of the land by providing both 'sabbatical' – i.e. one in seven years, and 'jubilee' years – one in 50 years – for the land to lie fallow, flocks and herds rested; along with a general re-establishing of a more equal and humane society. Jesus gave this fresh impetus in his Nazareth manifesto (Luke 4:18–19), but seemed to imply that the 'Jubilee Year' should be seen as the 'norm' for human living, and not relegated to observance once every 50 years.

Chapter forty one

1.	Kazantzakis, *Report to Greco*.
2.	Morris West, *The Shoes of the Fisherman* (New Milford, Toby Press, 2004) p.
3.	The United Society for the Propagation of the Gospel – now United Society of Partners in the Gospel – founded in 1701.
4.	Jubilee Debt Campaign is the successor to Jubilee 2000.
5.	The phrase 'moved with compassion' so often used to describe Jesus's approach to the harassed and dejected crowds who followed him, comes from the Greek verb *splangchnizomai* . Literally translated, this means 'moved to his guts' or entrails. Jesus' compassion is deep and basic, rooted in his very being. See references: Matthew 9:36; 14:14; Mark 8:2; Luke 7:13.
6.	'Soteriology' – the study of salvation.
7.	Felix Wilfred, 'Struggles for a More Equitable and Inclusive World', *Concilium* 2016/1, p. 21.
8.	Luke 4:16–20.
9.	Luke 4:20–30.
10.	Isaiah 25:1–9.

Chapter forty two

1.	Matthew 7:9–11.
2.	Hammarskjöld, *Markings*.
3.	Walter Wink, *Engaging the Powers: Discernment and Resistance in a World of Domination (Minneapolis,* Fortress, 1992), p. 85.
4.	John 8:23; and then again Jesus addresses first the religious prosecutors at his trial, John 18:20; and to Pilate, representative of the political powers (John 18:36).

Chapter forty three

1.	See Isaiah 52:7; Isaiah 9:5.
2.	Rudy Wiebe, *Blue Mountains of China* (Toronto, McClelland & Stewart, 1952).

3. Walter Wink, *Just Jesus: My Struggle to Become Human* (Shippensburg, Image, 2014), p. 165.
4. Matthew 10:40.
5. Richard Rohr with Mike Morrell, *The Divine Dance* (London, SPCK, 2016), pp.44–5.
6. John 14:11, translation mine.
7. Rohr with Morrell, *The Divine Dance*, p. 46.
8. Leonardo Boff in *Wait for the Light* (Robertsbridge, Plough Publishing, 2014), pp. 169–70.
9. James O'Halloran SDB, *Giving Life Away: Memories* (Dublin, A Little Book Company, 2015), p. 99.

Chapter forty four

1. Bloomfield, Accord Insight 3, *Transforming Broken Relationships*, p. 46.
2. The Burns Price Foundation set up in 2015 makes grants to 11–18-year-olds for community projects. See www.burnspricefoundation.org.uk
3. New Way is an open community and it would welcome your contribution to its life. See www.newway.org.uk/whatwedo
4. Martha C. Nussbaum, *Political Emotions: Why Love Matters for Justice* (Cambridge, Belknap-Harvard 2013), p. 2.
5. See Chapters 6 and 38 for more detailed definition of *shalom*.
6. Matthew 5:33, New Jerusalem Bible, italics mine.
7. Lapide, *Sermon on the Mount*, pp. 21–2. I was tempted to use the word *sedekah* throughout this section, but have opted for the more familiar, but less adequate, 'saving justice'.
8. Lapide, *Sermon on the Mount*, p. 22.
9. John 8:32.
10. Erik Borgman: 'The struggle against evil and dehumanisation in Europe, or how to deal with the other', *Concilium* 2008/1, Evil Today and The Struggle To Be Human, pp. 22–5.
11. Willard Swartley, op. cit., p.15.
12. David Cortright, *Peace: A History of Movement and Ideas* (Cambridge, Cambridge University Press, 2008), p. 339.
13. O'Halloran, *Giving Life Away*, p. 102.
14. Cortright, *Peace*, p. 339.
15. Luke 2:32.